WORKSHOPS IN COMPUTING
Series edited by C. J. van Rijsbergen

Also in this series

continued on back page...

Udo W. Lipeck and Bernhard Thalheim (Eds.)

Modelling Database Dynamics

Selected Papers from the Fourth
International Workshop on Foundations
of Models and Languages for Data and
Objects, Volkse, Germany
19–22 October 1992

Published in collaboration with the
British Computer Society

Springer-Verlag Berlin Heidelberg GmbH

Udo W. Lipeck, Dipl.-Inform.,
Prof. Dr. rer. nat. habil.
Institut für Informatik
Universität Hannover, Lange Laube 22
D-W 3000 Hannover 1, Germany

Bernhard Thalheim, Dipl.-Math.,
Prof. Dr. rer. nat. habil.
Fachbereich Informatik
Universität Rostock
Albert-Einstein-Straße 21
D-O 2500 Rostock 6, Germany

ISBN 978-3-540-19803-1

British Library Cataloguing in Publication Data
Modelling Database Dynamics: Selected Papers from the Fourth International
Workshop on Foundations of Models and Languages for Data and Objects,
Volkse, Germany, 19–22 October 1992. – (Workshops in Computing Series)
  I. Lipeck, Udo Walter
  II. Thalheim , Bernhard III. Series
005.74
ISBN 978-3-540-19803-1   ISBN 978-1-4471-3554-8 (eBook)
DOI 10.1007/978-1-4471-3554-8

Library of Congress Cataloging-in-Publication Data
A catalog for this book is available from the Library of Congress

Typesetting: Camera ready by contributors

34/3830-543210 Printed on acid-free paper

Preface

The series of International Workshops on Foundations of Models and Languages for Data and Objects was initiated by the working group "Foundations of Information Systems" of the GI (German Association for Informatics), and is organized in cooperation with EATCS (European Association for Theoretical Computer Science). The workshop timetable usually provides one hour slots for presentations and extensive time for discussions; thus it offers a unique opportunity for in-depth exchange of ideas and experiences.

This volume contains selected papers from the fourth workshop which took place at "Manor House" Volkse near Braunschweig, Germany, on 19–22 October 1992. Its particular focus was on modelling dynamic behaviour of database systems in formal frameworks.

The aim of database modelling is the design of databases which can be managed reliably and efficiently. Three different perspectives can be identified in modelling: the structure-oriented perspective focuses on what kinds of data are stored in the database, what constraints apply to these data, and what kinds of data are derivable. The process-oriented perspective is concerned with the processes or activities performed in the application area. The behaviour-oriented perspective is concerned with how events in the real world trigger actions in the database systems. Although database literature has traditionally emphasised the first perspective, it is now recognized that problems cannot be solved without an integrated consideration of all three perspectives. Therefore nowadays modelling database dynamics is considered to be as important as modelling static database structures.

This workshop covered new developments in theoretical aspects of this area, in particular:

Dynamics and behaviour: algebraic and logical mechanisms for computing dynamics and for reasoning on processes and database evolution, events, actions, triggers, active constraints, rules, and others.

Modelling aspects: the design, specification, and verification of database dynamics, the development of languages for representation of dynamics and behaviour of a database, classes of dynamic integrity constraints, models for supporting integrity enforcement during updates.

Formal frameworks: the theoretical fundamentals for modelling and reasoning on database dynamics, the development of appropriate logical and algebraic calculi.

Since most current work is utilizing object-oriented principles for treating database issues, a prominent emphasis of the workshop was on object dynamics. According to the above, the section topics of this volume are:

- Object creation
- Rule-based updates of objects
- Algebraic semantics of objects
- Logic approaches to updates and constraints
- Integrity enforcement

Additionally, there are two reports that summarize discussions on:

- Update languages
- Object migration and classification

There were 34 submissions by authors from 15 countries. After evaluation on the basis of originality, significance of contribution, quality of presentation, technical quality and suitability for discussion, 16 contributions were selected for presentation and discussion at the workshop and 12 of them for publication. To stimulate discussions further, each talk had at least one responder who knew the workshop version in advance – and the discussions were indeed very lively.

We thank all who submitted papers for consideration. We would like to sincerely thank the program committee members, as well as the external referees, for their care in evaluating the submissions and for the time they invested in reading them. We also acknowledge the continuous help of the members of the organization committee. The names of the persons involved in preparing the workshop, the names of the participants, and an author index are listed in this volume.

Last but not least we want to give our thanks to the participants in Volkse who have very actively contributed to the success of the workshop.

Hannover and Rostock   Udo Lipeck and Bernhard Thalheim
December 1992

Workshop Organization

Program Committee:

Serge Abiteboul   (INRIA Paris, France)
Janos Demetrovics   (HAS Budapest, Hungary)
José Fiadeiro   (INESC Lisboa, Portugal)
Georg Gottlob   (Technische Universität Wien, Austria)
Andreas Heuer   (Technische Universität Clausthal, Germany)
Udo W. Lipeck   (Universität Hannover, Germany, co-chair)
Jan Paredaens   (University of Antwerp UIA, Belgium)
Gunter Saake   (Technische Universität Braunschweig,
                            Germany)
Marc H. Scholl   (Universität Ulm, Germany)
Bernhard Thalheim   (Universität Rostock, Germany, co-chair)
Roel Wieringa   (Vrije Universiteit Amsterdam, Netherlands)

European Coordinator:

Jan Paredaens   (University of Antwerp UIA, Belgium)

Organization Committee:

Michael Gertz   (Universität Hannover, Germany)
Andreas Heuer   (Technische Universität Clausthal,
                            Germany, chair)
Carsten Hörner   (Technische Universität Clausthal, Germany)
Thorsten Hartmann   (Technische Universität Braunschweig,
                            Germany)

External Referees:

A. Benczùr   G. Kappel
S. Braß   A. Kiss
J. Carmo   L. Kozma
S. Conrad   G. Koschorreck
G. Denker   T. Markus
F. M. Dionisio   W. Nejdl
G. Friedrich   A. Oberweis
M. Gertz   J. Overbeck
T. Hartmann   G. Reichwein
K. Hülsmann   P. Spruit
R. Jungclaus   H. Zhou

Contents

Integrity Enforcement

Discussion Reports

List of Participants

Nader Azarmi
Intelligent Systems Research Section, BT Laboratories, Martlesham Heath, Ipswich IP5 7RE, UK

Catriel Beeri
Department of Computer Science, Hebrew University, Givat RAM, IL-91904 Jerusalem, Israel

Domenico Beneventano
Dipartimento di Electronica, Informatica e Sist., Università degli Studi di Bologna, Viale Risorgimento 2, I-40136 Bologna, Italy

Jan Chomicki
Department of Computing and Information Sciences, Kansas State University, 234 Nichols Hall, Manhattan, KS 66506-2302, USA

Karen C. Davis
Department of Electrical and Computer Engineering, University of Cincinnati, ML 30, Cincinnati, OH 45221-0030, USA

Guozhu Dong
Computer Science Department, University of Melbourne, Parkville, VIC 3052, Australia

Marcelo Finger
Department of Computing, Imperial College, 180 Queen's Gate, London SW7 2BZ, UK

Piero Fraternali
Dipartimento di Elettronica e Informazione, Politecnico di Milano, Via Lucini 3, I-22100 Como, Italy

Michael Gertz
Institut für Informatik, Universität Hannover, Lange Laube 22, D-W 3000 Hannover 1, Germany

Hele-Mai Haav
Software Department, Institute of Cybernetics, Estonian Academy of Sciences, Akadeemia tee 21, EE-0108 Tallinn, Estonia

Thorsten Hartmann
Institut für Programmiersprachen und Informationssysteme, Technische
Universität Braunschweig, Postfach 33 29, D-W 3300 Braunschweig,
Germany

Andreas Heuer
Institut für Informatik, Technische Universität Clausthal, Erzstraße 1,
D-W 3392 Clausthal-Zellerfeld, Germany

Carsten Hörner
Institut für Informatik, Technische Universität Clausthal, Erzstraße 1,
D-W 3392 Clausthal- Zellerfeld, Germany

Gerhard Knolmayer
Institut für Wirtschaftsinformatik, Universität Bern, Hallerstraße 6,
CH-3012 Bern, Switzerland

Christian Laasch
Institut für Informatik, Universität Ulm, Postfach 4066, D-W 7900 Ulm,
Germany

Georg Lausen
Fakultät für Mathematik und Informatik, Universität Mannheim,
Seminargebäude A5, D-W 6800 Mannheim, Germany

Udo W. Lipeck
Institut für Informatik, Universität Hannover, Lange Laube 22,
D-W 3000 Hannover 1, Germany

Danilo Montesi
Dipartimento di Informatica, Università di Pisa, Corso Italia 40, I-56125
Pisa, Italy

Jan Paredaens
Department of Mathematics and Computer Science, University of Antwerp,
Universiteitsplein 1, B-2610 Antwerp, Belgium

Georg Reichwein
Departamento de Matemática, IST, Rua Alves Redol 9, Apartado 10105,
P-1017 Lisboa Codex, Portugal

Gunter Saake
Institut für Programmiersprachen und Informationssysteme, Technische
Universität Braunschweig, Postfach 33 29, D-W 3300 Braunschweig,
Germany

Klaus-Dieter Schewe
Fachbereich Informatik, Universität Hamburg, Vogt-Kölln-Straße 30,
D-W 2000 Hamburg 54, Germany

Scarlet Schwiderski
Computer Laboratory, University of Cambridge, New Museums Site,
Pembroke Street, Cambridge CB2 3QG, UK

Paul Spruit
Department of Mathematics and Computer Science, Vrije Universiteit,
De Boelelaan 1081 a, NL-1081 HV Amsterdam, The Netherlands

Bernhard Thalheim
Fachbereich Informatik, Universität Rostock, Albert-Einstein-Straße 21,
D-O 2500 Rostock 6, Germany

Riccardo Torlone
IASI-CNR, Viale Manzoni 30, I-00185 Roma, Italy

Alexander Tuzhilin
New York University, 44 West 4th Street, Rm. 9-78, New York,
NY 10012-1126, USA

Jan Van den Bussche
Department of Mathematics and Computer Science, University of Antwerp,
Universiteitsplein 1, B-2610 Antwerp, Belgium

Roel Wieringa
Department of Mathematics and Computer Science, Vrije Universiteit,
De Boelelaan 1081 a, NL-1081 HV Amsterdam, The Netherlands

Elena Zucca
Dipartimento di Informatica, Università di Genova, Viale Benedetto
XV 3, I-16132 Genova, Italy

Object Creation

Non-Deterministic Aspects of Object-Creating Database Transformations

Jan Van den Bussche*
University of Antwerp
Antwerp, Belgium

Dirk Van Gucht†
Indiana University
Bloomington, IN, USA

Abstract

Various non-deterministic aspects of object creation in database transformations are discussed, from a modeling as well as from an expressive power point of view.

1 Introduction

In the past few years, a lot of attention has been paid to *database transformations* [5, 9, 10, 11, 15, 20, 21, 23]. Database transformations are binary accessibility relationships between database instances, and provide a simple, unifying model for the study of database query languages and important notions in database dynamics, such as updates, updatable views, and database restructurings.

In that study, the issue of *object creation* has attracted particular interest recently. After an object-creating database transformation (as opposed to a *domain-preserving* one), the output can contain domain elements that were not present in the input. Object creation differs from conventional insertion of a new value in that it contains an implicit form of *non-determinism*, i.e., the particular choice of the new domain value to be added is irrelevant, as long as it is new. This weak form of non-determinism is called *determinacy* [5].

Object creation finds an obvious application in object-oriented database systems, where, if a new object has to be added, the identity of this object must be distinct from those of all objects already present, but the particular choice of this new identifier is an implementation detail. Similarly, object creation is sometimes unavoidable to fully support updatable views in object-oriented database systems, i.e., derived information that is to be explicitly added in the database [1, 18], as well as database restructuring [5, 15].

The natural links between object-creating and non-deterministic database transformations [12] were recently explored by the authors [31], for the special case of queries and views (modeled as type-increasing transformations.) In the present paper, we widen our scope to arbitrary updates, present some new results and indicate some new open problems.

---

*Research Assistant of the N.F.W.O. Address: University of Antwerp (UIA), Dept. Math. & Comp. Science, Universiteitsplein 1, B-2610 Antwerp, Belgium. E-mail: vdbuss@uia.ac.be.

†Indiana University, Comp. Science Dept., Bloomington, IN 47405-4101, USA. E-mail: vgucht@cs.indiana.edu.

In Section 2, we define a simplified version of the IQL* model [5] for reasoning about object-creating database transformations. We discuss determinacy originally explored for the special case of queries, and show that some care must be taken when moving to arbitrary updates. We also compare the *determinate approach* to object-creation of [5] as used in this paper, to the *functional approach* proposed in [25]. There, newly created objects are interpreted as the result of functions applied to the existing objects. These functions are usually expressed as Skolem function terms, as is used in Logic Programming. We will show that the two approaches can be reconciled; in both approaches, object creation can be interpreted as untyped tuple and set construction. This reconciliation will also clarify the issue of the *completeness up to copies* of IQL* w.r.t. determinate transformations [5].

In Section 3, we discuss *semi-determinism*, a natural generalization of determinacy. We present a new result, linking object creation and non-determinism. More concretely, we show that object creation in function of sets is in a precise sense equivalent to a special semi-deterministic choice operation. Semi-determinism was again originally explored only for queries [31]. Extending the concept to arbitrary updates will turn out to yield several problems. First, it is not clear how the composition of two semi-deterministic transformations should be defined. Second, it is not clear what a language complete for all semi-deterministic transformations should look like. This contrasts sharply with the situation in the special case of queries, as considered in [31], where these two problems can be solved quite naturally. Perhaps we have encountered a fundamental distinction between queries and updates?

2 Determinate object-creating database transformations

For simplicity, we shall work in the relational model. Generalizations to richer complex object, semantic, or object-based models are straightforward.

Let S_{in}, S_{out} be database schemes. A *database transformation* of type $S_{in} \to S_{out}$ is a binary relationship $T \subseteq inst(S_{in}) \times inst(S_{out})$,[1] such that for some finite set C of constants, T is *C-generic*, meaning that for each C-permutation[2] f of the domain, $I \xrightarrow{T} J$ implies $f(I) \xrightarrow{T} f(J)$. (Transformations that are actually functions are called *deterministic*.)

Genericity is a consistency criterion, well-established in the database field [8]. Intuitively, it says that data elements should be treated uniformly (apart from a finite set of constants C that are particular to the application at hand). Pragmatically, it says that we are considering database computations, not arbitrary computations on bit streams.

We say that transformation T above is *object creating* if there are instances $I \xrightarrow{T} J$ for which the active domain of the output, J, contains elements that were not in the input, I, nor in C.

For example, if P is a relation containing person tuples, then the insertion:

$$P \stackrel{+}{\Longleftarrow} [\text{name} : \text{john}, \text{age} : 40, \text{address} : \text{new york}] \tag{1}$$

---

[1] For a scheme S, $inst(S)$ denotes the set of database instances over S.

[2] A C-permutation fixes every element of C.

name	age	address
jeff	20	dallas
john	40	new york

id	name	age	address
α	jeff	20	dallas
β	john	40	new york

id	name	age	address
α	jeff	20	dallas
β	john	40	new york
γ	john	40	new york

Figure 1: Object creation.

is not object-creating, but simply C-generic, with $C = \{$john, 40, new york$\}$. On the other hand, suppose PO is a class containing person objects, and we want to insert a new object with a new id. The update:

$$PO \overset{+}{\Longleftarrow} \textbf{new}[\text{id}] \, [\text{name} : \text{john}, \text{age} : 40, \text{address} : \text{new york}] \tag{2}$$

where **new**[id] stands for an arbitrary new id not yet present in the input database, is object-creating (and C-generic.)

We next define a simple language for expressing database transformations. Programs in the language are built from basic statements. Basic statements can be divided into relational statements and object-creating statements. Finally, programs can be iterated or called recursively. In this paper, we will not need to be concerned with the particular form of the iteration construct.

The *relational* statements are of the forms

$$P \overset{+}{\Longleftarrow} E, \; P \overset{-}{\Longleftarrow} E, \; \text{or} \; \textbf{drop} \; P$$

where P is a relation name and E is an expression in the relational algebra or calculus. The **drop** statement allows the destruction of an old relation with name P. For the $+$ and $-$ statements, the semantics is that E is evaluated, and the result is added to (in case of $+$) or deleted from (in case of $-$) relation P. In the case of $+$, P may be a new relation name, in which case a new relation with name P is created and initialized to the value of E. For example, the simple insertion statement (1) shown in the earlier example is a trivial example of a relational statement (the relational calculus expression is constant in this example.)

As just defined, relational statements are not object-creating. In order to express object creation, simple variations of these statements can be used. The **new** statement:

$$P \overset{+}{\Longleftarrow} \textbf{new}[A]E$$

creates a new object for each tuple in the value of E. More precisely, the value of the expression **new**[A]E is the relation obtained from the value of the expression E, after tagging each tuple with a different, new, A-attribute value.

To illustrate these concepts, consider the following example. Starting from the person relation P shown in Figure 1, left, we can create the set PO of person objects with identity shown in Figure 1, right, with the statement

$$PO \overset{+}{\Longleftarrow} \textbf{new}[\text{id}] \, P. \tag{3}$$

R_1	R_2
a	c c
b	d d

R_1	R_2
a	c a
b	d b

R_1	R_2
a	e a
b	f b

Figure 2: Composition does not preserve determinacy.

Note that this set PO contains a person object with attributes [name:john, age:40, address:new york]. If we now apply the earlier object insertion update statement (2), another person with these attributes will be added to PO, with another identity, as shown in Figure 1, middle. If we want to add a new person only if a person with the same attributes is not already present in the database, we must use a more elaborate statement:

PO $\overset{+}{\Longleftarrow}$ **new**[id] [name:john,age:40,address:new york] $\wedge$
    $(\not\exists t \in PO) : t(\text{name}) = \text{john} \wedge t(\text{age}) = 40 \wedge t(\text{address}) = \text{new york}$

We point out that the **new** operation is but a common denominator for many mechanisms for object creation considered in the literature [11, 5, 15, 19, 22, 25, 34].

An immediate consequence of genericity is that an object creating transformation must be non-deterministic. For example, in Figure 1, the particular choice of α and β as new id's is not crucial: we could have taken ε and δ as well. However, we can leave it to that, and restrict the non-determinism only to the particular choice of the newly created objects. This results in the notion of *determinate* transformation [5].

A transformation T is determinate if whenever $I \overset{T}{\longrightarrow} J_1$ and $I \overset{T}{\longrightarrow} J_2$, there exists an isomorphism $f : J_1 \to J_2$ that is the identity on the objects in I.

So, determinacy is determinism up to the choice of the new objects in the output.

Determinacy was originally considered in the context of queries (and views). These can be modeled as transformations that are *type-increasing*. A transformation T of type $\mathcal{S}_{\text{in}} \to \mathcal{S}_{\text{out}}$ is type-increasing if $\mathcal{S}_{\text{in}} \subset \mathcal{S}_{\text{out}}$, and for each $I \overset{T}{\longrightarrow} J$ and each relation name $R \in \mathcal{S}_{\text{in}}$, $R^J = R^I$.

For type-increasing transformations, determinacy is a robust notion: determinacy is preserved under composition. For arbitrary updates, however, this robustness property breaks down. For example, let $\mathcal{S}_{\text{in}}$ consist of two relations R_1, R_2. Consider transformation T_1, which erases relation R_2, and transformation T_2, which adds to relation R_2 as many new objects as there are in R_1. So, $T_1 \equiv R_2 \overset{-}{\Longleftarrow} R_2$ and $T_2 \equiv R_2 \overset{+}{\Longleftarrow} \text{new} R_1$. Then Figure 2, middle and right, shows two possible results of the composition $T_1; T_2$ applied to the instance shown in Figure 2, left. The determinacy requirement is clearly not satisfied, the reason being that in the middle instance, objects are created having belonged to R_2 in the past, while in the right instance, brand new objects are created.

This difficulty can be remedied by disallowing such situations: once an object has "died" (has been deleted), it can never be "reborn" (created). This is a commonly heard requirement in discussions on object identity, but the above discussion provides, to our knowledge, the first formal argument of why this is indeed necessary. Thus, rather than defining composition $T_1; T_2$ classically as: $\{(I, K) \mid (\exists J)T_1(I, J) \wedge T_2(J, K)\}$, we formally define it as: $\{(I, K) \mid (\exists J)T_1(I, J) \wedge T_2(J, K) \wedge$ for each object o appearing in I and K, o also appears in $J\}$. Using this new definition of composition, we can now show:

Theorem: If T_1, T_2 are determinate database transformations, then so is $T_1; T_2$.

Proof: We know that T_1, T_2 are C-generic for some C. To check whether $T_1; T_2$ is C-generic as well, assume $T_1; T_2(I, J)$, and let f be a C-permutation of the universe. We show that also $T_1; T_2(f(I), f(J))$. There exists a K such that $Q_1(I, K)$, $Q_2(K, J)$, and every object in $I \cap J$ is also in K. We have $T_1(f(I), f(K))$ and $T_2(f(K), f(J))$. Every object in $f(I) \cap f(J)$ is also in $f(K)$. Therefore, $T_1; T_2(f(I), f(J))$.

To check determinacy, assume $T_1; T_2(I, J_1)$ and $T_1; T_2(I, J_2)$. Then K_r, for $r = 1, 2$, exists such that $T_1(I, K_r)$, $T_2(K_r, J_r)$, and every object in $I \cap J_r$ is also in K_r. Since T_1 is determinate, there exists an isomorphism $f_1 : K_1 \to K_2$ such that f_1 is the identity on $I \cap K_1$. Since T_2 is generic, $T_2(K_2, f_1(J_1))$. Since T_2 is determinate, there exists an isomorphism $f_2 : f_1(J_1) \to J_2$ such that f_2 is the identity on $K_2 \cap f(J_1)$. Clearly, $f := f_2 \circ f_1 : J_1 \to J_2$ is an isomorphism. It remains to show that f is the identity on $I \cap J_1$. So, let $o \in I \cap J_1$. Then also $o \in K_1$, and hence $f_1(o) \in K_2 \cap f(J_1)$ as well as $f_1(o) = o$. Therefore, $f_2(f_1(o)) = f_1(o) = o$. $\square$

The **new** operation just introduced creates new objects in function of the tuples in some relation. One also needs a mechanism that creates objects in function of sets. This is provided by the *abstraction* operation in the following way. Let r be a binary relation. Then r can be viewed as a set-valued function, in the standard way. The result of $\mathbf{abstr}[A](r)$ is a ternary relation, obtained from r after tagging each tuple with a new A-attribute, such that two tuples (x_1, y_1) and (x_2, y_2) get the same tag if and only if the sets $r(x_1)$ and $r(x_2)$ are equal. This as opposed to the **new** operation, where *every* tuple gets a different tag.

The abstraction operation is determinate. We can incorporate abstraction in our language by allowing statements of the form: $P \overset{+}{\Leftarrow} \mathbf{abstr}[A]E$. For example, if PC is a parent-child relation, then the transformation:

$SPC \overset{+}{\Leftarrow} \mathbf{abstr}[S]PC;$
$SC \overset{+}{\Leftarrow} \pi_{S,C}(SPC)$

creates a unique object for each set of siblings and represents these sets in relation SC. See Figure 3. If we now also apply the statements

$PS \overset{+}{\Leftarrow} \pi_{P,S}(SPC);$
drop PC;
drop SPC

then the new relations PS and SC correspond to a useful *restructuring* of the original PC relation. See Figure 3.

Abstraction is the operational equivalent of the ability to treat set values as first-class citizens. As defined here, it was originally introduced in [15, 30], but it is a mechanism that has been considered frequently in the literature.

P	C
sam	toto
sam	zaza
mary	toto
mary	zaza
fred	nini

A	P	C
α	sam	toto
α	sam	zaza
α	mary	toto
α	mary	zaza
β	fred	nini

S	C
α	toto
α	zaza
β	nini

P	S
sam	α
mary	α
fred	β

Figure 3: Abstraction.

Abstraction corresponds to such concepts as grouping over sets [13], nesting [29], set-valued functions [4], and set-valued object assignments [5].

The transformation language with relational statements (giving us first-order logic), **new** (giving us tuple-id creation), **abstr** (giving us set-id creation) and recursion is essentially equivalent to the IQL* language, proposed in the seminal paper [5]. Therefore, we take the liberty to refer to it with the same name IQL*.

The semantics for object-creation considered above, has not been the only approach adopted in the literature. An alternative approach is the one proposed in [25], where object creation is interpreted as the construction of function terms over the existing objects, as is done in Logic Programming. We will call this the *functional* approach. The functional approach typically uses a calculus framework, where the relational calculus is extended with first-order function symbols. There is no need then for a special **new** operation.

For example, recall the **new** statement (3). The analogue in the functional approach would be:

$$PO \overset{+}{\Longleftarrow} \{[\text{id}: f(x, y, z), \text{name}: x, \text{age}: y, \text{address}: z] \mid P(x, y, z)\}$$

where f is a function symbol. Applying this statement to Figure 1 (left) will produce Figure 1 (right); however now, α and β are not arbitrary new values, but equal the first-order terms $f(\text{jeff}, 20, \text{dallas})$ and $f(\text{john}, 40, \text{new york})$, respectively. If g is another function symbol, applying the functional analogue of the insertion (1):

$$PO \overset{+}{\Longleftarrow} \{[\text{id}: g(\text{john}, 40, \text{new york}), \text{name}: \text{john}, \text{age}: 40, \text{address}: \text{new york}]\}$$

to Figure 1 (right) will produce Figure 1 (middle) with γ equal to $g(\text{john}, 40, \text{new york})$.

Note that if we would have used the same f, then no new object would have been created. This technical difference between the determinate approach and the functional approach is not really important, as we will see momentarily. In fact, there are no fundamental differences at all between the two approaches: we will next sketch how the one can simulate the other.[3]

We start with simulating the determinate approach by the functional one. For each relation name R that is used in the program, we have a different function symbol f_R. Then the statement:

$$R \overset{+}{\Longleftarrow} \textbf{new}[A]E$$

---

[3] A similar observation was made in [22], without proof.

is simulated by:

$$R \overset{\pm}{\Longleftarrow} \{[A : f_R(x_1, \ldots, x_n), A_1 : x_1, \ldots, A_n : x_n] \mid E(A_1 : x_1, \ldots, A_n : x_n)\}.$$

As just mentioned, this naive simulation fails in case object $f_R(x_1, \ldots, x_n)$ already exists in the database (because it was created by a previous **new** statement). This problem can be circumvented by storing in an auxiliary table Created$_R$ for each tuple $x_1, \ldots, x_n$ the last object o created in function of that tuple. The above statement is then modified to test first if there was already an object creation in function of $x_1, \ldots, x_n$; if yes, then $f_R(o, x_2, \ldots, x_n)$ is used instead of $f_R(x_1, \ldots, x_n)$.[4]

To simulate the functional approach by the determinate one, it suffices to store for each function symbol f used in the program, an auxiliary table R_f storing the current extension of f. If $f_R(x_1, \ldots, x_n)$ is created, then, using the **new** operation, a tuple $(o, x_1, \ldots, x_n)$ is stored in R_f with o an arbitrary new domain element playing the role of $f_R(x_1, \ldots, x_n)$. Further references to $f_R(x_1, \ldots, x_n)$ can then be handled by lookup in the auxiliary table.

The object-creation functions considered above are "syntactical" functions; they form first-order terms from their arguments. This is the standard Logic Programming approach. An alternative formalism for the functional approach to object creation, based on "semantical" functions, was presented in [16], where the so-called *tagging functions* are defined. There, all object creation happens through a single tagging function. The syntactical functional approach is a special case of the tagging functional approach, where this tagging function is simply the identity, mapping its arguments $x_1, \ldots, x_n$ to the tuple $(x_1, \ldots, x_n)$. (See also [33].) That there is one single tagging function is not a real restriction; if multiple function symbols are needed, one takes for each such symbol f a different constant c_f and simulates $f(x_1, \ldots, x_n)$ by $(c_f, x_1, \ldots, x_n)$.

So, object creation through the **new** operation, or, equivalently, functional object creation, amounts to tuple construction. Note that this tuple construction is necessarily *untyped*, since the nested structure of the various tuples is not fixed. Generalizing this observation to include the **abstr** operation, which creates objects representing sets, not tuples, means moving from tuples to sets. Indeed, tuples are a special case of sets by the well-known axioms: $(x, y) = \{\{x\}, \{x, y\}\}$ and $(x_1, \ldots, x_n) = (x_1, (x_2, \ldots, x_n))$. Including set-object creation in the functional approach could be done by introducing set-valued functions (as in [4]) or set-terms (as in [24]). We have thus arrived at the important insight that *object creation in IQL* can be interpreted as untyped-set construction*.

The use of untyped sets in database query languages has been studied in the literature [14, 17]. It is known that the relational calculus or algebra, extended with untyped sets and recursion or iteration, is computationally complete for all computable generic untyped-sets queries. It thus follows that IQL* can express exactly those determinate queries that correspond to a generic untyped-sets query. This has been made precise in [32], where the *constructive* queries were defined as a natural subclass of the determinate ones. Informally, a query is constructive if symmetries of the input database can be naturally extended to symmetries of the query result. It thus follows that IQL* can express exactly the constructive queries. This clarifies the incompleteness of IQL* w.r.t. the determinate queries; indeed, IQL* is known to be only determinate-complete

---

[4]This is only one trick to circumvent the problem; others can be used as well.

P	C
sam	toto
mary	zaza
fred	nini

P	C
sam	zaza
mary	zaza
fred	nini

Figure 4: Witness.

up to copies.[5] One possible philosophical interpretation of all this is that, a posteriori, the notion of determinacy is not quite restrictive enough. At any rate, there does not appear to be a *natural* example of a determinate, non-constructive query.

The foregoing discussion (and the presentation in [32]) went on for the special case of queries. However, it can be shown that everything goes through in general. In particular, one can consider general *constructive database transformations*, and prove that IQL* expresses exactly all constructive database transformations.

To conclude this section, we point out that in the functional approach, once the object-creating function(s) have been fixed, object-creation becomes ↑ *deterministic* operation. In other words, the non-deterministic characteristic f object creation is entirely captured in the particular *choice* of the function. s a consequence, there is no problem in using the classical composition of ɹatabase transformations, as in the determinate case. Also, it is interesting to observe that the function-terms semantics was adopted in [1] to study the view-update problem in the context of object-oriented database systems.

3   Semi-determinism

IQL* is a determinate, hence nearly deterministic language. In order to express arbitrarily non-deterministic transformations one can add the *witness* operation to the language. (See [2] for motivations for non-determinism, and [12] for a survey.)

Witness is a non-deterministic choice operation. Let r be a relation, and let X be a subset of its attributes. Then $W_X(r)$ evaluates to a sub-instance of r, obtained by choosing exactly one representative from each class of X-equivalent tuples of r. Here, two tuples are X-equivalent if they agree outside X.

For example, if r is the PC relation of Figure 3, then two possible results of $W_C(r)$ are shown in Figure 4. For every parent, an arbitrary child is chosen (as a "witness" for his/her parenthood.)

Witness can be incorporated in IQL* by allowing statements of the form: $P \overset{+/-}{\Longleftarrow} W_X E$. The resulting language will be called NIQL* (for non-deterministic IQL*). It is easy to see that NIQL* is equivalent to the languages TL [10] and DL* [11], which are known to express exactly all computable database transformations. So, NIQL* is well-understood, and also very powerful.

It is interesting to consider restrictions on the unlimited non-determinism that NIQL* programs allow. (For motivations we refer to [31].) To find sensible such restrictions, one can get inspiration from the definition of determinate

---

[5]In [5], it was conjectured that that IQL* is fully determinate-complete, but this was later shown to be false [3, 6].

transformation. That definition required that two possible outcomes of the transformations be isomorphic, *but* via an isomorphism that keeps the existing objects fixed. In [31], the present authors considered a weakened version of this qualification, for the special case of queries. The adopted qualification was to require that two possible outcomes of the query be isomorphic, *but* via an isomorphism that is an *automorphism* (also called *symmetry*) of the input database. Such queries were called *semi-deterministic*.

Denote by SNIQL^q, the sublanguage of NIQL* consisting of the programs that express semi-deterministic queries. The class of semi-deterministic queries exhibits a number of good properties [31]. It is therefore not surprising that membership in SNIQL^q is undecidable. Fortunately, we can replace the witness operation by a weaker choice construct, called *swap-choice*, which is guaranteed to be semi-deterministic (and still efficient to implement.) Swap-choice was already implicit in [31]; we next define it explicitly.

Let I be a database instance and R a relation name in the scheme of I. The *swap-choice* **swap**$[C](R, I)$ evaluates to a unary relation with attribute C, obtained by choosing from each equivalence class of *swap-equivalent* elements of the domain of R^I exactly one representative. Here, two domain elements o_1, o_2 are called swap-equivalent if the transposition $(o_1\ o_2)$ is a symmetry of I.

We can incorporate swap-choice in IQL* by allowing statements of the form: $P \overset{+/-}{\Longleftarrow} \mathbf{swap} E$. We will call the resulting language SIQL*, and its restriction to queries SIQL^q. It can be shown that queries expressed in SIQL^q are semi-deterministic.

While swap-choice may seem ad-hoc at first, the following theorem gives evidence for its naturalness. It says that in a semi-deterministic context, swap-choice, and the set-based object creation operation abstraction, are equivalent in expressive power. Since abstraction is naturally related to duplicate elimination in object creating languages, this result gives an intuitive technique to remove duplicates, i.e., retain only one version of otherwise indistinguishable objects. The theorem should also be contrasted with the result in [30] that abstraction is primitive in IQL*.

Theorem: *Swap-choice is expressible in SNIQL^q, using abstraction. Conversely, abstraction is not primitive in SIQL^q.*

Proof sketch: First, observe that swap-equivalence is definable in the relational calculus. Using abstraction, equivalence classes of swap-equivalent domain elements are grouped together and given a unique object identifier. These new identifiers are swap-equivalent, and using witness, representatives can be chosen in a semi-deterministic manner.

For the converse, observe that abstraction can be simulated using **new** with duplicates. These duplicates are swap-equivalent, yielding a simulation of abstraction using **new** and **swap**. □

The above theorem suggests that swap-choice, *in combination with object creation through* **new**, allows the specification of important data manipulation operations. This was also suggested in [31], where it was shown how a subclass of the *counting* queries (i.e., queries that involve the cardinality of certain sets) can be expressed in SIQL^q in PTIME. We have since then substantially extended the relevant techniques, and can prove that *all* counting queries can be expressed in this way. (We do not present this proof here.) The importance of this result stems from the observation that, unlike [7], we rely only on the very weak form of non-determinism allowed by the swap-choice operation. It is indeed well-known that *unrestricted* non-determinism offers efficient expressibility of all PTIME transformations. In other words, as far as counting applications are concerned, the usage of non-determinism can be heavily constrained, as to appear almost deterministic, however without sacrificing efficiency. It would be interesting to find other applications where this is possible.

As argued in [31] and further illustrate here, object-creation is vital in order to make semi-determinism feasible. This is especially true for queries, on which we have focused in our discussion up to now. We next turn to the question of how semi-determinism can be adapted to the general case of arbitrary database transformations. We will not give many answers, but rather indicate directions for further research.

We start with an example which, although trivial, demonstrates how the use of updates admits certain counting queries to be expressed semi-deterministically without a need for object creation. Let I be a database and consider a query based on the number of domain elements in a number of relations of I. This query can be solved semi-deterministically by first computing the active domain of these relations using a standard relational algebra expression. Subsequently every relation in I is dropped. We are now left with a unary relation containing the wanted active domain. We can now order this unary relation by repeatedly choosing elements from this unary relation. The choices are semi-deterministic, since we choose from an unstructed set of elements. Once the set is ordered, it is straightforward to test any PTIME-computable property of its cardinality.

Recall that for queries, which are modeled as type-increasing transformations, semi-determinism requires that two possible outcomes of the query to the same database I must be isomorphic, by an isomorphism that is a symmetry of I. But note that the latter condition on the isomorphism is actually voidly satisfied, since queries are type-increasing. When applying the same definition to arbitrary transformations, the condition becomes a real additional requirement. Formally, the requirement becomes: the isomorphism from J_1 to J_2 must map $I \cap J_1$ to $I \cap J_2$, where J_1 and J_2 are the two possible outcomes. For this definition to be workable, it needs to satisfy a reasonable compositionality criterion. At the end of Section 2 we gave such a criterion for determinate transformations. Since the semi-determinate transformations ought to include the determinate transformations, the searched for criterion needs to be at least as restrictive.

The following example puts a damper on the above proposal for semi-deterministic transformation. Let T_1 be the determinate transformation which adds to a unary relation S as many new elements as it originally contained:[6]

$$T_1 \equiv S \overset{+}{\Longleftarrow} \rho_{A \mapsto S} \pi_A \text{new}[A](S).$$

Furthermore, let T_2 be the transformation which deletes an arbitrary element from a unary relation S:

$$T_2 \equiv S \overset{-}{\Longleftarrow} \text{swap}(S).$$

---

[6] $\rho_{A \mapsto S}$ denotes a renaming.

Obviously, T_1 and T_2 are semi-deterministic according to the above proposal. However, when $T_1; T_2$ (defined as in the determinate case) is applied to a singleton relation $S = \{(a)\}$, a possible result of $T_1(S)$ is $\{(a), (b)\}$, and therefore two possible results of $T_1; T_2(S)$ are $\{(a)\}$ itself and $\{(b)\}$, which obviously violates the proposed requirement (since the intersection of S with the second result is empty, while the intersection with the first one is not).

Another possible natural generalization of the notion of semi-determinism from queries to updates is to simply require that two possible results are plainly isomorphic. In this case, compositionality is not a problem. In fact, even the classical composition can be used then.

Many other candidate definitions for semi-deterministic database transformation can be considered. For any of them, apart from the compositionality problem, there is another issue that must be taken into account: *completeness*.

Indeed, for the special case of queries, it can be shown that there exists a decidable sublanguage of SNIQL^q that is semi-deterministic-complete. This can be shown using the strategy to prove that IQL* is determinate-complete *up to copies* [5]. In contrast to the determinate situation, these copies do not pose a problem in a semi-deterministic setting, since they are isomorphic and can be eliminated in a semi-deterministic manner.[7] One can furthermore prove that the determinate strategy produces "sufficiently many" possible results; this is in turn not an issue in the determinate setting.[8]

Clearly, it is desirable to achieve semi-deterministic completeness also in the general database transformation case. This is a challenging open problem.

We conclude with the remark that in principle, semi-determinism can also be considered in the functional approach to object creation. However, in contrast to the determinate case, where the functional approach was not essentially different from the determinate approach, it is our belief that with respect to semi-determinism, there is is a fundamental difference between the two approaches. In particular, none of the main theorems presented here and in [31] seem to hold for the functional approach.

Acknowledgment

We are indebted to Marc Gyssens for inspiring discussions on the issues of compositionality of determinate database transformations and the completeness of SNIQL^q.

References

[1] S. Abiteboul and A. Bonner. Objects and views. In J. Clifford and R. King, editors, *Proceedings of the 1991 ACM SIGMOD International Conference on Management of Data*, volume 20:2 of *SIGMOD Record*, pages 238–247. ACM Press, 1991.

---

[7] This description is a gross simplification.

[8] We have indeed been able to settle the open problem mentioned in [31, page 198] affirmatively, contrary to the intuition expressed there.

[2] S. Abiteboul. Updates, a new frontier. In M. Gyssens, J. Paredaens, and D. Van Gucht, editors, *ICDT'88*, volume 326 of *Lecture Notes in Computer Science*, pages 1–18. Springer-Verlag, 1988.

[3] S. Abiteboul. Personal communication, 1990.

[4] S. Abiteboul and S. Grumbach. A rule-based langauge with functions and sets. *ACM Transactions on Database Systems*, 16(1):1–30, 1991.

[5] S. Abiteboul and P. Kanellakis. Object identity as a query language primitive. In J. Clifford, B. Lindsay, and D. Maier, editors, *Proceedings of the 1989 ACM SIGMOD International Conference on the Management of Data*, volume 18:2 of *SIGMOD Record*, pages 159–173. ACM Press, 1989.

[6] M. Andries and J. Paredaens. A language for generic graph-transformations. In *Graph-Theoretic Concepts in Computer Science*, volume 570 of *Lecture Notes in Computer Science*, pages 63–74. Springer-Verlag, 1992.

[7] S. Abiteboul, E. Simon, and V. Vianu. Non-deterministic languages to express deterministic transformations. In PODS [27], pages 218–229.

[8] A.V. Aho and J.D. Ullman. Universality of data retrieval languages. In *Proceedings of the ACM Symposium on Principles of Programming Languages*, pages 110–120, 1979.

[9] S. Abiteboul and V. Vianu. Equivalence and optimization of relational transactions. *Journal of the ACM*, 35:70–120, 1988.

[10] S. Abiteboul and V. Vianu. Procedural languages for database queries and updates. *Journal of Computer and System Sciences*, 41(2):181–229, 1990.

[11] S. Abiteboul and V. Vianu. Datalog extensions for database queries and updates. *Journal of Computer and System Sciences*, 43(1), 1991.

[12] S. Abiteboul and V. Vianu. Non-determinism in logic-based languages. *Annals of Mathematics and Artificial Intelligence*, 3:151–186, 1991.

[13] C. Beeri, S. Naqvi, R. Ramakrishnan, O. Shmueli, and S. Tsur. Sets and negation in a logic database language. In *Proceedings of the Sixth ACM Symposium on Principles of Database Systems*, pages 21–37. ACM Press, 1987.

[14] E. Dahlhaus and J.A. Makowsky. Computable directory queries. In *Logic and Computer Science: New Trends and Applications*, Rend. Sem. Mat. Univ. Pol. Torino, pages 165–197. 1987. An extended abstract appears in *LNCS 214*.

[15] M. Gyssens, J. Paredaens, and D. Van Gucht. A graph-oriented object database model. In PODS [27], pages 417–424.

[16] M. Gyssens, L.V. Saxton, and D. Van Gucht. Tagging as an alternative to object creation. In D. Maier and G. Vossen, editors, *Query Processing in Object-Oriented, Complex-Object and Nested Relation Databases*. Morgan Kaufmann, 1992. To appear.

[17] R. Hull and Y. Su. Untyped sets, invention, and computable queries In PODS [26], pages 347–359.

[18] A. Heuer and P. Sander. Classifying object-oriented query results in a class/type lattice. In B. Thalheim, J. Demetrovics, and H.-D. Gerhardt, editors, *MFDBS 91*, volume 495 of *Lecture Notes in Computer Science*, pages 14–28. Springer-Verlag, 1991.

[19] A. Heuer and P. Sander. Preserving and generating objects in the Living In A Lattice rule language. In *Proceedings Seventh International Conference on Data Engineering*, pages 562–569. IEEE Computer Society Press, 1991.

[20] R. Hull. Relative information capacity of simple relational schemata. *SIAM Journal on Computing*, 15(3):856–886, 1986.

[21] R. Hull, S. Widjojo, D. Wile, and M. Yoshikawa. On data restructuring and merging with object identity. *IEEE Data Engineering*, 14(2):18–22, June 1991.

[22] R. Hull and M. Yoshikawa. ILOG: Declarative creation and manipulation of object identifiers. In D. McLeod, R. Sacks-Davis, and H. Schek, editors, *Proceedings of the 16th International Conference on Very Large Data Bases*. Morgan Kaufmann, 1990.

[23] R. Hull and M. Yoshikawa. On the equivalence of database restructurings involving object identifiers. In PODS [28], pages 328–340.

[24] G. Kuper. Logic programming with sets. *Journal of Computer and System Sciences*, 41(1):44–64, 1990.

[25] M. Kifer and J. Wu. A logic for object-oriented logic programming (Maier's O-logic revisited). In PODS [26], pages 379–393.

[26] *Proceedings of the Eighth ACM Symposium on Principles of Database Systems*. ACM Press, 1989.

[27] *Proceedings of the Ninth ACM Symposium on Principles of Database Systems*. ACM Press, 1990.

[28] *Proceedings of the Tenth ACM Symposium on Principles of Database Systems*. ACM Press, 1991.

[29] S. Thomas and P. Fischer. Nested relational structures. In P. Kanellakis, editor, *The Theory of Databases*, pages 269–307. JAI Press, 1986.

[30] J. Van den Bussche and J. Paredaens. The expressive power of structured values in pure OODB's. In PODS [28], pages 291–299.

[31] J. Van den Bussche and D. Van Gucht. Semi-determinism. In *Proceedings 11th ACM Symposium on Principles of Database Systems*, pages 191–201. ACM Press, 1992.

[32] J. Van den Bussche, D. Van Gucht, M. Andries, and M. Gyssens. On the completeness of object-creating query languages. In *Proceedings 33rd Symposium on Foundations of Computer Science*, pages 372–379. IEEE Computer Society Press, 1992.

[33] D. Van Gucht. *Theory of unnormalized relational structures*. PhD thesis, Vanderbilt University, 1985.

[34] C. Zaniolo. Object identity and inheritance in deductive databases—an evolutionary approach. In W. Kim, J.-M. Nicolas, and S. Nishio, editors, *Proceedings 1st International Conference on Deductive and Object-Oriented Databases*, pages 2–19. Elsevier Science Publishers, 1989.

Rule-Based Updates of Objects

Specifying the Dynamics
of Complex Object Databases*

Luigi Palopoli

DEIS, Università della Calabria

87036 Rende (CS), Italy.

2102pal@csccuc.bitnet

Riccardo Torlone

IASI–CNR

Viale Manzoni 30, 00185 Roma, Italy.

torlone@iasi.rm.cnr.it

Abstract

In this paper, a rule-based language for specifying the evolution of a complex object database is defined. Several update operators are introduced, which correspond to basic manipulations of data entities with object identity. These operators can be used in rules bodies for specifying complex update transactions. The syntax and the semantics of the language is given with reference to a simple data model for complex objects with identity. The issues of integrity constraints maintenance and language expressibility is also discussed.

1   Introduction

Only very recently the fundamental issue of specifying the evolution of data in the framework of advanced data models have received a sufficient deal of attention in the specialized literature, although an adequate support of the update activity is a very important task that any database system has to carry out [2, 8, 9, 12, 17].

In this paper we are concerned with the design of an update language for manipulating a complex object database. Our data model of reference, which we shall refer to as CO, is a complex object database model deriving from the model of reference of Logidata+ [7], an advanced database system currently under development. Existing proposals in this field either refer to classical (relational) frameworks [11, 14, 15] or are based on interpreting the heads of logical rules as the specifications of updates defined on the classes associated to the head predicate symbols [1, 3, 5, 6]. Conversely, we will study the problems related to the design of an update language for complex objects having a top-down (i.e., procedure-call) oriented computational model.

An important point in dealing with objects is that equality of values does not imply identity. This is implemented by means of *object identifiers* which are generally invisible to the users. It follows that updates can only be specified referring to values and this fact could raise some problems. For instance, consider a database storing several objects identical in all their attribute values. Since these objects cannot be distinguished on the basis of their attribute values, to eliminate just one of them in this situation it is necessary to have the possibility to non-deterministically select just one object to be deleted. At the same time it can be useful to allow the elimination of all the objects sharing the

---

*This work has been partially supported by Consiglio Nazionale delle Ricerche, within "Progetto Finalizzato Sistemi Informatici e Calcolo Parallelo, LRC Logidata+".

same attribute values. Thus, we have defined a number of basic update operators corresponding to the primitive manipulations of data, which seem needed
to express updates, taking into account the presence of object identifiers. Such
basic operators are used for the definition of complex transactions, which are
organized in the form of sets of (possibly recursive) *update rules*. The language
has a non-deterministic semantics in the following sense: *(i)* it includes invention of object identifiers; *(ii)* it allows partially specified information to be used;
(iii) it includes two inherently finitely non-deterministic update operators; *(iv)*
when more than one update transaction can be activated at a time, just one
of them is non-deterministically chosen and executed. The rational underlying this choice is that non-determinism has several theoretical and pragmatical
advantages over determinism (refer to [4] for a clean discussion on this point),
without taking into account that the manipulation of data with identity is inti-
mately related to invention, and so to non-determinism. The main contribution
of this paper are:

- the complete definition of an operator based logic update language for
  complex object databases with a procedure-call oriented execution model,
  as opposed the bottom-up model of other well known logic update languages for databases;

- the characterization of the language expressive power;

- a discussion about how, within the update language, integrity constraints
  can be defined and maintained throughout update execution.

The paper is organized as follows. Section 2 illustrates, by some examples,
the capability of the language for specifying update transactions. In Section 3
the data model of reference is briefly described. Section 4 and Section 5 contain
the update language formal syntax and semantics, respectively. In Section 6,
the issue of maintaining integrity constraints throughout database evolution
is discussed. In Section 7 the expressibility of the language is investigated.
Finally, in Section 8 we summarize our conclusions. Because of space limitation
the proofs of the results are just sketched and can be found in [16].

2 Overview: the update language by examples

All the examples of this section refer to the database instance reported in
Figure 1: it is possible to see that a CO scheme is a collection of classes, each of
which denotes a set of objects. Each object is uniquely identified by its object
identifier (oid), which is not visible to the user, and is-a relationships can be
defined amongst classes. Further, attribute values of objects can be built from
explicit references to other objects. This is obtained using oid's as (components
of) attribute values. The attributes of an object for which the value is unknown
have associated the null value $\perp$.

In designing our update language, we have considered three basic update
activities, namely, insertions, deletions and modifications of objects. Being
the data model of reference object based, we can have different stored objects,
which are identical in the values of all the attributes (e.g., objects $\#p2$ and $\#p4$

person

	name	birthdate			sons
		dd	mm	yy	
#p2	Tom	[1	6	58]	∅
#p4	Tom	[1	6	58]	∅
#p5	Tom	[4	10	58]	{#p6}
#p6	John	[12	3	80]	⊥

student (isa person)

	st-code	follows
#p2	11056	{#c1,#c3}
#p6	23974	{#c2}

worker (isa person)

	salary	seniority
#p4	22000$	⊥
#p5	19500$	2

course

	duration	name
#c1	140	oper. syst.
#c2	⊥	compilers
#c3	160	databases

professor (isa worker)

	position	teaches	advises
#p4	full	{#c1}	{#p2}
#p5	associate	∅	{#p6}

Figure 1: A CO database instance

in person, Figure 1). Thus, for each basic update activity, the user is given the mean to specify whether a multiple-object execution (denoted by a ϕ subscript) or a single-object execution (denoted by a 1 s ubscript) is to be carried out. A resulting set of six basic update operators is hence obtained: INS_1, one object is inserted with a (new) system invented oid; INS_ϕ, a new object is inserted only if there does not already exist some object matching all the specified attribute values; DEL_ϕ, all the objects matching the specified attribute values are deleted; DEL_1, one non-deterministically chosen object matching the specified attribute values (if any) is deleted; MOD_ϕ, all the objects matching the specified attribute values are modified; MOD_1, one non-deterministically chosen object matching the specified attribute values (if any) is modified. The set of basic update operations further includes the "null effect" update operator, denoted by SKIP.

Example 1 *Assume we want to store a new person in the database, with name John, and we want this new person to be stored in any case, even if there is another person having John as the name; in this case we use:*

$\leftarrow INS_1(person(X, [name : john]))$.

We point out that the variable with no associated attribute label, X in this case, denotes the object as a whole: this variable takes the (system invented) value of the oid of the new object as its value. The deletion of one person named Tom, born on 1-6-58 and without sons can be specified with:

$\leftarrow DEL_1(person(X, [name : Tom, birthdate : [dd : 1, mm : 6, yy : 58], sons :\emptyset]))$.

In this case one object, out of #p2 and #p4, is non-deterministically chosen and deleted from the database. Finally, we can use:

$\leftarrow MOD_\phi(worker(X, [seniority : 2, salary : S])|[salary : S * 1.1]))$.

to raise of the salary of all the workers having a seniority of two years.

Updating a database is, to a major extent, an inherently sequential activity. This procedurality explicitly reflects in the language, and updates are executed in goals from left to right, in the order in which they appear. Thus, in $\leftarrow u_1, u_2$, the update u_1 is executed first, and then u_2 is executed. It is possible to specify also conditional updates. A conditional update is one which is executed only if some logical guard is satisfied. For instance, consider the update $\leftarrow c_1, u, c_2$ where c_1 and c_2 are conditions (i.e., conjunctions of logical literals) and u is an update predicate. The effect of executing the above conditional update coincides with the execution of the simple update $\leftarrow u$ if and only if: *(i)* the condition c_1 is true with respect to the database status at the time of execution, and *(ii)* the condition c_2 is true with respect to the status the database would assume if u were run. Thus, c_1 stands for a pre-condition whereas c_2 is a post-condition to the execution of u. The evaluation of c_1 produces bindings which can be used to supply values to update operators following it into the left to right order (only u in the case at hand) and also to specify join conditions to other literals.

Example 2 *Assume we want to add the information that if there is a person with name Jim and birthdate 1-1-91 then he is the son of a person named Tom, born on 1-6-58. This can be accomplished by:*

```
← person(Y,[name:jim,birthdate:[dd:1,mm:1,yy:91]]),
   MOD₁(person(Z,[name:tom,birthdate:[dd:6,mm:1,yy:58],sons:S])|
                  [sons:S∪{Y}])).
```

where the first literal of the goal returns the binding for the variable Y, that is, the oid of a person named Jim and born on 1-1-91. Recall that the choice on which person (out of #p2 and #p4) is to be modified is taken by the system nondeterministically.

We point out that we have decided to treat updates as denoting pure "db-state transformations", and therefore, basic operators do not produce bindings.

Updates can be organized in the form of rules which implement complex manipulations. Rules are activated calling the execution of the corresponding head predicates. The head predicate of an update rule may include variables in its arguments which are used to supply input data to the transaction.

Example 3 *Assume that each professor has his salary incremented by 100$ for each advised student, and that we can assign one professor as advisor of a student if the student follows one of his courses, and if, after the assignment, the average of professors' salary is less than 40000$. Then, a transaction assigning an advisor to a student can be implemented as follows:*

```
assign-advisor(S) ← student(X,[st-code:S,follows:C1]),
                    professor(Y,[teaches:C2]),C1∩C2<>∅,
                    MOD₁(professor(Y,[advises:A,salary:S])|
                                   [advises:A∪{X},
                                    salary:S+100]),
                    average(salary.professor)<40000.
```

Thus, if we want to assign an advisor to a student whose code is 11056, we can activate the transaction with: ←assign-advisor(11056).

Once an update predicate has been defined it can be used in the body of other update rules. In particular, the head update predicate can be used in the body of rules transitively associated with it, henceforth obtaining a set of recursive update rules. The execution of a set of update rules proceeds as follows. One of the rules associated with the update predicate is activated nondeterministically, and its body is executed. On fail (when some guard condition is not satisfied), another update rule associated with the called update predicate is tried, and so on until no more executions can be activated.

Example 4 *Assume we have decided to level-up the salary of the workers having a certain seniority given as input. This can be accomplished by a recursive update, as follows:*

```
level-up(Y) ← worker(X,[seniority:Y,salary:S]),
              worker(Z,[seniority:Y,salary:T]),S>T,
              MOD₁(worker(X,[salary:T])|[salary:S]),level-up(Y).
level-up(Y) ← ¬(worker(X,[seniority:Y,salary:S]),
              worker(Z,[seniority:Y,salary:T]),S>T),SKIP().
```

Intuitively, the update works as follows: a pair of workers with the same se-niority given as input but with different salaries are searched for. If such a pair exists, then the precondition in the first rule is satisfied and therefore its body is executed and so the salary of the worker that earns less is changed to the higher salary; otherwise, the second rule is activated and so the transac-tion terminates. In the first case the update is recursively called to perform the same operations again. Thus, if we want to level-up the salary of the workers having a seniority of 2 years, then the whole transaction can be activated using ←level-up(2).

3 A model for complex objects with identity

For a formal definition of the update language we shall refer to a simple data model, called $\mathcal{CO}$, which is object based in the sense that the only allowed struc-ture construct is the *class*. A $\mathcal{CO}$ class is a set of objects, complex entities for which value equality of objects does not imply identity – this is implemented by means of object identifiers, which are not visible to the user. An object is built from base values and oid's using set and tuple constructors. Moreover, gener-alization hierarchies among classes can be built by means of *is-a* relationships with inherited properties.

Let $\mathcal{B}$ be a finite set of *base type names* with associated to each $B \in \mathcal{B}$ a set of *base values* $\mathrm{V}(B)$ in such a way that the sets of values are pairwise disjoint. We shall denote with DOM the union of the sets of base values: $\mathrm{DOM} = \cup_{B \in \mathcal{B}} \mathrm{V}(B)$. A $\mathcal{CO}$ *scheme* is a triple $\mathbf{S} = (\mathbf{C}, \mathrm{TYP}, \mathrm{ISA})$ with associated a set $\mathrm{TYPES}(\mathbf{S})$ of *types*, where:

- $\mathbf{C}$ is a set of symbols called *class names*;

- A *type* of $\mathbf{S}$ is one of the following: (1) if B is a base type name in $\mathcal{B}$, then B is a type of $\mathbf{S}$; (2) if C is a class name in $\mathbf{C}$, then C is a type of $\mathbf{S}$; (3) if τ is a type of $\mathbf{S}$, then $\{\tau\}$ is also a type of $\mathbf{S}$, called a *set* type; (4) if $\tau_1, \ldots, \tau_k$, with $k > 0$, are types of $\mathbf{S}$ and $A_1, \ldots, A_k$ are distinct labels, then $[A_1 : \tau_1, \ldots, A_k : \tau_k]$ is also a type of $\mathbf{S}$ (called a *tuple* type) in which the order of components is immaterial; (5) $\{\}$ and $[]$ are types of $\mathbf{S}$, called the *empty set* type and the *empty tuple* type respectively (they are useful for technical reasons);

- TYP is a function that associates to each symbol in $\mathbf{C}$ a tuple type of $\mathbf{S}$;

- ISA is a partial order over $\mathbf{C}$, with the condition that if $C_1 \mathrm{ISA} C_2$, then $\mathrm{TYP}(C_1)$ is a refinement of $\mathrm{TYP}(C_2)$ according to the definition given below.

A type τ is a *refinement* of a type τ' (in symbols $\tau \preceq \tau'$) if and only if at least one of the following conditions hold: (1) $\tau = \tau'$; (2) $\tau, \tau' \in \mathbf{C}$ and $\tau \mathrm{ISA} \tau'$; (3) $\tau = \{\tau_1\}$ and either $\tau' = \{\}$ or $\tau' = \{\tau'_1\}$ with $\tau_1 \preceq \tau'_1$; (4) $\tau = [A_1 : \tau_1, \ldots, A_k : \tau_k, \ldots, A_{k+p} : \tau_{k+p}]$, $\tau' = [A_1 : \tau'_1, \ldots, A_k : \tau'_k]$, with $k \geq 0$, $p > 0$, and $\tau_i \preceq \tau'_i$, for $1 \leq i \leq k$. It can be shown that the refinement relationship $\preceq$ induces a lower semilattice on $\mathrm{TYPES}(\mathbf{S})$, defined as the set of types of $\mathbf{S}$ augmented with a special type τ_ϵ, such that $\tau_\epsilon \preceq \tau$, for every

$\tau \in \text{TYPES}(\mathbf{S})$; therefore, we can speak of *greatest lower bound (glb)* of a finite set of types.

Let $\mathcal{O}$ a countable set of oid's and $\perp$ be a special symbol (called the *null value*) denoting an undefined value regardless of its type. Then, we associate with each type τ of $\mathbf{S}$ the set $\text{VAL}(\tau)$ of its possible values, called the *value-set* of τ, as follows: (1) if $\tau = B \in \mathcal{B}$, then $\text{VAL}(\tau) = \text{v}(B) \cup \{\perp\}$; (2) if τ is a class name $C \in \mathbf{C}$, then $\text{VAL}(\tau) = \mathcal{O} \cup \{\perp\}$; (3) if τ is a set type, that is, it has the form $\{\tau'\}$, then its value-set is the family of the finite subsets of $\text{VAL}(\tau')$ augmented with the null value $\perp$; (4) if τ is a tuple type $[A_1 : \tau_1, \ldots, A_k : \tau_k]$, $k > 0$, then $\text{VAL}(\tau) = \{t : \{A_1, \ldots, A_k\} \to \cup_{i=1}^{k}\text{VAL}(\tau_i) \mid t(A_i) \in \text{VAL}(\tau_i), \text{for } 1 \leq i \leq k\} \cup \{\perp\}$; (5) $\text{VAL}(\{\})$ is the empty set and $\text{VAL}([\,])$ is the empty tuple.

Let $\text{CDOM}(\mathbf{S}) = \cup_{\tau \in \text{TYPES}(\mathbf{S})}\text{VAL}(\tau)$, that is, the union of all the value-sets of the types of $\mathbf{S}$. A *potential instance* $\mathbf{s}$ of a $\mathcal{CO}$ scheme $\mathbf{S} = (\mathbf{C}, \text{TYP}, \text{ISA})$, is a pair $\mathbf{s} = (\mathbf{c}, \mathbf{o})$, where: *(i)* $\mathbf{c}$ is a function that associates with each class name $C \in \mathbf{C}$ a finite set of oid's $(\mathbf{c}(C) \subseteq \mathcal{O})$, *(ii)* $\mathbf{o}$ is a partial function from $\mathcal{O}$ to $\text{CDOM}(\mathbf{S})$ with the conditions that for every $C \in \mathbf{C}$ and for every $o \in \mathbf{c}(C)$, $\mathbf{o}(o)$ is defined and belongs to the value-set of a type τ that is a refinement of the type $\text{TYP}(C)$.

An instance $\mathbf{s} = (\mathbf{c}, \mathbf{o})$ of a $\mathcal{CO}$ scheme $\mathbf{S} = (\mathbf{C}, \text{TYP}, \text{ISA})$ is *oid-coherent* if and only if: (1) for every $C_1 \text{ ISA } C_2$, it is the case that $\mathbf{c}(C_1) \subseteq \mathbf{c}(C_2)$; (2) if $\mathbf{c}(C_1) \cap \mathbf{c}(C_2) \neq \emptyset$ then there is a class C in $\mathbf{C}$ such that $C_1 \text{ISA} C$ and $C_2 \text{ISA} C$; (3) for the value sets, if C is a class, then $\text{VAL}(C) = \mathbf{c}(C) \cup \{\perp\}^1$.

4   Update language syntax

Let $\mathbf{S} = (\mathbf{C}, \text{TYP}, \text{ISA})$ be a $\mathcal{CO}$ scheme, $\mathbf{U}$ be a set of symbols called *update predicate names* such that each $u \in \mathbf{U}$ has a fixed arity and each argument of u has associated a fixed type of $\mathbf{S}$, $\mathbf{B} = \{\text{INS}_\phi, \text{INS}_1, \text{DEL}_1, \text{DEL}_\phi, \text{MOD}_1, \text{MOD}_\phi, \text{SKIP}\}$ be the set of the *basic update operators* and, for each type τ of $\mathbf{S}$, let $\mathbf{V}_\tau$ be a countable set of *variable names* of type τ. We assume to have at disposal a predefined set $\mathbf{F}$ of interpreted built-in functions on sets (union, intersection and difference), and a set of typed equality predicates $\mathbf{P}$, with each argument (and range for functions) of a fixed type of $\mathbf{S}$.

A *constant* is a value from the union of the base values of $\mathbf{S}$; since the base values are pairwise disjoint, each constant has a unique type.

An *(ordinary) term* is one of the following:

- a variable or a constant;

- if $f \in \mathbf{F}$ with arity $l > 0$ and t_i is a term of the same type associated with the i-*th* argument of f, for $1 \leq i \leq l$, then $f(t_1, \ldots, t_l)$ is a *function* term whose type is the type of the range of f;

- if t_i is a term of type τ_i, for $1 \leq i \leq m$, $m \geq 0$, then $\{t_1, \ldots, t_m\}$ is a *set* term whose type is $\{glb(\tau_1, \ldots, \tau_m)\}$ if $m > 0$, and $\{\}$ if $m = 0$ (in this case it denotes the empty set);

---

[1]The notion of coherent instance refines the notion of potential instance in the sense that it prevents possible inconsistencies among occurrences of oid's in an instance.

- if t_i is a term of type τ_i, for $1 \leq i \leq n$, $n \geq 0$, and $A_1, \ldots, A_n$ are distinct labels, then $[A_1 : t_1, \ldots, A_n : t_n]$ is a *tuple* term whose type is $[A_1 : \tau_1, \ldots, A_n : \tau_n]$ if $n > 0$, and $[\,]$ if $n = 0$ (in this case it denotes the empty tuple).

A term is *ground* if no variable occurs in it. A term is *closed* if either it is a ground function term or all the function terms occurring in it are ground. Note that since we have considered only interpreted functions, in a closed term all the function applications can be replaced by their actual images.

An *atom* is one of the following:

- if $C \in \mathbf{C}$, X is a variable of a class type τ such that $C \preceq \tau$ (so that the possible values for X are oid's for C or for a superclass of C) and t is a tuple term of a type τ' such that $\text{TYP}(C) \preceq \tau'$ (so that, in the case of partial information, there is no need to specify all the possible attributes of $\text{TYP}(C)$ but just some them), then $C(X, t)$ is an *object* atom, where X and t are called the *object variable* (it denotes the oid of an object) and the *object specification* of the atom respectively; for simplicity, if t is the empty tuple, $C(X)$ will be used instead of $C(X, [\,])$;

- if $p \in \mathbf{P}$ with arity $m > 0$ and, for $1 \leq i \leq m$, t_i is a term of the same type associated with the i-*th* argument of p, then $p(t_1, \ldots, t_m)$ is a *built-in* atom.

A *literal* can be static or dynamic. A *static* literal can be in turn simple or composed. A *simple* static literal is an atom (positive atom) or an atom preceded by the symbol $\neg$ (negated atom). A *composed* static literal is a conjunction of static literals delimited by brackets and preceded by the symbol $\neg$ (it is used to express complex negative conditions). A *dynamic* literal can be instead basic or defined. A *basic* dynamic literal can be built using the basic update operators as follows:

- if O is an object atom, then $\text{INS}_1(O)$ and $\text{INS}_\phi(O)$ are basic *inserting* literals;

- if O is an object atom, then $\text{DEL}_1(O)$ and $\text{DEL}_\phi(O)$ are basic *deleting* literals;

- if $O = C(X, t)$ is an object atom and t' is a tuple term such that the type of t is a refinement of the type of t', then $\text{MOD}_1(O \mid t')$ and $\text{MOD}_\phi(O \mid t')$ are basic *modifying* literals;

- $\text{SKIP}()$ is the *null-effect* basic update literal.

A *defined* dynamic literal (also called for simplicity an *update literal*) has the form $u(t_1, \ldots, t_l)$ where $u \in \mathbf{U}$ with arity $l \geq 0$ and, for $0 \leq i \leq l$, t_i is a term of the same type associated with the i-*th* argument of u.

An *(update) rule* is an expression of the form $U \leftarrow L_1, \ldots, L_n$. where U (the *head*) is an update literal and $L_1, \ldots, L_n$ (the *body*) is a conjunction of (static or dynamic) literals, with at least one dynamic literal occuring in it. An *update goal* is a rule which has an empty head, that is, an expression of the form $\leftarrow L_1, \ldots, L_m$. An *UCO program* (a short-hand for Updating Complex

Objects) for the scheme **S** is a finite set of rules. Finally, let P be a program and G a goal; we say that G is a goal for P if each update literal occuring in G also occurs in the head of some rule in P.

5 Update language semantics

In this section we formally define a semanitcs of $\mathcal{UCO}$ programs. Before that, we shall introduce some preliminary concept.

5.1 Preliminaries

Let **S** be a $\mathcal{CO}$ scheme, an *extended term* on **S** is defined as an ordinary term with the only difference that the oid's and the null value are also terms. In the sequel we will consider only *extended atoms* and *extended literals* which are built from extended terms instead of ordinary terms.

Let $\text{VAR}(\mathbf{S}) = \cup_{\tau \in \text{TYPES}(\mathbf{S})} \mathbf{V}_\tau$. A *substitution* θ is a function from $\text{VAR}(\mathbf{S})$ to $\text{VAR}(\mathbf{S}) \cup \text{CDOM}(\mathbf{S})$, We shall denote with $\theta_\perp$ the ground substitution such that $\theta_\perp(X) = \perp$, for every $X \in \text{VAR}(\mathbf{S})$, and with θ_{new}^s the ground substitution which associates to each object variable a (new) oid in $\mathcal{O}$ not already appearing in the instance s.

Let t be a closed term whose type is $\tau \in \text{TYPES}(\mathbf{S})$ and let τ' be another type of **S** such that $\tau' \preceq \tau$. We say that the *extension* of t to τ' (in symbols $\text{EXT}_{\tau'}(t)$) is the term obtained as follows:

- if t is a variable then $\text{EXT}_{\tau'}(t)$ is a variable in $\mathbf{V}_{\tau'}$ not appearing elsewhere;

- if t is a constant then $\text{EXT}_{\tau'}(t) = t$;

- if t is a set term of the form $t = \{t_1, \ldots, t_m\}$, $m \geq 0$, and $\tau' = \{\tau_1'\}$, then $\text{EXT}_{\tau'}(t) = \{\text{EXT}_{\tau_1'}(t_1), \ldots, \text{EXT}_{\tau_1'}(t_m)\}$;

- if t is a tuple term of the form $t = [A_1 : t_1, \ldots, A_n : t_n]$, $\tau = [A_1 : \tau_1, \ldots, A_n : \tau_n]$ and $\tau' = [A_1 : \tau_1', \ldots, A_n : \tau_n', A_{n+1} : \tau_{n+1}', \ldots, A_{n+p} : \tau_{n+p}']$, $n \geq 0$, $p \geq 0$, then we have $\text{EXT}_{\tau'}(t) = [A_1 : \text{EXT}_{\tau_1'}(t_1), \ldots, A_n : \text{EXT}_{\tau_n'}(t_n), A_{n+1} : X_{n+1}, \ldots, A_{n+p} : X_{n+p}]$, where, for $1 \leq i \leq p$, X_{n+i} is a variable in $\mathbf{V}_{\tau_{n+i}'}$ not appearing elsewhere.

Let t be a ground term of type $\tau \in \text{TYPES}(\mathbf{S})$ and $\gamma \in \text{CDOM}(\mathbf{S})$ an element from the value sets of **S**. We say that t *matches* with γ (in symbols $t \mapsto \gamma$) if and only if $\gamma \in \text{VAL}(\tau)$ and one of the following conditions hold: *(i)* t is a constant and $\gamma = t$; *(ii)* $t = \{t_1, \ldots, t_m\}$, $m \geq 0$, and for each $\gamma_1 \in \gamma$ there is a term t_i, $1 \leq i \leq m$, such that $t_i \mapsto \gamma_1$, and vice versa; *(iii)* $t = [A_1 : t_1, \ldots, A_n : t_n]$, $\gamma = [A_1 : \gamma_1, \ldots, A_n : \gamma_n]$, $n \geq 0$, and, for $1 \leq i \leq n$, $t_i \mapsto \gamma_i$ ($\gamma = []$ for $n = 0$).

Finally, let $O = C(\hat{t}, t)$ be a closed object atom; we can associate a truth value to O ($\neg O$) with respect to an instance s of **S** as follows: O is true in s if there exists (not exists) an element $o \in \text{c}(C)$ and a ground substitution θ such that $o = \hat{t}\theta$ and $\text{EXT}_\tau(t)\theta \mapsto \text{o}(o)$, being τ the type of $\text{o}(o)$, and it is false otherwise. If an atom O is true in an instance s, then we say that a substitution verifying the condition above is a *valuation* of O in s.

Example 5 *Let O = worker(X,[name:Tom,birthdate:[yy:58],salary:Y])
and s be the instance in Figure 1. Then we have that O is true in s because of the
object #p4 that matches with the tuple term in O. In fact, the extension of such
a term to the type worker is:* [name:Tom,birthdate:[dd:V,mm:W,yy:43],
sons:Z,salary:Y,seniority:T]], *and a valuation of O in s is the substitution:* $\theta = \{X/\#p4, V/1, W/6, Z/\emptyset, Y/22000, T/\perp\}$.

5.2 The semantics

Let **S** be a $\mathcal{CO}$ scheme. We start by considering the basic dynamic literals of
the language: we say that a basic dynamic literal B, is *workable* if (1) B is
either an inserting or a deleting literal and it is closed, (2) $B = u(C(X,t) \mid t')$
is a modifying literal and: *(a)* $C(X,t)$ is closed, and *(b)* each variable in t'
occuring in a function term also occurs in t.

The semantics of the basic operators is based on the notion of *set of potential
solutions* for the application of a workable basic dynamic literal B to an instance
s of **S**, denoted with $\Upsilon_B(s)$, and defined as follows:

- $\Upsilon_{\mathbf{INS}_1(C(\hat{\imath},t))}(s)$ is the singleton $\{s\}$ if $\hat{\imath} \in o(C)$, otherwise it is the set
  of pairs of functions $s' = (c',o')$ such that $c' = c$ and $o' = o$ except
  that: *(i)* let $o = \hat{\imath}\theta^s_{new}$, then $c'(C') = c(C') \cup \{o\}$, for each class C'
  such that $C\mathrm{ISA}C'$, and *(ii)* o' is also defined on o as follows: $o'(o) =$
  $\mathrm{EXT}_{\mathrm{TYP}(C)}(t)\theta_\perp$;

- $\Upsilon_{\mathbf{INS}_\phi(C(\hat{\imath},t))}(s)$ is the singleton $\{s\}$ if either $\hat{\imath} \in o(C)$ or $C(\hat{\imath},t)$ is true in
  s, otherwise it coincides with $\Upsilon_{\mathbf{INS}_1(C(\hat{\imath},t))}(s)$;

- $\Upsilon_{\mathbf{DEL}_\phi(C(\hat{\imath},t))}(s)$ is the singleton $\{s\}$ if $C(\hat{\imath},t)$ is false in s, otherwise it
  is the set of pairs of functions $s' = (c',o')$ such that $c' = c$ and $o' = o$
  except that: *(i)* for each valuation θ of $C(\hat{\imath},t)$ in s and for each class C'
  such that $\hat{\imath}\theta \in c(C')$, $c'(C') = c(C') - \{\hat{\imath}\theta\}$, *(ii)* o' is no longer defined
  on $\hat{\imath}\theta$, *(iii)* in the co-domain of o', $\hat{\imath}\theta$ is replaced by $\perp$;

- $\Upsilon_{\mathbf{DEL}_1(C(\hat{\imath},t))}(s)$ is the singleton $\{s\}$ if $C(\hat{\imath},t)$ is false in s, otherwise it is
  the set of pairs of functions $s' = (c',o')$ such that $c' = c$ and $o' = o$ except
  that: *(i)* let θ be a valuation of $C(\hat{\imath},t)$ in s, then $c'(C') = c(C') - \{\hat{\imath}\theta\}$,
  for each class C' such that $\hat{\imath}\theta \in c(C')$, *(ii)* o' is no longer defined on $\hat{\imath}\theta$,
  (iii) in the co-domain of o', $\hat{\imath}\theta$ is replaced by $\perp$;

- $\Upsilon_{\mathbf{MOD}_\phi(C(\hat{\imath},t)|t')}(s)$ is the singleton $\{s\}$ if $C(\hat{\imath},t)$ is false in s, otherwise it
  is the set of pairs of functions $s' = (c',o')$ such that $c' = c$ and $o' = o$
  except that: for each valuation θ of $C(\hat{\imath},t)$ in s, $o'(\hat{\imath}\theta) = \mathrm{EXT}_\tau(t')\theta$, where
  τ is the type of $o(\hat{\imath}\theta)$;

- $\Upsilon_{\mathbf{MOD}_1(C(\hat{\imath},t)|t')}(s)$ is the singleton $\{s\}$ if $C(\hat{\imath},t)$ is false in s, otherwise it
  is the set of pairs of functions $s' = (c',o')$ such that $c' = c$ and $o' = o$
  except that: let θ be a valuation of $C(\hat{\imath},t)$ in s, then $o'(\hat{\imath}\theta) = \mathrm{EXT}_\tau(t')\theta$,
  where τ is the type of $o(\hat{\imath}\theta)$;

- $\Upsilon_{\text{SKIP}()}(s)$ is the singleton $\{s\}$.

Let $\alpha = B_1, \ldots, B_n$ be a sequence of basic dynamic literals. Then, the set of potential solutions for the application of $\leftarrow \alpha$ to an instance s of S coincides with the set of pairs of functions $s_n = (c_n, o_n)$, such that, for $1 \leq i \leq n$ and $s_0 = s$, $s_i \in \Upsilon_{B_i}(s_{i-1})$.

Let $\beta = D_1, \ldots, D_n$ be a conjunction of closed static literals (the order in which they appear is immaterial here). We say that β $(\neg(\beta))$ is true in s if there exists (there not exists) a set of valuations $\theta_1, \ldots, \theta_p$, $1 \leq p \leq n$, of all the positive object literals (i.e., the object atoms) of β such that, being $D'_1, \ldots, D'_{n-p}$ the other literals of β, the conjunction $(D'_1, \ldots, D'_{n-p})\theta_1, \ldots, \theta_p$ is true, and it is false otherwise. If β is true, then the composition of the valuations $\theta_1, \ldots, \theta_p$ is called a *valuation* of β in s.

Now, let $\mu = \beta_1, \alpha_1, \beta_2, \ldots, \beta_{n-1}, \alpha_n, \beta_{n+1}$, $n > 1$, be a sequence of literals such that β_i is a sequence of static literals and α_i a sequence of basic dynamic literals, for $1 \leq i \leq n$. Then, we say that the goal $\leftarrow \mu$ is *applicable* to an instance s of $\bar{S}$ if, for $1 \leq i \leq n$ and $s_0 = s$, there exists a valuation θ_i of $\beta_i \theta_1 \ldots \theta_{i-1}$ in s_{i-1}, such that $\beta_{i+1} \theta_1 \ldots \theta_i$ is true in s_i, where s_i is a potential solution for the application of $\leftarrow \alpha_i \theta_1 \ldots \theta_i$ to s_{i-1}. If $\leftarrow \mu$ is applicable, there is associated to it a notion of set of potential solutions for the application $\leftarrow \mu$ to s.

Let P be an $\mathcal{UCO}$ program for S and $G = \leftarrow L_1, \ldots, L_n$ be a goal for P. An *expansion* G^* of G with respect to P is the last element of a sequence of goals $G = G_0, G_1, \ldots, G_k = G^*$ such that: if U_j is an update literal occurring in G_{i-1} and there is (a variant of) a rule R in P (in such a way that R does not have any variable which already appears in G_{i-1}), such that U_j and the head of R unify with unifier σ, then G_i is derived from G_{i-1} and R using σ, for $1 \leq i \leq k$. If G^* does not contain update literals, then we say that it is a *full* expansion of G with respect to P.

Finally, let s be an instance of S, if there exists a full expansion G^* of G with respect to P that is applicable to s, then a *(possible) result* for the application of $P \cup \{G\}$ to s is a potential solution for the application of G^* to s, otherwise the result is s itself.

Theorem 1 *Let s be a coherent instance of S, then a result for the application of $P \cup \{G\}$ to s is also a coherent instance of S.*

Sketch of Proof. The proof is based on the observation that, by definition, the potential solutions of the application of a single basic dynamic literal to a coherent instance are coherent instances themselves, and that the application of a full expansion of a goal to an instance corresponds to the application of a goal containing only (bounded occurences of) basic dynamic literals. Thus, the claim follows by induction on the number of basic dynamic literals in the goal. $\square$

It should be noted that for simplicity, but by abuse of notation, the same punctuation symbol "," is used here with two meanings; it stands for sequential composition if it preceeds or follows a dynamic literal, it stands for logical 'and' otherwise.

We point out that, in verifying for applicability of a sequence of literals, some problems may arise. In particular it may be the case that at a certain point an object literal needs to be evaluated but it is not closed, or that a potential solution for the application of a basic dynamic literal needs to be found but the the literal is not workable. In [16] we show that opportune safety conditions can be given in order to overcome such difficulties.

6 Maintaining integrity constraints

In Section 3 we defined the concept of oid-coherent instance, as one which verifies the constraints induced by the presence of is-a relationships and references amongst objects through oid's (the so called "inherent constraints" of the model). The semantics of basic operators is defined in such a way to implicitly maintain inherent constraints (see Section 5). In general, also other constraints could be explicity defined on a database schema, describing several sorts of dependencies amongst data. In this section we shall discuss the maintenance of explicit constraints, adopting a rather informal presentation style.

For instance, assume the presence of a set of functional dependencies from the attribute st-code to all the others in the class student (i.e., in relational terms, st-code is a *key* for student). For these constraints to be dynamically maintained, two different politics can be adopted:

1. a tight politics, which consists in imposing that any insertion and modification on the class student can take place only if the newly inserted object does not violate them;

2. a loose politics, which consists in allowing a (complex) update to temporarily violate the constraints and in restoring a consistent database state as soon as the update halts.

In the example at hand, the former politics can be implemented by defining two new update predicates, $\text{INS}_\phi^{\text{student}}$ and $\text{INS}_1^{\text{student}}$ which are to be used in the place of INS_ϕ and INS_1 when applied to student. The definition of the new predicates is as follows:

$$\text{INS}_\phi^{\text{student}}(X,t) \leftarrow \text{INS}_\phi(\text{student}(X,t)), \neg(\text{student}(Z,[\text{st-code}:C]),$$
$$\text{student}(Y,[\text{st-code}:C]),Y<>Z).$$

$$\text{INS}_1^{\text{student}}(X,t) \leftarrow \text{INS}_\phi(\text{student}(X,t)), \neg(\text{student}(Z,[\text{st-code}:C]),$$
$$\text{student}(Y,[\text{st-code}:C]),Y<>Z).$$

The negative condition in the rules above causes the update to fail (i.e., to produce a null effect) if the functional dependencies are violated by the newly inserted objects. A similar technique can be used to assure constraint maintenance through modification executions. So, two new modification predicates on student are defined, which are to be executed in the place of the corresponding basic ones.

To adopt the latter politics, a number of update rules have to be defined which check and possibly restore a consistent database state. With reference to our example, the following recursive rule can be defined:

```
restore() ← student(X,[st-code:C]),student(Y,[st-code:C]),
            X<>Y,DEL₁(student(Y,[st-code:C])),restore().
restore() ← ¬ (student(X,[st-code:C]),student(Y,[st-code:C]),
            X<>Y),SKIP().
```

The restoring update literal restore() is then to be called immediately after any update including modifications or insertions on student.

In a similar way any constraint could be taken care of either by "coding" in the language suitable modifications of the appropriate update operators or by programming the proper restoring update rules. We note that restoring rules could also be specialized to optimize the restoring phase or to implement particular restoring politics. The reference [16] contains a more detailed discussion about the constraint maintenance issue.

7 Expressibility

In this section we shall discuss the computational power of the $\mathcal{UCO}$ language. In particular we shall show that it allows to express all the non-deterministic database transformations between instances, with the limitations that invention regards object identifiers only. Before showing this, several concepts are needed, which are recalled next.

The semantics of an $\mathcal{UCO}$ program and goal, can be described as a set of pairs (s, s') of input/output instances. This is called the *effect* of the program and the goal [5]. Thus, given a $\mathcal{UCO}$ program P for a $\mathcal{CO}$ scheme S and a goal G for P, the *effect* of P and G with respect to S, denoted $\text{EFF}(S, P, G)$, is defined as: $\text{EFF}(S, P, G) = \{(s, s') \mid s, s' \in \text{INST}(S)$ *and* s' *is a result for the application of* $P \cup \{G\}$ *to* $s\}$. However, when speaking about the expressive power of a database transformation language it is worth referring to an input and an output schema. So, let R and S be the $\mathcal{CO}$ input and output schema respectively, P be a $\mathcal{UCO}$ program for $R \cup S$ and G be goal for P. The effect of P and G with respect to R and S, denoted $\text{EFF}((R, S), P, G)$, is the following subset of $\text{INST}(R) \times \text{INST}(S)$: $\{(r, s) \mid \exists (r', s') \in \text{EFF}(R \cup S, P, G), \pi_R(r') = r, \pi_S(s') = s$ *and* $\pi_S(r')$ *contains only empty classes*$\}$.

Now, we consider the class of transformations defined by our language. So, the *transformations defined by* $\mathcal{UCO}$, denoted by $\text{TRANS}(\mathcal{UCO})$, is defined as: $\text{TRANS}(\mathcal{UCO}) = \{\text{EFF}((R, S), P, G) \mid R$ *and* S *are* $\mathcal{CO}$ schemas, P *is a* $\mathcal{UCO}$ *program for* $R \cup S$, *and* G *is a goal for* $P\}$. The *active domain* of an instance s ($\text{ADOM}(s)$) is that subset of DOM which occurs in s. In our context, we allow invention of values to take place only relatively to oid's. So we say that a binary relation $\varphi \subseteq \text{INST}(R) \times \text{INST}(S)$ is *without constants invention* if there exists a finite set $C \subseteq \text{DOM}$ such that for each pair $(r, s) \in \varphi$, $\text{ADOM}(s) \subseteq \text{ADOM}(r) \cup C$. It is usually requested that database mappings do not interpret domain values except, at most, for a finite set. This concept is formalized next. Let K be a finite subset of DOM. A binary relation $\varphi \subseteq \text{INST}(R) \times \text{INST}(S)$ is K−generic if for each bijection ρ over $\text{DOM} \cup \mathcal{O}$ which is the identity on K, it is the case that $(r, s) \in \varphi$ if and only if $(\rho(r), \rho(s)) \in \varphi$.

We shall next define the concept of non-deterministic database transformation [5], in our context. Clearly not any instance can be the result of a transformation of complex object database instances. For example, type constraints have to be verified. Therefore, following other authors [5, 3, 13], we define a the notion of database transformation which accounts for the legal input-output correspondences between instances.

Definition 1 *A binary relation φ over CO instances is a* non-deterministic database update transformation *if there exists two CO schemata $\mathbf{R}$ and $\mathbf{S}$ and a set $K \subseteq \text{DOM}$ such that:*

1. $\varphi \subseteq \text{INST}(\mathbf{R}) \times \text{INST}(\mathbf{S})$,

2. φ *is recursively enumerable,*

3. φ *is without constants invention,*

4. φ *is K-generic.*

In the above definition, the first condition is used to fix the input and the output schemata. The second condition restricts allowed mappings to effectively computable ones. The third condition disallows the invention of values which are not oid's. Finally, the fourth condition stands for the requirement that all the constants but a finite set, and also all the oid's in our context, are uninterpreted. We note that our definition of database transformation generalizes, in the context of complex object databases, analogous definitions known in the literature [3, 5].

We are now in the position of defining the notion of completeness for an update language in a complex object framework.

Definition 2 *A language $\mathcal{L}$ is* non-deterministic update complete *if $\text{TRANS}(\mathcal{L})$ coincides with the set of non-deterministic database update transformations.*

We are now ready to present the results stating the expressibility of the UCO language.

Theorem 2 *UCO is non-deterministic update complete.*

Sketch of Proof. The proof has two parts. The first part consists in showing that any transformation in $\text{TRANS}(UCO)$ is a non-deterministic database update transformation. The latter part consists in showing that any non-deterministic database update transformation is in $\text{TRANS}(UCO)$. The proof of the former stems quite easily from definitions. As for the latter, the proof consists in: (1) showing that UCO can compute a standard encoding of the input database; this is done by selecting some ordering of values domain and then compute a Goedel number corresponding to the input database; (2) showing that UCO is capable to simulate a Turing machine; (3) showing that the result instance can be computed from the standard encoding of the output. □

Consider now the language obtained from UCO by allowing only the operators INS_1 and DEL_1 to be used in update programs. Call UCO^{red} the resulting language. Then we have the following.

Theorem 3 *$\text{TRANS}(UCO^{red}) = \text{TRANS}(UCO)$.*

Sketch of Proof. Since the semantics is the same for the two language, the proof can be easily carried out by showing that each basic operator of $\mathcal{UCO}$ can be programmed using the operators in $\mathcal{UCO}^{red}$. As an example, we show how the operators SKIP and DEL$_\phi$ can be obtained in $\mathcal{UCO}^{red}$:

$$\text{SKIP}() \leftarrow C(X), \text{INS}_1(C(X)), \text{DEL}_1(C(X)).$$
$$\text{DEL}_\phi^C(X, t) \leftarrow C(X, t), \text{DEL}_1(C(X, t)), \text{DEL}_\phi^C(C(Y, t)).$$
$$\text{DEL}_\phi^C(X, t) \leftarrow \neg C(X, t), \text{SKIP}().$$

The proof can be then completed by showing that the programmed updates have the same semantics as the simulated basic ones. □

Therefore the reduced language turns out to be equivalent to the full one as far as the expressive power is concerned. It immediately follows from theorem 2 and theorem 3 that also the reduced language is capable to express any transformation.

Corollary 1 $\mathcal{UCO}^{red}$ *is non-deterministic update complete.*

Sketch of Proof. The corollary immediately follows from the previous theorems. □

The full language can be also reduced differently, obtaining languages with different expressive powers. See [16] for more on this subject.

8   Conclusions

In this paper, a rule based non-deterministic update language for complex object databases has been presented. The language, called $\mathcal{UCO}$, is built around a set of basic update operations which, we argue, correspond to a reasonable set of basic manipulations of data stored in a complex object database. The managed data are always in the form of objects, and thus identity on values does not imply identity (this is obtained using object identifiers). This fact had strongly impacted the choice of basic update operations.

Basic update operations can be used to build complex transactions, which are defined in the form of rules, and which are activated by calling the corresponding head literal. The defined update literals can in turn be used in other update rules bodies, even recursively. Thus, the language has a procedure-call based (i.e., top-down) computational model, as opposed to other languages which use a bottom-up model [3, 10]. Rule bodies are executed strictly from left to right. In rule bodies, conditions can be specified which serve the two purposes of controlling computations as pre- and post-conditions and constructing unifications.

The presented language has been the framework within which a number of aspects of updating complex object databases through a top-down oriented non-deterministic logic language have been investigated.

References

[1] S. Abiteboul. Towards a deductive object-oriented database language. *Data and Knowledge Engineering*, 5:263–287, 1990.

[2] S. Abiteboul. Updates, a new frontier. In *ICDT'88 (Second International Conference on Data Base Theory), Bruges, Lecture Notes in Computer Science 326*, pages 1–18, Springer-Verlag, 1988.

[3] S. Abiteboul and P. Kanellakis. Object identity as a query language primitive. In *ACM SIGMOD International Conf. on Management of Data*, pages 159–173, 1989.

[4] S. Abiteboul, E. Simon, and V. Vianu. Non-deterministic languages to express deterministic transformations. In *Ninth ACM SIGACT SIGMOD SIGART Symp. on Principles of Database Systems*, pages 218–229, 1990.

[5] S. Abiteboul and V. Vianu. Datalog extensions for database queries and updates. *Journal of Comp. and System Sc.*, 43(1):62–124, August 1991.

[6] S. Abiteboul and V. Vianu. Procedural and declarative database update languages. In *Seventh ACM SIGACT SIGMOD SIGART Symp. on Principles of Database Systems*, pages 240–250, 1988.

[7] P. Atzeni and L. Tanca. The LOGIDATA+ model and language. In *Next Generation Information Systems Technology, Kiev, USSR, Lecture Notes in Computer Science 504*, pages 294–310, Springer-Verlag, 1990.

[8] P. Atzeni and R. Torlone. Updating databases in the weak instance model. In *Eigth ACM SIGACT SIGMOD SIGART Symp. on Principles of Database Systems*, pages 101–109, 1989. Full version to appear in *ACM Trans. on Database Syst.*

[9] F. Bancilhon and N. Spyratos. Update semantics of relational views. *ACM Trans. on Database Syst.*, 6(4):557–575, 1981.

[10] F. Cacace, S. Ceri, S. Crespi-Reghizzi, L. Tanca, and R. Zicari. Integrating object oriented data modelling with a rule-based programming paradigm. In *ACM SIGMOD International Conf. on Management of Data*, pages 225–236, 1990.

[11] C. de Maindreville and E. Simon. Modelling non-deterministic queries and updates in deductive databases. In *Fourteenth International Conference on Very Large Data Bases, Los Angeles*, 1988.

[12] R. Fagin, J.D. Ullman, and M.Y. Vardi. On the semantics of updates in databases. In *Second ACM SIGACT SIGMOD Symp. on Principles of Database Systems*, pages 352–365, 1983.

[13] R. Hull and M. Yoshikawa. ILOG: declarative creation and manipulation of object identifiers. In *Sixteenth International Conference on Very Large Data Bases, Brisbane*, pages 455 – 468, 1990.

[14] S. Manchanda and D.S. Warren. A logic-based language for database updates. In J. Minker, editor, *Foundations of Deductive Databases and Logic Programming*, pages 363–394, Morgan Kauffman, Los Altos, 1988.

[15] S.A. Naqvi and R. Krishnamurthy. Database updates in logic programming. In *Seventh ACM SIGACT SIGMOD SIGART Symp. on Principles of Database Systems*, pages 251–262, 1988.

[16] L. Palopoli and R. Torlone. *Extended update operations for complex objects databases*. Rapporto R.327, IASI-CNR, Roma, 1991.

[17] M. Winslett. A framework for the comparison of update semantics. In *Seventh ACM SIGACT SIGMOD SIGART Symp. on Principles of Database Systems*, pages 315–324, 1988.

A Possible World Semantics for Updates by Versioning

Georg Lausen

Fakultät für Mathematik und Informatik, Universität Mannheim

W-6800 Mannheim, Germany

Gunter Saake

Informatik, Abt. Datenbanken, Technische Universität Braunschweig

W-3300 Braunschweig, Germany

Abstract

Recently a rule-language for updating objects based on versioning has been proposed [1]. The units for update are base properties of the objects. Updates are defined by rules; several rules may be used to implement a specific update. Rules are evaluated in a bottom-up way according to a certain stratification. Up to now semantics is defined by the fixpoint resulting from the bottom-up evaluation procedure. In this paper a possible-world semantics is introduced to give a declarative semantics to the rule-language.

1 Introduction

Several rule-based approaches for updates have been proposed in the literature. Some of them rely on SLD-, SLDNF-Resolution or Abduction (e.g. [2, 3, 4, 5], or Prolog). Other approaches assume a bottom-up evaluation of the rules. In [6] various extensions of Datalog including deletions are investigated, and the language *RDL1* [7] provides a separate component for explicit control of the bottom-up evaluation. Moreover, updates in production systems (e.g. OPS5 [8]) and corresponding extensions of relational databases by rules (e.g. [9, 10, 11]) are realized by applying the rules in a bottom-up way, and, finally, also some database programming languages which incorporate rules follow this way (e.g. [12, 13]).

In this paper we continue research started in [1]; in this work an approach to update objects by rules is presented. During bottom-up evaluation of the rules explicit control is achieved in a rather intuitive way by introducing object-versions. More specifically, control is based on so called *version-identities* (VIDs), which are special object-identities, built-up by function symbols denoting types of updates (*insert, delete, modify*) in such a way, that they admit tracing back the history of updates performed on each object. The idea to use terms to identify versions is borrowed from [14, 15]. VIDs have temporal characteristics, denoting different versions of an object during its update-process. Each object-version can be considered as a single stage – corresponding to a certain time-step – of the entire process of updating the object. A set of update-rules forms an *update-program*. Update-programs have fixpoint semantics; the fixpoint can be computed by a bottom-up evaluation according to a certain stratification.

The language has several attractive features: deterministic and non-deterministic bottom-up evaluation produce the same results, and, if there are no arithmetic expressions used in the rules, bottum-up evaluation is guaranteed to terminate. Moreover, versions support thinking in states in a rather intuitive way. The contribution of the current paper is a possible world semantics for the rule-language. The purpose of the new semantics is to give a declarative modal semantic justification for the already proposed fixpoint semantics. The relationship of the possible world semantics introduced in the current paper and the fixpoint semantics introduced in [1] can only be sketched in this paper due to space limitations; however, the new semantics is an interesting aspect by itself.

The paper is organized as follows: In Section 2, we introduce the syntax of the rule-language. A discussion of the underlying intuition and some interesting examples is the topic of Section 3. In Section 4 the possible worlds semantics is introduced. Finally, a discussion of open topics and a short summary conclude the paper.

2 Syntax of the Rule-Language

The following definitions, with little modifications, come from [1]. We consider a language for objects, by which we can define updates using rules. The alphabet of our update language consists of (1) a nonempty set O of *object-identities* (OIDs) to denote the relevant objects, (2) an infinite set V of *variables* to denote objects, (3) an infinite set M of *method-names*, and (4) a set $U := \{+, -, \mp\}$ of function symbols of arity one denoting certain *update types*. Here $+, -, \mp$ stand for *insert/delete/modify*, respectively. Methods are functions to express properties of objects. The result of a method-application either is a *value*, or is an OID which denotes an object to describe a *relationship* between objects. For formal simplicity, we do not introduce types for values - we consider values as specific OIDs in O.

To give a first example, in the following expression a method *salary* is applied on an object with OID *henry* and gives as result (the OID) 250:

$henry.salary \rightarrow 250.$

Now we will introduce terms, atoms and rules. As usual, when one of these does not contain a variable, it will be called *ground*. The basic constructs of our language are object-id-terms and version-id-terms. An *object-id-term* either is a variable or an OID. To each object there may exist several versions. To be able to distinguish the different version we introduce version-id-terms.[1] A *version-id-term* is defined as follows: (1) any object-id-term is also a version-id-term; (2) let V be a version-id-term, then $\alpha(V)$ with $\alpha \in \mathcal{U}$ is a version-id-term. The set of all ground version-id-terms is denoted by $\mathcal{O}_v$; its elements are called *version-identities* (VIDs). VIDs are used to denote specific versions of the respective objects. Notice that $\mathcal{O} \subset \mathcal{O}_v$. In the sequel we denote non-ground object-id-terms and version-id-terms by names starting with an upper-case letter; ground terms are denoted by names starting with a lower-case letter.

An *atom* in our language either is a usual arithmetic *built-in predicate* ($<$, $>$, $=$, etc.) or a *version-term* or an *update-term*. The arithmetic predicates may contain usual arithmetic expressions. We consider update- and version-terms, because it is important for our approach to distinguish between (1) whether a certain update is applied on a version to create a new version with different properties, or (2) whether a version which has been created by the application of a certain update has a certain property. For the former we introduce *update-terms*, for the latter *version-terms*.

Let m be a name of a method, V a version-id-term, and $A_1, ..., A_k$, R object-id-terms. Consider '@' to be an indicator for method arguments; it is omitted if there are no arguments. A version-term is any expression of the form $V.m@A_1, ..., A_k \rightarrow R$, where $k \geq 0$.

A set of ground version-terms is called an *object-base*. An expression $m@A_1, ..., A_k \rightarrow R$ is also called a *method-application*. The *state* of a version w.r.t. a certain object-base is given by the set of all ground method-applications, which can be derived from its version-terms in the respective object-base.

Update-terms are the means to express changes of the states of the versions. Let m be a name of a method, V a version-id-term, and $A_1, ..., A_k$, R, R' object-id-terms. An update-term now is any expression of one of the following: $+[V].m@A_1, ..., A_k \rightarrow R$, $-[V].m@A_1, ..., A_k \rightarrow R$, or $\mp[V].m@A_1, ..., A_k \rightarrow (R \rightsquigarrow R')$, where $k \geq 0$. Each of these updates expresses a transition from the state of a version V to the state of a version $\alpha(V)$, where $\alpha \in \mathcal{U}$. Syntactically, updates are indicated by the braces '[', ']'. Note, that these braces are replaced by '(', ')' when referring to the version being the result of the state transition. In case of an insert, the state of version $+(V)$ the respective method-application becomes an element of the state of the version $+(V)$, in case of a delete, the state of version V contains a method-application, which is no longer contained in the state of version $-(V)$, and, finally, in case of a modify, both states of the versions $\mp(V)$ and V contain a method-application w.r.t. the same method and the same arguments, however the results may be different.

For example the *version-term*

$$\mp(henry).salary \rightarrow 275$$

states that the method *salary* applied to the version $\mp(henry)$ of object *henry*

---

[1] On the result-position of a method only object-id-terms will be allowed, not version-id-terms. We choose this way because versions are only introduced for the purpose of the update-process; a relationship is considered to be a more stable concept in comparison to the concept of versions in our approach.

yields the result 275. Here $\mp(henry)$ is a VID; *henry* and 275 are OIDs. We consider $\mp(henry)$ to be the version of *henry* after an update of type *modify* has been applied to *henry*. On the other hand, the *update-term*

$$\mp[henry].salary \rightarrow (250 \rightsquigarrow 275)$$

defines an update of type *modify* changing the result of *salary* applied to *henry* from 250 to 275. The new value will hold in the state of $\mp(henry)$.

An **update-rule** is written as

$$H \Longleftarrow B_1 \wedge ... \wedge B_k \ , \ k \geq 0,$$

where H is an update-term called the *head* of the rule, and $B_1, \ldots, B_k$ are positive or negated atoms forming the rule's *body*. H and the B_i's are also called *literals*. If $k = 0$, then the rule is called an *update-fact*. Rules are considered to be $\forall$-quantified; the domain of quantification is the set $\mathcal{O}$, i.e. the set of all OIDs. Let R be an update-rule and let r be an update-rule which is derived from R by replacing variables by OIDs. We call r a *ground instance* of R. We require that rules are *safe* (cf. [16]). A set of update-rules forms an **update-program**. The evaluation of an update-program is called **update-process**. From now on when talking about "rules", "programs" or "processes", we always mean "update-rules", "update-programs" or "update-processes", respectively.

As a first example, demonstrating the power of our language, consider the following rule:

$$\mp[E].sal \rightarrow (S \rightsquigarrow S') \ \Longleftarrow E.isa \rightarrow empl \ \wedge \ E.sal \rightarrow S \ \wedge \ S' = S * 1.1$$

To every employee a 10% salary-raise has to be performed. It is worthwhile noticing that this intuitive version of the *salary-update* terminates, when evaluated bottom-up. In the above example each employee gets his salary raised exactly once (as intended), because the rule only applies to "initial" (i.e. non-updated) employees. (Remember, that a variable can only be instantiated by a OID, not VID.) Thus versions help to avoid non-terminating update-loops.

3 Intuition of the Language

We conceive an update as a mapping from an (old) object-base into a (new) object-base. The update is defined by a certain update-program; it is realized by a bottom-up evaluation of the latter. Our update-approach bases on the idea of object-versions at different time-steps, where the first version of an object (denoted by an OID) is the one found in the current to-be-updated object-base. Updating an object is done by carrying-out on it a sequence of updates of type *insert*, *delete* or *modify*. The updates are implemented by one or several update-rules which all together form the update-program.

An update either affects an already existing version without creating a new version, or transforms an object-version into the next (further updated) version of the respective object. The former is only possible if the respective version was created by an update of the same type. The transformation of object-versions shall be understood as follows: Consider an object o. Assume that some updates of a type α $(\in \{+, -, \mp\})$ are to be performed on o. The updates of type α "defined on version o" are performed by changing the state of o accordingly. To this end, first a copy of the state of o is performed to initialize the state of the $\alpha(o)$-version. On this initial state all updates of type α are realized. After all $\alpha(o)$-updates have been performed, $\alpha(o)$ is the α-updated version of o which then might be the basis for some β-type updates, where again $\beta \in \{+, -, \mp\}$, by which a new version denoted $\beta(\alpha(o))$ is derived, etc. Again, before the first update of type β is applied, a copy of the state of the previous version is performed to initialize the state of the $\beta(\alpha(o))$-version. On this initial state all updates of type β are realized. Once an update-program has terminated, the last version becomes the result of the complete update and is denoted by o again.

In the following example we use the version concept in a rather extensive, however, in our opinion, intuitive way, to perform some kind of hypothetical reasoning. In the example we intend to determine if after a hypothetical salary-raise (non-linear) to all employees, the employee *peter* would be the richest employee of the enterprise:

$$\mp[E].sal \rightarrow (S \rightsquigarrow S') \quad\quad \Longleftarrow \quad E.sal \rightarrow S \wedge E.\ factor \rightarrow F$$
$$\wedge\ S'=S*F$$
$$\mp[\mp(E)].sal \rightarrow (S' \rightsquigarrow S) \quad\quad \Longleftarrow \quad \mp(E).sal \rightarrow S' \wedge E.sal \rightarrow S$$
$$+[(\mp(\mp(peter)))].richest \rightarrow yes \quad \Longleftarrow \quad true$$
$$\mp[+(\mp(\mp(peter)))].richest \rightarrow (yes \rightsquigarrow no) \quad \Longleftarrow \quad \mp(E).sal \rightarrow SE\ \wedge$$
$$\mp(peter).sal \rightarrow SP$$
$$\wedge\ SE > SP$$

Here the first two rules realize the hypothetical salary-raise by performing and revising it right away. For each employee e the $\mp(\mp(e))$-version is identical to the e-version and the $\mp(e)$-version contains the raised salary. The third and fourth rule determine — by using the version after the first modify — whether *peter* would be the richest employee of the enterprise. As it is described in detail in [1], bottom-up evaluation is based on a stratification of the rule-program. In our example, each rule is put in a separate stratum, because each rule introduces a new version of the respective object.

4 A Possible World Semantics

As interpretation structures for update rules we use a *Kripke structure* following the ideas introduced in [17]. A Kripke structure is defined by a set of *possible worlds* and an *accessibility relation* between those worlds. To give a semantics to database updates, we consider allowed database states as worlds and express correct updates as accessibility relation between worlds. We start with defining such a structure fitting to our rule framework.

With $\mathcal{F}$ we denote the set of *possible ground base terms* (or *base facts*) of the form $o.m \rightarrow v$. For keeping the definitions simpler we omit method parameters in the following considerations. With $2^{\mathcal{F}}$ we denote all possible subsets of $\mathcal{F}$.

The set of possible *worlds* $\mathcal{W}$ is defined as the largest subset of all possible collections of base terms, $\mathcal{W} \subseteq 2^{\mathcal{F}}$, satisfying the model-inherent integrity constraints of our data model, i.e.

- methods are functions,

$$(\forall w \in \mathcal{W})((o.m \rightarrow v \in w \wedge o.m \rightarrow v' \in w) \Rightarrow (v = v')).$$

We now define a relation $\mathcal{R}$ between worlds called *modification relation*. The modification relation consists of a family of relations mapping sets of deleted resp. inserted facts to state transitions, i.e.

$$\mathcal{R} : 2^{\mathcal{F}} \times 2^{\mathcal{F}} \rightarrow (\mathcal{W} \times \mathcal{W})$$

where for worlds $I, J \in \mathcal{W}$ and parameters $F_d, F_i \in 2^{\mathcal{F}}$ the relation $\mathcal{R}$ is defined as

$$(I, J) \in \mathcal{R}(F_d, F_i) \iff J = (I - F_d) \cup F_i.$$

The relation $\mathcal{R}$ is a partial function between database states realizing arbitrary updates consisting of first removing a set of base facts F_d and then inserting a set of base facts F_i. This update function is partial because of the model-inherent integrity constraints, i.e. no update is allowed leading to an inconsistent database state. In the following definitions, we will denote with F_d the first parameter of $\mathcal{R}$ and with F_i the second, respectively. For defining the semantics of local updates in the language presented in Section 2, this update relation is too general. Therefore we restrict $\mathcal{R}$ to an *update relation* $\mathcal{R}^u$ as follows:

$$\mathcal{R}^u = \mathcal{R}^+ \cup \mathcal{R}^- \cup \mathcal{R}^{\mp}$$

where

- the *insert relation* $\mathcal{R}^+$ is defined as $\mathcal{R}$ where $F_d = \{\}$,

- the *delete relation* $\mathcal{R}^-$ is defined as $\mathcal{R}$ where $F_i = \{\}$, and

- the *modification relation* $\mathcal{R}^{\mp}$ is defined as $\mathcal{R}$ where

$$\forall(o.m \rightarrow b \in F_d)\exists(b')(o.m \rightarrow v') \in F_i$$

(each removed method value is replaced by a modified fact) and

$$\forall(o.m \rightarrow b' \in F_i)\exists(v)(o.m \rightarrow b) \in F_d$$

(each inserted fact replaces a deleted fact).

The set of worlds $\mathcal{R}$ and the relation $\mathcal{R}^u \subseteq \mathcal{W} \times \mathcal{W}$ define the *update structure* $\mathcal{K} = \langle \mathcal{W}, \mathcal{R}^u \rangle$ as interpretation structure for update programs.

The structure $\mathcal{K}$ constitutes the interpretation domain for arbitrary update programs. The worlds of $\mathcal{K}$ are defined as possible database extensions, i.e. as consisting of base facts only. However, we can generalize this approach to integrate the handing of an intensional part, i.e. of *rules R* to define derived facts. We give this extended definition because intensional facts (for example derived views) are commonly used in database technology. Our language proposal given in Section 2 assumes only base facts for defining possible database states.

A rule program R for intensional facts defines the intensional part of a deductive database containing neither version terms nor update terms, i.e. rules in R are defined and evaluated with respect to single database states only. We assume stratified rule programs R (see [16]) allowing the following definition, which defines when a ground term g (i.e. a ground fact of the form $o.m \rightarrow v$) is valid for a world $w \in \mathcal{W}$:

$$w \models_R g \ \text{ iff } \ g \in \mathcal{M}^*(\mathcal{W} \cup R)$$

where $\mathcal{M}^*$ denotes the perfect model of a stratified rule program.

We are now able to define the semantics of update programs in terms of the update structure $\mathcal{K}$. Before we define the validity of formulae containing update terms, we first sketch the basic idea of the inductive definition. The intended meaning of an update program is a *path* in $\mathcal{K}$ corresponding to the structure of version ID terms occurring in this program. We will start with observing such paths locally for one object.

A given update program **prog** characterizes a set of paths all satisfying the update program (corresponding to a set of models satisfying a usual rule program). Out of this set a path corresponding to a somehow 'minimal performed update' has to be chosen. The local object paths can afterwards be combined to a global update by interleaving of the local paths such that there are no cyclic dependencies between object versions. This can be syntactically guaranteed by analyzing update programs similar to a stratification test. In this paper, we will mainly concentrate on the local semantics of object updates.

A *(finite) path P* is defined as a triple $\langle \sigma, \tau, \mathbf{u\_type} \rangle$ where

- σ is a sequence of states, $\sigma : \{0 \ldots n\} \rightarrow \mathcal{W}$,

- τ is a sequence of update transitions, $\tau : \{1 \ldots n\} \rightarrow 2^{\mathcal{F}} \times 2^{\mathcal{F}}$, and

- $\mathbf{u\_type}$ characterizes the sequence of updates as a sequence of insertions, deletions or modifications, $\mathbf{u\_type} : \{1 \ldots n\} \rightarrow \{+, -, \mp\}$.

The value n is called *length* of the path P. As for modification relations, we can select the first and second value of an update transition $\tau(i)$ as $\tau(i).F_d$ and $\tau(i).F_i$. A path P is called *valid in $\mathcal{K}$* iff

$$\forall (0 < i \leq n) \ (\sigma(i-1), \sigma(i)) \in \mathcal{R}^{\mathbf{u-type}(i)}(\tau(i)).$$

The set of all valid paths is denoted by $\mathcal{P}$. Valid paths correspond to sequences in $\mathcal{K}$ build by transitions following the update relation. In the following we will always mean valid paths if we talk about paths.

The interpretation of version identifiers $v \in \mathcal{O}_V$ plays an important role in the following definitions. We use the following functions to simplify definitions handling version IDs:

- **degree** : $\mathcal{O}_V \to I\!N_0$ giving the depth of nesting of a version identifier.

- **oid** : $\mathcal{O}_V \to \mathcal{O}$ giving the corresponding object identifier for a version identifier.

- **u_seq** : $\mathcal{O}_V \to (\{1 \ldots \mathbf{degree}(v)\} \to \{+, -, \mp\})$ giving the sequence of update modifications induced by a version identifier.

We define the satisfaction of an update program as usual in an inductive way. The interpretation of ground facts (containing version identifiers) and ground update terms is the interesting part because it differs from the corresponding definitions for rule satisfaction in deductive databases. The interpretation of conjunction, rules and variable substitution necessary for defining the semantics of positive rule programs directly follows the usual definitions and is left out in the following. Since we assume a proper stratification for update-programs, when processing programs stratum by stratum, negation in rule bodies can be handled according to CWA (just in analogy to the stratified datalog case [16]).

For a given valid path $P = \langle \sigma, \tau, \mathbf{u\_type} \rangle \in \mathcal{P}$ of length n we define the *satisfaction of formulae* (denoted in the following as usual with the $\models$ symbol) containing version IDs and update terms as follows:

1. A ground term $v.m \to b$ is true in P iff

$$n \geq \mathbf{degree}(v)$$
$$\wedge \quad \forall (0 < i \leq \mathbf{degree}(v)) \; \mathbf{u\_seq}(v)(i) = \mathbf{u\_type}(i)$$
$$\wedge \quad \sigma(\mathbf{degree}(v)) \models_R \mathbf{oid}(v).m \to b$$

2. A ground update term $u[v].m \to b$ with $u \in \{+, -\}$ or $\mp[v].m \to (b \rightsquigarrow b')$ is true in P iff

$$n \geq \mathbf{degree}(v) + 1$$
$$\wedge \quad \forall (0 < i \leq \mathbf{degree}(v)) \; \mathbf{u\_seq}(v)(i) = \mathbf{u\_type}(i)$$
$$\wedge$$

in case of

(a) an insertion $+[v].m \to b$:

$$\mathbf{u\_type}(\mathbf{degree}(v)) = +$$
$$\wedge \quad \mathbf{oid}(v).m \to b \in \tau.F_i$$

(b) a deletion $-[v].m \to b$:

$$\mathbf{u\_type}(\mathbf{degree}(v)) = -$$
$$\wedge \quad \mathbf{oid}(v).m \to b \in \tau.F_d$$

(c) a modification $\mp[v].m \to (b \rightsquigarrow b')$:

$$\mathbf{u\_type}(\mathbf{degree}(v)) = \mp$$
$$\wedge \quad \mathbf{oid}(v).m \to b \in \tau.F_d$$
$$\wedge \quad \mathbf{oid}(v).m \to b' \in \tau.F_i$$

3. Negation, conjunction, implication, quantification is defined as usual. For negation a suitable CWA is assumed.

A given update program **prog** characterizes the set of paths $\mathcal{P}_{\mathbf{prog}}$ satisfying **prog**, i.e. $\mathcal{P}_{\mathbf{prog}} = \{P \mid P \models \mathbf{prog}\}$. For a given current state σ_c, we are interested in those paths $\mathcal{P}_{\mathbf{prog}}(\sigma_c)$ which satisfy **prog** and start at σ_c:

$$\mathcal{P}_{\mathbf{prog}}(\sigma_c) = \{P \mid P \models \mathbf{prog} \wedge \sigma(0) = \sigma_c\}$$

Our definition of the satisfaction of update terms allows update transition performing more updates than necessary (and intended!) — if, for example, an insert transition satisfies a insertion rule, each insert transition inserting a superset of this transition satisfies the same rule. This corresponds to the frame problem in characterizing updates: our aim is to perform a minimal update satisfying our update program. However, it is not suitable to compute the straightforward intersection of all paths satisfying a program, because for example an additional unintended insert in the first transition may influence the rest of the transition sequence in an arbitrary way.

To define minimal update paths, we therefore define a *partial order* $\preceq$ on paths being stepwise evaluated starting from the beginning of paths:

$$P \preceq P' \iff \quad P.\sigma(0) = P'.\sigma(0) \wedge P.\mathbf{u\_type} = P'.\mathbf{u\_type}$$
$$\wedge \quad \exists c \forall (i < c)\ (P.\tau(i) = P'.\tau(i))$$
$$\wedge \quad P.\tau(c) \subseteq P'.\tau(c)$$

Now we can define the *semantics of a program* **prog** evaluated w.r.t. a current state σ_c as follows:

$$[\mathbf{prog}](\sigma_c) := \min_{\preceq}(\mathcal{P}_{\mathbf{prog}}(\sigma_c))$$

The function '$\min_{\preceq}$' denotes the set of minimal elements w.r.t. the partial order $\preceq$ on states. Our special interest lays on programs where $[\mathbf{prog}](\sigma_c)$ is non-empty (meaning **prog** is a consistent and allowed update for σ_c) and contains exactly one element (the update is deterministic). We will shortly discuss these questions together with the combination of local paths to a global update in the following discussion section.

5 Discussion of Open Topics

The semantics of an update program was defined as the set of minimal paths with respect to the partial order $\preceq$. We are interested in those cases where this set contains exactly one path defining intended update transition. For arbitrary formulae containing update terms this is of course not always the case, for example in the presence of disjunctions. A general characterization of programs for which uniqueness is guaranteed is an interesting research topic.

Until now, we have discussed the semantics of updates locally to objects. A path is constructed based on the versioning of *one* object identifier. Update programs typically effect several objects, and may generate different version for different objects during evaluation. If the different paths for single objects are independent, we can construct a global update path simply by a suitable interleaving of the local paths as known from process theory. Interleaving means to construct a new update path from several local paths where the restriction of the constructed path to local objects delivers the original local paths again (maybe with some additional dummy transitions to handle different path lengths).

The independence of paths is guaranteed if update rules do only depend on unversioned facts of other objects. This property can be checked syntactically. However, this syntactical property is too restrictive — for example, the update program realizing the hypothetical salary-raise in Section 3 can not be formulated under this restriction.

If we allow arbitrary versioned facts in rule bodies, we have to check for *cyclic dependencies* between versions of several objects. A cyclic dependency occurs if for example a version $\alpha(o)$ depends on $\beta'(\alpha'(o'))$ and the version $\alpha'(o')$ depend on $\beta(\alpha(o))$. If such dependencies do not exist, we can construct a sound interleaving respecting the dependencies defining the global update semantics. Again, a characterization of programs for which such cyclic dependencies cannot occur is an interesting research topic.

To keep the framework simple, we restricted our language more than necessary. More expressive power can be gained for example by allowing to quantify over VIDs in addition to OIDs. This does not affect the presented semantics definition using Kripke structure because only ground VID terms are interpreted. However, allowing quantification over VIDs may lead to update programs being only satisfied by infinite paths (corresponding to non-terminating update processes).

Future work will concentrate on combining the evaluation technique presented in [1] with the declarative semantics defined in this paper to show their equivalence. The interpretation structure for updates by versioning resembles concepts known from modal and temporal logics. The investigation of the relationship especially to temporal logics seems to be an interesting field for further research.

6 Acknowledgement

We would like to thank Michael Kramer for contributing to the design of the update-language.

References

[1] M. Kramer, G. Lausen, and G. Saake. Updates in a Rule-Based Language for Objects. In Li-Yan Yuan, editor, *Proc. 18th Int. Conf. on Very Large Databases, Vancouver*, pages 251—262, 1992.

[2] Paolo Atzeni and Riccardo Torlone. Updating Deductive Databases with Functional Dependencies. In C. Delobel, M. Kifer, and Y. Masunaga, editors, *Proc. 2nd Int. Conf. on Deductive and Object-Oriented Databases DOOD'91*. Springer-Verlag, 1991.

[3] Hendrik Decker. Drawing updates from derivations. In S. Abiteboul and P. C. Kanellakis, editors, *Proc. of the Intl. Conf. on Database Theory, Paris, LNCS 470*. Springer, 1990.

[4] A. Kakas and P. Mancarelle. Database Updates Through Abduction. In D. McLeod, R. Sacks-Davis, and H. Schek, editors, *Proc. of the Int. Conf. on Very Large DataBases, Brisbane*, pages 650–661, 1990.

[5] Anthony Tomasic. View Update Translation via Deduction and Annotation. In M. Gyssens, J. Paredaens, and D. Van Gucht, editors, *Proc. of the Intl. Conf. on Data Base Theory, Bruges, LNCS 326*, pages 338–352. Springer, 1988.

[6] Serge Abiteboul and Victor Vianu. Datalog extensions for database queries and updates. *Journal of Computer and System Sciences, Vol.43*, pages 62–124, 1991.

[7] Christophe de Maindreville and Eric Simon. A production rule based approach to deductive databases. In *Proc. of the Intl. Conf. on Data Engineering, Los Angeles*, 1988.

[8] Lee Brownstone, Robert Farell, Elaine Kant, and Nancy Martin. *Programming Expert Systems in OPS5*. Addison Wesley, 1986.

[9] M. Stonebraker, A. Jhingran, J. Goh, and S. Potamianos. On rules, procedures, caching and views in data base systems. In H. Garcia-Molina and H. V. Jagadish, editors, *Proc. of the ACM SIGMOD Symp. on the Management of Data*, pages 281–290, 1990.

[10] Jennifer Widom and Sheldon J. Finkelstein. Set-oriented production rules in relational database systems. In *Proc. of the ACM SIGMOD Symp. on the Management of Data*, pages 259–264, 1990.

[11] Y. Zhou and M. Hsu. A theory for rule triggering systems. In F. Bancilhon, C. Thanos, and D. Tsichritzis, editors, *Proc. of the Intl. Conf. on Extending Database Technology*, pages 407–421. Springer, 1990.

[12] Geoffrey Phipps, Marcia A. Derr, and Kenneth A. Ross. Glue-Nail : A deductive database system. In J. Clifford and R. King, editors, *Proc. of the ACM SIGMOD Conf. on Management of Data*, pages 308–317, 1991.

[13] Richard Hull and Dean Jacobs. Language Constructs for Programming Active Databases. In G. M. Lohman, A. Sernadas, and R. Camps, editors, *Proc. of the Intl. Conf. on Very Large Data Bases, Barcelona*, pages 455–468, 1991.

[14] Michael Kifer and James Wu. A logic for object-oriented logic programming (maier's o-logic revisited). In *Proc. of the ACM SIGACT-SIGMOD-SIGART Symposium on Principles of database Systems*, pages 379 – 393, 1989.

[15] Michael Kifer and Georg Lausen. F-logic: A higher-order language for reasoning about objects, inheritance and scheme. In *Proc. of the ACM SIGMOD Conf. on Management of Data*, pages 134 – 146, 1989.

[16] Jeffrey D. Ullman. *Principles of Database and Knowledge-Base Systems, Volume I*. Computer Science Press, New York, 1988.

[17] S.A. Kripke. Semantical Considerations on Modal Logic. *Acta Philosophica Fennica*, 16:83–94, 1963.

Specifying Semantics of Evolution in Object-Oriented Databases Using Partial Deduction

Hele-Mai Haav

Software Department, Institute of Cybernetics
Estonian Academy of Sciences
Tallinn, EE0108, ESTONIA

Abstract

In this paper, we propose a methodology for specification of semantics of evolution in object-oriented databases. Our methodology is based on Horn logic as metalanguage for specification of semantics of both schema and object evolution in object-oriented databases. Partial Deduction is used as technique for specialization of a set of general constraints on database and its schema and to derive conditions that must be satisfied to guarantee the validity of managing evolution in object-oriented databases. Implementation principles of the methodology are discussed on the basis of the object-oriented language NUT. Different types of transformations are defined that allow derivation of predicates from the descriptions of classes and objects used in the NUT system.

1 Introduction

It is now widely recognized in the object-oriented database (OODB) research community that modelling evolution of objects and classes is as important as dealing with static aspects of OODB. However, research along modelling evolution in OODB tends to focus on one particular feature instead of investigating the whole complexity of problems.

Most of proposals are dealing with managing evolution of database objects only. There are three basic approaches used to model the dynamics of the database objects as follows [1, 2]:

1. Design versioning.
2. Modelling history of objects.
3. Specifying integrity constraints defined by a set of logical rules.

Usually the specification languages used for these approaches are based on the first order logical language. For instance, history of objects is specified using language based on temporal or modal logic [3, 4]. Much work has been done incorporating object-oriented features into deductive databases for supporting object-oriented concepts, as objects, classes and inheritance, in deductive languages [5, 6, 7]. Only a few approches in this framework consider updates of objects. For example, the Logres language [8] supports object-oriented concepts and allows updates that can be expressed in rule-heads. Logical rules are also used to place certain restrictions on database objects to reflect only possible evolutions of the real world in the database [9].

Less attention is payd to the modelling schema evolution in OODB and to propagation schema changes to the database objects [10].

On the other hand, research on object-oriented languages and systems is dealing with problems of class evolution very intensively because of growing need for reusable software components. Automatic class reorganization methods proposed in this field [11] may be useful for implementation of schema evolution in OODBs as well.

The approaches proposed are mostly implementation issues. A formal framework for reorganizing class hierarchies and modelling schema evolution in OODBs is still missing. No good declarative semantics of this evolution has been defined.

Current object-oriented database systems and corresponding data models provide a limited dynamic abstraction capability. They include only few kinds of dynamic features. For example, VISION [12] implements historical information, whereas ORION [13] and ObjectStore [14] implement design versioning. Some of them support schema evolution (e.g. O2 [15], GemStone [16]), some others support "active" values known from active database systems [8, 9]. Up to now, there are no results in integration of these various features in a single system.

We are interested in the specification of semantics of both object and class evolution as well as propagation schema changes to database objects. In this paper we present approach where logical language is used as uniform metalanguage for specifying semantics of different types of evolution in OODB. The approach is based on incorporation of Horn logic into an object-oriented specification language.

The purpose of this paper is to propose a new methodology for specification of semantics of evolution in OODB. Our approach is based on transformations of object-oriented specifications to a corresponding set of predicates, Horn logic as metalanguage for defining evolution in OODB and Partial Deduction (PD) [17] used to guarantee the validity of propagation of changes. Although using PD is unusual in OODB, it allows to make deduction on incomplete specifications. The latter is normal case when we transform object-oriented specifications to the predicate form.

The rest of the paper is organized as follows. In Section 2 we present a brief survey of the results of the research on Partial Deduction used in our methodology. Section 3 describes the methodology proposed in this paper. In Section 4 we discuss implementation principles of the methodology on the basis of the object-oriented language and system NUT [18]. Finally, Section 5 presents our conclusions.

2 Issues in Partial Deduction

The process of performing part of the computations of a program at compile time rather than at run time is called partial evaluation. In the context of logic programming, where computations can be viewed as logical deduction, this process might be called partial deduction.

Initial work in partial evaluation in logic programming and introduction of the notion of partial deduction was done by J. Komorowski [17], and work on the formal foundation is presented by J. W. Lloyd and J. C. Shepherdson in [19]. During the last five years the importance of PD has been realized and applications of PD have been described [19].

PD is a source-to-source transformation technique which, given a program P and a goal G, produces a new program P', which is more specific and in many cases more efficient than P and has the same set of answer substitutions for the goal G and its instances. The computed and correct answers for G in P' should be equal to answers for G in P. The basic technique for producing P' from P is based on constructing partial derivation trees for G in P and extracting P' from the definitions associated with the leaves of these trees.

We recall the basic concepts for partial deduction required for presentation of the methodology proposed in this paper. The definitions of the basic concepts follow Lloyd and Shepherdson [19].

Definition 1. A partial deduction of an atom A in a program P is the set of all non-failing leaves of an SLD-tree of A <- A. A failing leaf is a selected atom which does not unify with any clause of the program.

If $A = \{A_1,...,A_n\}$ is a finite set of atoms, then a partial deduction of A in P is the union of partial deductions of $A_1,...,A_n$ in P.

Definition 2. A partial deduction of P with respect to (wrt) A is a program P' obtained from P by replacing the set of clauses in P whose heads contain one of the predicate symbols appearing in A with partial deduction of A in P.

Let us illustrate above definitions with an example. Consider the definite program P as follows:

```
inherits(Subclass,Class)  <-    super(Class,Subclass)
inherits(Subclass,Class)  <-    inherits(Subclass,Subclass1),
                                super(Class,Subclass1)
add_method(Method,Class)  <-    not_defined(Method,Subclass),
                                inherits(Subclass,Class)
add_method(Method,Class)  <-    leaf(Class)
super(vehicle,aircraft)<-
super(aircraft,short)<-
leaf(short)<-
```

Let G be the goal <-add_method(draw,Class). In this case a partial deduction of P wrt {add_method(draw,Class)} produces the following definition for the predicate *add_method*, where the atom selected by computation rule was always the leftmost atom, unless the predicate in the atom was *not_defined*, in which case the derivation was terminated.

```
add_method(draw,vehicle)  <-   not_defined(draw,aircraft)
add_method(draw,vehicle)  <-   not_defined(draw,short)
add_method(draw,aircraft) <-   not_defined(draw,short)
add_method(draw,short)<-
```

The above program P', consisting of the definition for predicate *add_method* together with the one for the predicate *not_defined*, can be used to answer goals of the form <-add_method(draw,Class). In the following Sections, we show that according to our methodology the result of partial deduction is not used for answering goals as traditionally but this specialization is considered as a set of conditions for managing evolution in OODB.

The main foundational questions are concerned with the soundness and completeness of partial deduction. Soudness of the partially evaluated program P' wrt the original program P and goal G for the declarative (resp., procedural) semantics means that correct (resp., computed) answers for G and P' are correct answers for G and P. Completeness is the converse of this. Lloyd and Shepherdson [19] studied conditions under which P' is sound and complete wrt P for the goal G. They have shown that for definite programs and goals partial deduction is always sound, but may not be complete. For normal programs and goals partial deduction in general is incomplete and unsound.

To ensure completeness in the case of definite programs and goals, Lloyd and Shepherdson defined a closedness condition on the program resulting from the partial deduction.

Definition 3. Let S be a set of first order formulae and A a finite set of atoms. We say S is A-closed if each atom in S containing a predicate symbol occuring in an atom in A is an instance of an atom in A.

The main theorem of partial deduction formulated by Lloyd and Shepherdson is as follows.

Let P be a program, G a goal, A a finite set of atoms and P' a partial deduction of P wrt A (using SLD-trees). Then the following hold:

1. P' is sound wrt P and G
2. If P' U {G} is A-closed , then P' is complete wrt P and G.

J. Komorowski has defined opening and abbreviating tactics for PD in [20]. Informally, the purpose of opening is to identify where PD steps take place. That is in contrast to another research concerning PD that advocates processing entire programs rather than their fragments. The main idea used in PD with opening tactics is as follows. The initial program is divided into two disjoint sets of clauses: source and axiomatization. Computational rules are defined in such a way that the predicates of the atoms selected by this rule are predicates of the heads of the clauses in the axiomatization part. In this case the local goal for each step of the deduction is defined in the process of PD.

Definition 4. Let A be a finite set of atoms, G a definite goal, and P a definite program where $P = P_1 \cup S$ for some disjoint P_1 and S, where S is a set of definitions of some predicate symbols. We call P_1 a source, and S an axiomatization. Let P' be a partial deduction of P wrt A such that P' U {G} is A-closed, where predicates of the atoms selected by the computation rule are the predicates of the heads of the clauses in S. Such partial deduction is called opening of predicates S in P wrt A.

For example, consider the following specification of *change_class* predicate:

```
change_class (X, long) <- aircraft(X, Xrange), gt(Xrange,2.0), inherits(long,aircraft)
change_class(X, short) <- aircraft(X, Xrange), le(Xrange,1.0), inherits(short,aircraft)
```

If the axiomatization is aircraft(jak11, 2.5) <- , then the result of opening the axiomatization in the source program is as follows:

```
    change_class (jak11, long)    <-  gt(2.5, 2.0), inherits(long,aircraft)
    change_class (jak11, short)   <-  le(2.5, 1.0), inherits(short,aircraft)
```

Choosing another axiomatization, for example,

```
    inherits(Subclass,Class) <-   super(Class,Subclass)
    inherits(Subclass,Class) <-   inherits(Subclass,Subclass1),
                                  super(Class,Subclass1)
    super(aircraft,short) <-
    super(aircraft,long) <-
```

leads to another program as follows:

    change_class (X, long) <- aircraft(X, Xrange), gt(Xrange,2.0)
    change_class(X, short) <- aircraft(X, Xrange), le(Xrange,1.0)

In the next Sections, we show how results on PD can be used for managing object and schema evolution in OODB.

3   The methodology

Allowing schema evolution in addition to evolution of object base within object-oriented databases makes it necessary to manage the following types of modifications:

1. Modifications on the class lattice, i.e. on inheritance relationships and class definitions (schema evolution).
2. Reflection of schema changes on database objects.
3. Modifications on object base.
4 Propagation of changes on semantically related objects.
5. Dynamic change of object class.

In general, all the changes listed above are dependent on inheritance lattice, especially on its problem-oriented semantics. Modelling evolution in OODB creates the problem of preserving consistence of database schema and object base. Another problem that arises is along preserving correctness of reflection of schema changes on database objects. Thus, conceptual data model used for modelling evolution in OODB must allow to specify constraints that define the desired evolution of database schema and objects as well as propagation of schema changes to objects. Besides this, it must include tools for representation of semantics of inheritance lattice of classes.

Usually, in current OODBs and in the corresponding data models the logical rules are used at the level of object base for checking integrity constraints when updating object states. These rules are embedded into class description and are activated by update operations. No rules on the more general class lattice level are described and used.

The goal of our proposal is to provide the user with conditions which must be satisfied to guarantee the validity of managing evolution in OODB. We propose to use logical language, especially Horn clauses as an uniform language for specification of integrity constraints on database objects and class lattice as well as for representing semantics of inheritance lattice. In this case, the Horn logic is considered as a metalanguage. Certain transformations for generation of a set of predicates from descriptions of classes and object states must be introduced for producing problem-oriented logical language. The collection of transformations for the NUT language is defined in the next Section of this paper.

For derivation of specialized conditions for managing evolution in OODB we propose to use PD besides the traditional deduction. In general, incomplete specification of the semantics of evolution is taken into account because it is supposed that not all possible predicates are generated from the description of classes and objects. There exist a lot of reasons why the complete set of predicates is not generated. First of all, the predicates produced from object states are unknown on the schema level, i.e. at the compile time of classes. But following the partial evaluation method we can do a part of deduction at compile time. Second, not all facts needed for checking constraints on schema evolution may be known or it is unefficient to add them to the specification. Nevertheless, using PD allows to make deduction before knowing all of these facts.

Incompleteness of the specification of semantics of evolution in OODB was the main reason why our proposal uses PD instead of traditional deduction. Under the circumstances PD allows us to make deductions on incomplete specifications. The result of PD can be considered as a specialized condition with respect to the particular problem that is arisen in the process of managing evolution in OODB. For example, it allows to generate conditions for modifications of objects and classes or derive specialized constraints on database objects. Consider the following partially deduced program presented already in the previous Section:

```
add_method(draw,vehicle)   <-  not_defined(draw,aircraft)
add_method(draw,vehicle)   <-  not_defined(draw,short)
add_method(draw,aircraft)  <-  not_defined(draw,short)
add_method(draw,short)<-
```

This program can be considered as a set of conditions for adding the method **draw** to class descriptions. It specifies that the method **draw** can be added to the description of the class **vehicle** only if it is not defined in the classes **aircraft** and **short**. The **draw** method can be added to the **aircraft** class only if it is not defined in the **short** class and it can be always added to the **short** class. Validity of these conditions can be checked before performing the real changes on the class descriptions.

In the following Section we show how PD allows to transform the initial set of rules given on the schema level to corresponding set of more specific rules for object level .

Another problem is that in general case it is not very clear how to formulate a goal with respect to the deduction has to be performed. Then the PD is not applied straightforwardly, but local opening strategy is used.

4   Implementation principles of the methodology

An object-oriented language NUT [18] is used to describe the conceptual model of database. This language was our tool at the previous stages of research on conceptual modelling [21] when we had to deal with database quering only. The main feature of the NUT language is automatic synthesis of methods based on proof-as-program paradigm, where intuitionistic propositional calculus has been used as underlying formalism. But the modelling power of this language is too restricted for modelling dynamical aspects of the OODB. Naturally, NUT includes procedural language for defining methods, but using logical language on the meta level gives us the possibility to increase descriptive power of our modelling tool. The latter was one of our goals.

According to the approach implemented in the NUT system [18] the class description may contain production rules considered as metalanguage for representation of knowledge about manipulation of classes and objects. We have proposed using production rules on more general level than level of class description in [22], where rules have been used for specifying propagation of changes in OODB. The production system is not a part of the program synthesizer used for synthesis of methods, but it can be invoked during synthesis in the case of an unsolvable task. It automatically allows to extend class description on the basis of given production rules and in this way gives more information to the synthesizer for problem solving. A variant of resolution method is used for derivation on production rules.

Specifications of production rules can be considered as formulas of the following form:

$$A_1 \ \& \ A_2 \& ... A_n \to A_0,$$

where A_i, $i=0,...,n$ are atomic formulae. An atomic formula consists of the predicate symbol and a list of parameters. Functional symbols are not allowed. We use Prolog like notation to present predicates and rules in this paper. In the NUT language Horn clauses are written as implications. Three types of predicates have been defined in [23] as follows:

1. **Abstract predicates** which are used to represent abstract associations between objects. For example, $inherits(@x,@y) <- $super(@y,@x)$. Abstract predicates are denoted by symbol $ and names of variables by symbol @ in the rule description.

2. **Computable predicates** which are names of preprogrammed procedures. They are denoted by symbol !. For example, !ask("Enter a new name",@x).

3. **Defining predicates** which are derived from a class description when invoking a production system. The NUT system can transform any description of a component of a class to the form of predicate and vice versa. Predicate symbol corresponds to the name of the class of the component and arguments to names of components, i.e. the following transformation is allowed:

$$P(z, x_1,...,x_n) <-> z{:}P \ a_1{=}x_1,...,a_n{=}x_n \ ,$$

where P is the class name, z is a name of component of the class P , $a_1,...,a_n$ are names of subcomponents of the class P, and $x_1,...,x_n$ are names of objects which are equal to subcomponents of the class P.

New transformation for derivation of predicates, which correspond to objects have to be added to those described above. The transformation is as follows:

$$P(z, x_1,...,x_n) <-> z{:=} \underline{new} \ P \ a_1{=}x_1,...,a_n{=}x_n \ ,$$

where P is the class name, z is a name of object of the class P , $a_1,...,a_n$ are names of subcomponents of the class P, and $x_1,...,x_n$ are names of objects which are equal to subcomponents of the class P.

Let us consider as running example the database that consists of objects from an area of design of vehicles. The following fragment of description of classes in the NUT language illustrates the technique used. In this example, three classes named **aircraft**, **long** and **medium** are presented in the NUT language as follows:

aircraft
 <u>var</u> type:text;
   range:num;
   l_distance:num;

long
    <u>super</u>   aircraft;
    <u>initialization</u> l_distance := 2000;

medium
    <u>super</u>   aircraft;
    <u>initialization</u> l_distance := 1500;

For creation of the object Jak11 that belongs to the class **aircraft** the following statements can be used:

Jak11:= <u>new</u> aircraft range:=2.5, type:='turboprop';

The following defining predicate can be derived from this statement by corresponding transformation rule:

aircraft(Jak11, 2.5, 'turboprop', nil)<- ;

where predicate symbol *aircraft* corresponds to the name of the class of the object Jak11.

To demonstrate the usefulness of PD let us continue to consideration this example. The rule for class level can be the following:

!change_class(@x, long) <-   aircraft(@x, @x.range, @x.type, @x.l_distance),
                       !gt(@x.range, 2.0),

Using this rule and defining predicate the following atom can be derived:

!change_class(Jak11, long);

The problem is that the above rule does not guarantee the correctness of the object base because the dynamic changing the class of the object is safe only if some additional conditions are held. For example, changing the class of the object preserves correctness if the new class inherits from the old one:

!change_class(@x, long) <- aircraft(@x, @x.range, @x.type, @x.l_distance),
                      !gt(@x.range, 2.0), $inherits(long, aircraft);

Traditional deduction is not possible in this case because of incompleteness of specification (there are no clauses containing atom $inherits(long, aircraft) in their left part). However PD allows us to derive the following specialized condition:

!change_class(Jak11, long)<-$inherits(long, aircraft);

Interpretation of the derived rule is obvious.

The following example demonstrates how the methodology is used to propagate changes on the schema level and to preserve the consistency of objects. This example describes conditions for the addition of a new method to classes. General specification of inheritance lattice is as follows:

(1) $inherits(@subclass,@class) <- $super(@class,@subclass)
(2) $inherits(@subclass,@class) <- $inherits(@subclass,@subclass1),
$super(@class,@subclass1)

The predicate *$super(@class,@subclass)* means that the class @class is an immidiate superclass of class @subclass and the predicate *$inherits(@subclass,@class)* says that the class @subclass inherits its properties from class @class through sub/superclass chain.

Suppose that for adding a new method the following restrictions are used:

(3) !add_method(@method,@class)<- $not_defined(@method,@subclass),
$inherits(@subclass,@class)
(4) !add_method(@method,@class) <- $leaf(@class)

These rules say that adding a new method to class desription is allowed if it is not already defined in its subclasses.

Predicates corresponding to database schema of vehicle design database can be derived from inheritance hierarchy as follows:

$super(vehicle,aircraft)<-
$super(aircraft,long)<-
$super(aircraft,medium)<-
$super(aircraft,short)<-
$leaf(long)<-
$leaf(medium)<-
$leaf(short)<-

Let the goal be <- add_method(print,@class). Then PD of specification (i.e. rules 1,2,3,4) and axiomatization wrt {add_method(print,@class)} produces the following definition, where the atom selected by the computation rule was always the leftmost atom, unless the predicate in the atom was *$not_defined*, in which case the derivation was terminated:

!add_method(print,vehicle) <- $not_defined(print,aircraft)
!add_method(print,vehicle) <- $not_defined(print,long)
!add_method(print,vehicle) <- $not_defined(print,medium)
!add_method(print,vehicle) <- $not_defined(print,short)
!add_method(print,aircraft) <- $not_defined(print,long)
!add_method(print,aircraft) <- $not_defined(print,medium)
!add_method(print,aircraft) <- $not_defined(print,short)
!add_method(print,short) <-
!add_method(print,medium) <-
!add_method(print,long) <-

This definition can be interpreted as a set of specialized conditions for adding the method **print** to the definition of classes of the database schema. It is not supposed to use for answering goals like <- add_method(print,@class), but for checking validity of adding the method **print** to the class descriptions..

So far only schema evolution was considered. Suppose that following constraints on schema and data objects are specified for vehicle design database in addition to those described for database schema and inheritance relationships:

```
!change_class(@x,long)     <-  aircraft(@x,@x.range, @x.type, @x.l_distance),
                               !gt(@x.range,2.0),$inherits(long,aircraft)
!change_class(@x,medium) <-  aircraft(@x, @x.range, @x.type,@x.l_distance),
                               !le(@x.range,2.0), !gt(@x.range,1.0),
                               $inherits(medium,aircraft)
!change_class(@x,short)    <-  aircraft(@x,@x.range, @x.type, @x.l_distance),
                               !le(@x.range ,1.0),$inherits(short,aircraft)
```

The predicate *!change_class(@x,class_name)* means that the class of object @x can be changed to the class **class_name**. In the case, when a set of different predicates for specification of constraints is described, it is difficult to select a particular goal for PD. That is why we propose application of the opening tactics instead of full PD in general case. For division of sources and axiomatization we have used different types of predicates. Defining predicates together with inheritance conditions can specify axiomatization.

After the application of opening tactics the specification of general constraints on aircrafts is as follows (the result of opening of the predicate *!add_method(@method, @class)* is not presented due to space limitation of this paper):

```
!change_class(@x,long)     <-  aircraft(@x,@x.range, @x.type, @x.l_distance),
                               !gt(@x.range,2.0)
!change_class(@x,medium) <-  aircraft(@x, @x.range, @x.type,@x.l_distance),
                               !le(@x.range,2.0), !gt(@x.range,1.0),
!change_class(@x,short)    <-  aircraft(@x,@x.range, @x.type, @x.l_distance),
                               !le(@x.range ,1.0)
```

We can use these specialized constraints on the level of objects. For example, creating a new aircraft and desribing it by the following statement:

Jak11:= <u>new</u> aircraft range:=2.5, type:='turboprop';

the following defining predicate can be derived:

aircraft(Jak11, 2.5, 'turboprop', nil)<- ;

By adding this defining predicate to rules above we can deduce that the class of the object Jak11 can be changed to the class **long**. On the other hand, changing the class of object to a more specialized allows one the use of additional methods for query evaluation.

This approach can be used for propagation of schema changes to database objects. Changing constraints influences classification of objects. Adding or deleting classes changes database schema and correspondence between classes and existing objects. New constraints can be specified to propagate schema changes to objects.

Propagation of changes on semantically related objects can be also specified in a similar way.

5 Conclusion

In this paper, the methodology for specification of semantics of evolution in object-oriented databases was presented. It is based on the following proposals:

1. On the meta level Horn clauses can be used as an uniform language for specification of integrity constraints on database objects and class lattice as well as for representing semantics of inheritance lattice.
2. Partial Deduction can be used as technique for specialization of a set of general constraints on database and its schema and to derive conditions that must be satisfied to guarantee the validity of managing evolution in object-oriented databases.
3. Transformations of descriptions of classes and objects into predicate form and vice versa can be defined. It is shown on the basis of the NUT language.

Implementation of the proposals allows specification of dynamic aspects of databases, deduction and specialization of constraints on database and combination of knowledge from objects and classes with logical rules for managing evolution in OODB.

Application of the methodology was illustrated for specification of semantics of evolution of class lattice, for propagation of schema changes and for dynamic modification of object-base (propagation of changes on semantically related objects could be implemented in the similar way).

The further work is needed to investigate problems concerning incremental specifications and reusability of partially deduced programs.

Acknowledgements

I sincerely acknowledge Dr. M. Matskin for many fruitful discussions on the topic presented.

References

1. Sciore E. Using Annotations to Support Multiple Kinds of Versioning in an Object-Oriented Database System. ACM Transactions on Database Systems, 1991, 16:417-438

2. Ariav G. Temporally oriented data definitions: Managing schema evolution in temporally oriented databases. Data & Knowledge Engineering 1991, 6:451-467

3. Jungclaus R, Saake G, Hartmann T, Sernadas C. Object-Oriented Specification of Information Systems: the T_{ROLL} Language, Braunschweig, 1991

4. Saake G, Jungclaus R. Specification of Database Applications in the T_{ROLL} Language, In: Proceedings of Int Workshop on the Specification of Database Systems, Glasgow, 1991, Springer-Verlag, London, 1991

5. Abiteboul S. Towards a deductive object-oriented database language. Data & Knowledge Engineering 1990, 5:263-287

6. van de Riet R. P. MOKUM: An object-oriented active knowledge base system, Data & Knowledge Engineering 1989, 4:21-42

7. Potter W. D, Trueblood R. P and Eastman C. M. Hyper-semantic data modeling, Data & Knowledge Engineering 1989, 4:69-90

8. Tanca L. (Re-)action in Deductive Databases, In: Proceedings of Second Int. Workshop On Intelligent and Cooperative Information Systems: Core Technology For Next Generation Information Systems, Italy, October 28-30, 1991, pp 55-61

9. Lohman G. M, Lindsay B, Pirahesh H, and Schiefer K. B. Extentions to Starburst: Objects, Types, Functions, and Rules. Communications of ACM 1991, 34:94-110

10. Nguyen G. T, Rieu D. Schema evolution in object-oriented database systems. Data & Knowledge Engineering 1989, 4:43-67

11. Casais E. An Incremental Class Reorganization Approach, In: Madsen L.(ed) Proceedings of the ECOOP'92 European Conference on Object-Oriented Programming, The Netherlands, Springer-Verlag, 1992, pp 114-131

12. Caruso M. and Sciore E. Meta-Functions and Contexts in an Object-Oriented Database Language. In: Proceedings of the ACM-SIGMOD Conference, Chicago III, June 1988, pp 56-68

13. Banerjee J, Kim W, et al., Semantics and Implementation of Schema Evolution in Object-Oriented Databases, In: SIGMOD Record, 1987, 16(3), pp 311-322

14. Lamb C, Landis G, Orenstein J, and Weinreb D. The ObjectStore Database System. Communications of ACM 1991, 34:50-64

15. Deux O, et al., The O2 System. Communications of ACM 1991, 34:34-50

16. Butterworth P, Otis A, and Stein J. The GemStone Object Database Management System. Communications of ACM 1991, 34:64-78

17. Komorowski J. A Specification of an Abstract Prolog Machine and Its Application to Partial Evaluation. PhD thesis, Linköping University, Sweden, 1981

18. Tyugu E, Matskin M, Penjam J, Eomois P. NUT-An object-oriented language, Computers and Artificial Intelligence 1986, 6:521-542

19. Lloyd J. W and Shepherdson J. C. Partial evaluation in logic programming. Technical Report CS-87-09, Department of Computer Science, University of Bristol, England, 1987

20. Komorowski J. Elements of a Programming Methodology Founded on Partial Deduction-Part 1, In: Proceedings of the Fifth International Symposium on Methodologies for Intelligent Systems, Tennessee, 1990, North-Holland, pp 514-521

21. Haav H-M. An Object-oriented approach to conceptual data modelling. In: Information Modelling and Knowledge Bases III: Foundations , Theory and Applications, IOS Press, Amsterdam, 1992 pp 333-347

22. Haav H-M, Matskin M. Using Partial Deduction for automatic propagation of changes in OODB. In: Information Modelling and Knowledge Bases IV: Foundations , Theory and Applications, IOS Press, Amsterdam, 1993 (in print)

23. Eomois P. Knowledge Representation and Deduction in Extended PRIZ. In: Plander J. (ed) Artificial Intelligence and Information Control Systems of Robots, Elsevier Science Publishers B. V., North-Holland, 1984, pp 123-127

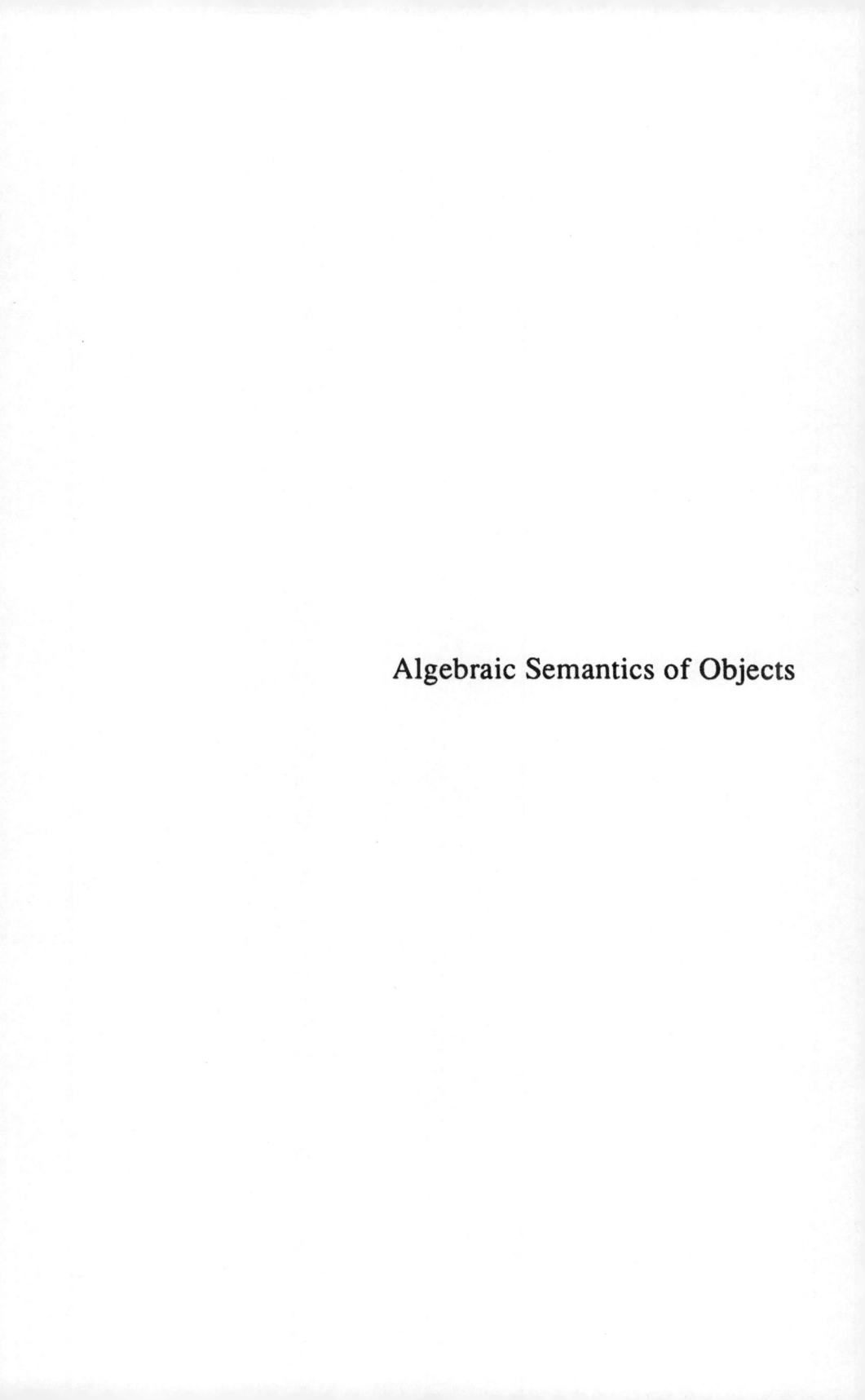

Algebraic Semantics of Objects

A Semantic Model for Dynamic Systems*

Egidio Astesiano and Elena Zucca

Dipartimento di Informatica e Scienze dell'Informazione,

Università di Genova

Genova (Italy)

E-Mail: {astes, zucca}@cisi.unige.it

Abstract

We present a new formal structure, called d-oid, for modelling systems of evolving objects. In our view, d-oids are the dynamic counterpart of many-sorted algebras, in the sense that they can model dynamic structures as much as algebras can model static data types. D-oids are a basis for giving syntax and semantics for kernel languages for defining methods; these languages are built over what we call method expressions, like applicative kernel languages are built over terms. Moreover some hints are given towards modelling classes and inheritance.

1 Introduction

The main aim of this paper is to present a modelization of systems of objects by means of a new formal structure, *d-oid*, which could play in the dynamic case the role played by classical algebras for modelling static data types.

D-oids may model classes of objects as universes of dynamic systems. A system here is viewed as having both a static (say also "horizontal") and dynamic (say also "vertical") structure. The horizontal structure concerns an instant state which is represented as an instant algebra: by its carriers and operations the structure of the auxiliary values and of the existing objects at that time is given. The vertical structure is related to the evolution of a system, which is formalized by the notion of dynamic operation or method, as we say. A method applied to a tuple of values in an instant algebra transforms an instant algebra into another one, possibly giving a result; moreover the transformation consists also in a map between the carriers of the corresponding algebras; this map is called *tracking map*, because intuitively it keeps track of the object identities, showing how a single object is transformed into another one. The notion of tracking map is essential not only for defining relationships between structures (morphisms), but also to give a rigourous semantics to method expressions.

First we present our semantic model, which is illustrated by means of a toy example, inspired by the language used in [11]. Then we concentrate our attention on the semantics of a kernel language for defining methods. The kernel language is built on top of what we call method expressions, adding

---

*This work has been partially supported by ESPRIT BRA WG n.6071 ISCORE, Progetto Finalizzato Sistemi Informatici e Calcolo Parallelo of C.N.R. and MURST-40% Modelli e Specifiche di Sistemi Concorrenti

conditional and recursion; method expressions are the correspondent of terms in the case of algebras. Finally we briefly explain the connection with typical object oriented features like inheritance, for which we have a formalization via a reduct operation. In the conclusion we relate our to other approaches and outline ongoing work.

2 The model

In the following we assume for simplicity that static data types are formalized in the usual framework of total algebras. Actually our work can be framed in a parameterized way on the top of any chosen algebraic framework for static data types. Also we assume known the notions of signature (metavariable Σ) and Σ-algebra; $Alg(\Sigma)$ denotes the class of Σ-algebras.

2.1 From data types to d-oids

Analogously to the static case, we first introduce signatures (i.e. syntactic symbols for dynamic operations with their functionalities) and then the models over a signature (i.e. semantic structures). However in the dynamic case the interpretation of a symbol, that we call *method* (or *dynamic operation*), is not just a function. The concept of method, which is defined in terms of the transformation that it induces over a configuration, with its associated tracking map, is central to our approach.

The following notation is easily understood in terms of Pascal-like procedures and functions: a procedure with parameters of type $s_1, \ldots, s_n$ has functionality $s_1 \ldots s_n \Rightarrow \bullet$, also written $s_1 \ldots s_n \Rightarrow$; a function with the same types of the arguments and with result of type s has functionality $s_1 \ldots s_n \Rightarrow s$. In particular a parameterless procedure (resp. function) has functionality $\Rightarrow$ (resp. $\Rightarrow s$). Note however that we have also constant operation symbols (functionality s or $\bullet$), to be distinguished from parameterless operations.
If A is a set, then $[A]$ denotes $A \cup \{\bullet\}$, for some $\bullet \notin A$, which is called *null*.

Def. 2.1 A *dynamic signature* is a couple $D\Sigma = (\Sigma, DOP)$ where

- Σ is a signature (called *instant signature*); set $S = Sorts(\Sigma)$;

- DOP is a $(S^* \times [S]) \cup [S]$-family of symbols called *dynamic operation symbols*; if $dop \in DOP_{w,s}$, then w, s are called *arity* and *sort* of dop, respectively, and for $w = s_1 \ldots s_n$, we write

$$dop: s_1 \ldots s_n \Rightarrow s,$$

  if s is non-null, and

$$dop: s_1 \ldots s_n \Rightarrow,$$

  if s is null; if $dop \in DOP_s$, then dop is called a *constant* dynamic operation symbol, and s is called *sort* of dop; we write $dop: s$, if s is non-null, and $dop:$, if s is null. □

Let in what follows $D\Sigma = (\Sigma, DOP)$ be a dynamic signature and set $S = Sorts(\Sigma)$. Assume $D \subseteq Alg(\Sigma)$; for every $w = s_1 \ldots s_n \in S^*$, set

$$D_w = \{<A, a_1, \ldots, a_n> \mid A \in D, a_i \in A_{s_i}, \forall i = 1, \ldots, n\}.$$

We also assume, for simplifying the notation, that dynamic signatures have no overloading, i.e. , for every dynamic signature $D\Sigma = (\Sigma, DOP)$, if $dop \in DOP_{w,s}$, and $dop \in DOP_{w',s'}$, then $w = w'$ and $s = s'$.

Def. 2.2 For every $D \subseteq Alg(\Sigma)$ and for every $A \in D$, a *transformation of A in D* is a triple $<A, f, B>$ where $B \in D$, $f : |A| \rightarrow |B|$, denoted by $f: A \Rightarrow B$. ($|A|$ denotes as usual the family of the carriers of an algebra A.) The map $f : |A| \rightarrow |B|$ is called *tracking map*.

For every $D \subseteq Alg(\Sigma)$, $w = s_1 \ldots s_n \in S^*$, and $s \in [S]$, a *(non-constant) method (or dynamic operation) m over D*, of arity $s_1 \ldots s_n$ and sort s, written $m: D_{s_1 \ldots s_n} \Rightarrow D_{[s]}$ (we write simply D for $D_\bullet$), associates with every $<A, a_1, \ldots, a_n> \in D_w$ a transformation of A in D, say $f: A \Rightarrow B$, and, if s is non-null, a value $b \in B_s$. The result of applying m to $<A, a_1, \ldots, a_n>$ is denoted by $m_{<A, a_1, \ldots, a_n>}$, and we write $m_{<A, a_1, \ldots, a_n>} = <f: A \Rightarrow B[, b]>$.

For every $D \subseteq Alg(\Sigma)$, $s \in [S]$, a *constant method (or constant dynamic operation) m over D*, of sort s, written $m : D_{[s]}$ (we write simply D for $D_\bullet$), consists of an algebra $B \in D$, and, if s is non-null, a value $b \in B_s$, and we write $m = <B[, b]>$. $\square$

Note that the tracking map is not required to be a homomorphism, since in general the effect of applying a method is to change the structure of a configuration; that will be illustrated by the following examples.

We give now the formal definition of d-oids (d stands for "dynamic").

Def. 2.3 A *d-oid over* $D\Sigma = (\Sigma, DOP)$ is a couple $\mathcal{D} = (D, \{dop^{\mathcal{D}}\}_{dop \in DOP})$ where:

- $D \subseteq Alg(\Sigma)$ (the algebras in D are called *instant algebras*);

- $dop^{\mathcal{D}}: D_{s_1 \ldots s_n} \Rightarrow D_{[s]}$, for $dop: s_1 \ldots s_n \Rightarrow [s]$;

- $dop^{\mathcal{D}}: D_{[s]}$, for $dop: [s]$. $\square$

If one wants to stress the difference between objects and usual values, then a specialized version of d-oids can be adopted, where an explicit "value part" is introduced, as shown below.

Def. 2.4 A *dynamic signature with value part* is a couple $(D\Sigma, \Sigma_V)$ where $D\Sigma = (\Sigma, DOP)$ is a dynamic signature and Σ_V is a signature s.t. $\Sigma_V \subseteq \Sigma$. $\square$

Def. 2.5 Given a dynamic signature with value part $D\Sigma_V = (D\Sigma, \Sigma_V)$, a *d-oid with value part* over $D\Sigma_V$ is a couple $(\mathcal{D}, A_V)$ where $\mathcal{D} = (D, \{dop^{\mathcal{D}}\}_{dop \in DOP})$ is a d-oid over $D\Sigma$, A_V is a Σ_V-algebra s.t. the following conditions hold:

- for each $A \in D$, $A_{|\Sigma_V} = A_V$

- for each dop: $s_1 \ldots s_n \Rightarrow [s]$, $<A, a_1, \ldots, a_n> \in D_{s_1 \ldots s_n}$,
  if $dop^{\mathcal{D}}_{<A, a_1, \ldots, a_n>} = <f: A \Rightarrow B[, b]>$,
  then f is the identity over $A_{|\Sigma_V}$. $\square$

Here $A'_{|\Sigma_V}$ denotes the Σ_V-reduct of A, i.e. intuitively the algebra obtained from A "forgetting" sorts and operations which are not in Σ_V. The formal definition is delayed to sect.4 (Def.4.10), where we will need the reduct notion for modelling inheritance.

Finally, we introduce the notion of *d-oid morphism*. The basic idea is simple: a morphism from $\mathcal{D}$ into $\mathcal{D}'$ consists of a family of homomorphisms, one for every instant algebra in D into some instant algebra in D', which are compatible with the methods. We recall that a Σ-homomorphism f from a Σ-algebra A into a Σ-algebra B, written $f: A \rightarrow B$, is a S-family of functions $\{f_s: A_s \rightarrow B_s\}_{s \in S}$ which are compatible with the operations, i.e.
for every op: $s_1 \ldots s_n \rightarrow s$, $a_1 \in A_{s_1}, \ldots, a_n \in A_{s_n}$,

$$f_s(op^A(<a_1, \ldots, a_n>)) = op^B(f_{s_1}(a_1), \ldots, f_{s_n}(a_n)).$$

Def. 2.6 Given two d-oids on $D\Sigma$,

$$\mathcal{D} = (D, \{dop^{\mathcal{D}}\}_{dop \in DOP}),$$

$$\mathcal{D}' = (D', \{dop^{\mathcal{D}'}\}_{dop \in DOP}),$$

a *$D\Sigma$-morphism ϕ from $\mathcal{D}$ into $\mathcal{D}'$*, written $\phi: \mathcal{D} \rightarrow \mathcal{D}'$, associates with every instant algebra $A \in D$, a Σ-homomorphism $\phi_A: A \rightarrow A'$, with $A' \in D'$, and has the following properties:

- for every dop: $[s]$,

  if $dop^{\mathcal{D}} = <A[, a]>$, $dop^{\mathcal{D}'} = <A'[, a']>$,
  then $\phi_A: A \rightarrow A'$, $[\phi_A(a) = a']$;

- for every dop: $s_1 \ldots s_n \Rightarrow [s]$, $<A, a_1, \ldots, a_n> \in D_{s_1 \ldots s_n}$,

  if
  $$dop^{\mathcal{D}}_{<A, a_1, \ldots, a_n>} = <f: A \Rightarrow B[, b]>, \ \phi_A: A \rightarrow A',$$
  $$\phi_A(a_1) = a'_1, \ldots, \phi_A(a_n) = a'_n,$$
  $$dop^{\mathcal{D}'} <A', a'_1, \ldots, a'_n> = <g: A' \Rightarrow B'[, b']>$$
  then
  $$\phi_B: B \rightarrow B',$$
  for every $a \in A$, $\phi_B(f(a)) = g(\phi_A(a))$;
  $$[\phi_B(b) = b']. \ \square$$

The second condition can be expressed by the commutativity of a diagram[1]:

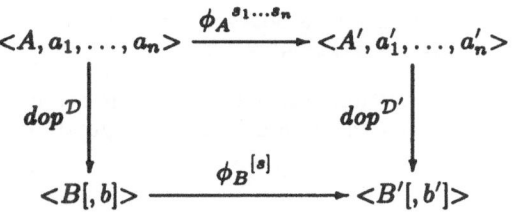

where $\phi_A{}^{s_1\cdots s_n}$ is defined by:

$$\phi_A{}^{s_1\cdots s_n}(<A, a_1, \ldots, a_n>) = <A', \phi_A(a_1), \ldots, \phi_A(a_n)> \text{ for } \phi_A\colon A \to A'.$$

D-oids over $D\Sigma$ and their morphisms form a category.

We show now some examples of d-oids modelling objects and object systems. Let us consider the following object type in the language EasyOBL defined in [11].

```
object type LEGAL_ENTITY is
instance variables
    TelNo: NUMBER; Name: STR;
operations
    getTelNo () : NUMBER { return TelNo };
    putTelNo (n : NUMBER) { TelNo := n };
    getName () : STR { return Name };
    putName (s : STR) { Name := s };
end LEGAL_ENTITY
```

This declaration defines a legal entity as a dynamically evolving object which has, at every stage in its evolution, a telephone number and a name (which is a string); these two components can be read (as an effect of calling the operations getTelNo, getName) and updated (as an effect of calling the operations putTelNo, putName).

Such an object can be modelled as a d-oid $\overline{\mathcal{LE}}$ in a very natural way. Each intermediate configuration of a legal entity can be formalized by an algebra over the following signature (an instant algebra):

```
sig Σ_LE =
    sorts number, str
    opns ... operations on natural numbers and strings
        TelNo: → number
        Name: → str
```

More precisely, an instant algebra in $\overline{\mathcal{LE}}$ is an algebra over $\Sigma_{\overline{\mathcal{LE}}}$ such that the interpretation of sorts *number*, *str* are natural numbers and char strings, respectively, operations on natural numbers and strings are interpreted in the usual way, while the interpretation of the operations *TelNo*, *Name* is free and models the current values of these instance variables. Formally, denoting by $\overline{LE}$ the class of such algebras:

---

[1]This diagram has been produced using Paul Taylor's package.

$$\overline{LE} =$$
$$\{ A \mid \quad A \text{ algebra over } \Sigma_{\overline{LE}},$$
$$\text{operations on numbers and strings as usual,}$$
$$A_{number} = \mathbb{N}, \; A_{str} = Char^* \}.$$

Accordingly to the definition above, the dynamic evolution of a legal entity can be modelled by four dynamic operations, corresponding to read/update the telephone number and the name, respectively.

$getTelNo: \Rightarrow number$
$putTelNo: number \Rightarrow$
$getName: \Rightarrow str$
$putName: str \Rightarrow$

Consider for example $putTelNo$; it takes an instant algebra A in $\overline{LE}$, corresponding to an entity configuration, a natural number n' (a new telephone number) and gives a transformation of A, say $f: A \Rightarrow B$, as follows.

$B \in \overline{LE}$,
$TelNo^B = n'$, $Name^B = Name^A$.
The tracking map is the identity map from $|A|$ into $|B|$.

Note that A and B are different as algebras but have the same carriers.

2.2   Object identity and sharing

Of course the purpose of an object type declaration like the one in our example is not only to define what is a single legal entity, but a system where many legal entities may coexist. We define here below three versions of a d-oid LE modelling such a system; that allows us also to show how object identity is handled in a very natural way in our approach.

The instant signature and the dynamic operations must change their functionality, taking into account the legal entity to which an operation is referred, as follows:

sig $\Sigma_{LE} =$
    sorts $legEnt, number, str$
    opns ... operations on natural numbers and strings
        $TelNo: legEnt \rightarrow number$
        $Name: legEnt \rightarrow str$

$getTelNo: legEnt \Rightarrow number$
$putTelNo: legEnt \; number \Rightarrow$
$getName: legEnt \Rightarrow str$
$putName: legEnt \; str \Rightarrow$

The different versions of d-oids modelling legal entities correspond to different ways of representing in a carrier a legal entity.

An abstract view of legal entities. In each intermediate configuration in the life of the system, there is a finite number of existing legal entities, each one with a given telephone number and name. However, different legal entities with the same telephone number and name may exist in the system. In order to express that, all the possible configurations of the system can be modelled as $\Sigma_{\mathcal{LE}}$-algebras A such that:

(*)
$$LE = \{\; A \mid$$
A algebra over $\Sigma_{\mathcal{LE}}$, operations on numbers and strings as usual,
$A_{number} = \mathbb{N}, A_{str} = Char^*,$
A_{legEnt} finite$\}$.

We denote in the following by LE a class of such algebras. Note that we do not fix which is the carrier of the sort $legEnt$ in an instant algebra, since we do not want to define what legal entities actually are: the only requirement we want legal entities to meet is that we can observe which is the telephone number and the name of a legal entity; moreover we require that A_{legEnt} is a finite set since we want that only a finite number of legal entities exist in each configuration.

For example, a configuration in which two legal entities exist, say le_1, le_2, with telephone number n_1, n_2 and name s_1, s_2, respectively, is modelled by a $\Sigma_{\mathcal{LE}}$-algebra $\overline{A}$ in LE defined by (*) and $\overline{A}_{legEnt} = \{le_1, le_2\}$, $TelNo(le_1) = n_1$, $TelNo(le_2) = n_2$, $Name(le_1) = s_1$, $Name(le_2) = s_2$. Note that it does not matter what le_1, le_2 are.

We consider now the dynamic evolution of the system. Consider for example $putTelNo$; it takes a system configuration, say $\overline{A}$ above, a legal entity in $\overline{A}$, say le_1, and a natural number n' (a new telephone number), and gives a transformation of $\overline{A}$, say $f: \overline{A} \Rightarrow \overline{B}$, as follows.

$$f_{number} = id_{\mathbb{N}}$$
$$f_{str} = id_{Char^*}$$
$$f_{legEnt} \text{ injective}$$
$$\overline{B}_{legEnt} = \{f(le) \mid le \in \overline{A}_{legEnt}\}$$
$$TelNo^{\overline{B}}(f(le_1)) = n', \; TelNo^{\overline{B}}(f(le)) = TelNo^{\overline{A}}(le), \forall le \in \overline{A}_{legEnt}, le \neq le_1$$
$$Name^{\overline{B}}(f(le)) = Name^{\overline{A}}(le), \forall le \in \overline{A}_{legEnt}.$$

Here and in what follows, if A is a set, then id_A denotes the identity of A.

In this way object identity is modelled in a very abstract way by means of the tracking map; there is no need of an explicit notion of "identity". (In the sequel we will show some particular case of the above model in which we use explicit identities for legal entities.) The tracking map keeps trace of object identity, allowing to recognize different states of a single object during the evolution of the system. More precisely, the state of a single object in a configuration (e.g. of a legal entity) is modelled by an element in a carrier of the corresponding instant algebra (e.g. le_1) together with the current interpretation of the operations, giving the relationship with other objects (e.g. $TelNo$, $Name$).

Note moreover that in this approach usual values (e.g. natural numbers) can be viewed as "constant" objects, i.e. objects which always exist and never change. If one wants to stress the difference between usual values and objects, then the specialized version of d-oids can be used in which values (immutable objects) are a-priori distinguished from mutable objects (see Def. 2.4 and 2.5), while in the general approach the fact that some objects are constant is discovered in an a-posteriori way.

Our notion of dynamic operation includes also *object creation*: indeed the tracking map is not required to be surjective. Consider for example a dynamic operation *newLE* which models the creation of a new legal entity with a given telephone number and name. For each instant algebra A in LE, telephone number n, name s

$$newLE^{\mathcal{LE}}_{<A,n,s>} = <f: A \Rightarrow B, \overline{le}>$$

where:

$\overline{le} \notin A_{legEnt}$;
$B_{legEnt} = \{f(le) \mid le \in A_{legEnt}\} \cup \{\overline{le}\}$;
$TelNo^B(\overline{le}) = n$, $Name^B(\overline{le}) = s$;
$TelNo^B(f(le)) = TelNo^A(le)$, $\forall le \neq \overline{le}$;
Name analogously.

Finally we show an example of constant operation. In the d-oid $\mathcal{LE}$ described until now we can add a constant operation symbol *Empty* whose interpretation is the configuration in which no legal entity exists.

$$Empty^{\mathcal{LE}} = A \text{ where } A \in LE, A_{legEnt} = \emptyset.$$

We recall that in the d-oid $\mathcal{LE}$ described until now LE may be any class of $\Sigma_{\mathcal{LE}}$-algebras satisfying (*) and closed w.r.t. dynamic operations. We show now two choices of LE which lead to two concrete models which are particularly interesting from the intuitive point of view.

Legal entities as couples with name. In the first model, we define LE, the class of the instant algebras, as the class of all the $\Sigma_{\mathcal{LE}}$-algebras A such that (*) holds and moreover

$A_{legEnt} \subseteq Id \times \mathbb{N} \times \mathbb{N}$,
$\forall <id, n, s> \in A_{legEnt}$,
$\qquad TelNo^A(<id, n, s>) = n$,
$\qquad Name^A(<id, n, s>) = s$,
(**) if $<id, n, s>, <id, n', s'> \in A_{legEnt}$, then $n = n'$, $s = s'$

where Id is some set of names. This model corresponds to the intuitive view of a legal entity as a triple consisting of current telephone number and name and of an "identity" which must be unique in the system (as guaranteed by the assumption (**) above). It is easy to adapt the above definitions to this particular case; for example, in the interpretation of the dynamic operation *putTelNo* applied to $<\overline{A}, le, n'>$, with $le = <id, n, s>$, the tracking map f becomes as follows:

f maps $le = <id, n, s>$ into $<id, n', s>$,
f is the identity elsewhere.

With this choice, all the states of the same legal entity in different configurations of the system keep the same identity.

Legal entities as pure identities. Note that in the preceding model the information modelled by n and s in the triple $<id, n, s>$ is "redundant" since the fact that the legal entity whose name is id has current telephone number n and name s is already modelled by the current interpretation of the operations in A. Hence a different model can be defined fixing LE as the class of all the $\Sigma_{\mathcal{LE}}$-algebras A such that (*) holds and moreover

$$A_{legEnt} \subseteq Id$$

This model corresponds to the intuitive view of a legal entity as just an "identity", while the information about the two instance variables is "stored" in the structure. The other definitions must change consistently; for example, in the interpretation of the dynamic operation $putTelNo$, the tracking map becomes the identity.

These two models (and other particular cases obtained by fixing the choice of LE and the tracking maps) look equivalent, and indeed can be proved to be *isomorphic* w.r.t. to the morphism notion given above (Def. 2.6).

We present one more example, whose aim is to illustrate how objects with object subcomponents and object sharing can be handled in this framework in a very natural way.

Let us consider the following class definition:

```
class ACCOUNT is
attrs
    ...
    holder: LEGAL_ENTITY;
...
end ACCOUNT
```

In this case, an object in the system (an account) has an object subcomponent (a legal entity). We can model a system containing legal entities and accounts by a d-oid defined analogously to $\mathcal{LE}$ above. A configuration in which, for example, two accounts a_1 and a_2 share the same holder le can be modelled by an instant algebra A as follows

$$a_1, a_2 \in A_{account},$$
$$le \in A_{legEnt},$$
$$holder^A(a_1) = le,\ holder^A(a_2) = le.$$

3 Languages for defining methods

In the static case the *expressions* or *terms* over a signature are the basis for building (applicative) kernel languages for defining functions; typically one starts from terms over the signature and then uses constructs such as if-then-else (conditional), let-in and recursion. We plan to do the same for the dynamic case, i.e. we want to define the analogous of terms, that we call *method expressions*, in order to have a basis for building a language for defining methods.

It will be seen that for the semantics of method expressions an essential role is played by the tracking map, which finds here its deepest technical motivation, accordingly to the intuitive motivation of keeping track of object identities.

3.1 Method expressions

The aim of this subsection is to define (the syntax and semantics of) the dynamic counterpart of terms over a signature, i.e. *method expressions* over a dynamic signature.

We start from the case of constant method expressions. In the static algebraic framework constant (ground) terms are just terms without free variables and are syntactic representations of values in an algebra. In the dynamic case, constant method expressions have to denote instant algebras and values in an instant algebra. We have two essential constructs for (creating and) denoting instant algebras: applying a dynamic operation to an algebra and a tuple of values denoted by terms: $dop(t_1, \ldots, t_n)$; and concatenating method expressions, say $me_1; me_2$. However whenever dop has result sort s, with $s \in S$, then $dop(t_1, \ldots, t_n)$ denotes also a value in an instant algebra, which can be used later via a tracking map in another instant algebra. Thus we need to denote this value and we use for this the construct let $x = dop(t_1, \ldots, t_n)$ in me endlet. Of course the basis for denoting instant algebras is given by the constant operations.

For example, referring to the preceding example of legal entities, the following is a constant method expression over the dynamic signature $\Sigma_{\mathcal{LE}}$:

(*)   *Empty*;
    let $y = newLE(n_1, s_1)$ **in**
        let $z = newLE(n_2, s_2)$ **in**
            $putTelNo(y, n_1'); putTelNo(z, n_2')$
        endlet
    endlet

where y, z are variables of sort *legEnt*, n_1, n_2, n_1', n_2', s_1, s_2 are constant terms over $\Sigma_{\mathcal{LE}}$.

In the d-oid $\mathcal{LE}$ defined in the preceding section, this method expression denotes the instant algebra obtained as follows:

- starting from the algebra in which no legal entity exist;

- creating a new legal entity, which will be denoted from now on by y;

- creating another new legal entity, which will be denoted from now on by z;

- changing to n_1' the telephone number of y;

- changing to n_2' the telephone number of z.

Considering now the case of non-constant method expressions, we again do a comparison with the static case. In the static framework, a non-constant (open) term (i.e. a term with free variables) can be evaluated in an algebra A if we fix the values in A to be associated with the variables. Hence a term with variables, say x_1 of sort s_1, ..., x_n of sort s_n, denotes no longer a value in A (as in the constant case), but a *function* from $A_{s_1} \times \ldots \times A_{s_n}$ into A_s where s is the sort of the term.

In the dynamic framework, a non-constant method expression can be evaluated in a d-oid, say $\mathcal{D}$, if we fix an initial instant algebra A and the values in A to be associated with the variables. Hence a method expression with free variables, say x_1 of sort s_1, ..., x_n of sort s_n, denotes no longer an instant algebra in D (as in the constant case), but a *method* from $D_{s_1...s_n}$ into D_s where s is the sort of the method expression.

Formally, a non-constant method expression is like a constant one, except that it does not start with a constant operation.

Referring to the preceding example of legal entities, a non-constant method expression over the dynamic signature $\Sigma_{\mathcal{LE}}$ with a free variable h of sort $legEnt$ is e.g. :

> **let** $y = newLE(n_1, s_1)$ **in**
>   **let** $z = newLE(n_2, s_2)$ **in**
> $putTelNo(y, n_1')$;
> $putTelNo(z, n_2')$;
> $putTelNo(h, n_3)$;
>   **endlet**
> **endlet**

where h is a variable of sort $legEnt$, n_3 is a constant term over $\Sigma_{\mathcal{LE}}$.

The intuitive meaning is that the evaluation of this method expression needs to fix an initial configuration of the system of legal entities (formally, instant algebra), in which h denotes an existing legal entity.

Note that, due to the above definitions, constant method expressions are different from those non-constant method expressions whose set of free variables is the empty set; indeed, in the last case it is still necessary to fix an initial instant algebra, as illustrated by the example:

> **let** $y = newLE(n_1, s_1)$ **in**
>   **let** $z = newLE(n_2, s_2)$ **in**
> $putTelNo(y, n_1')$;
> $putTelNo(z, n_2')$
>   **endlet**
> **endlet**

in which the new legal entities added to the system depend on which are the already existing legal entities. Hence we have the apparently counterintuitive fact that non-constant method expressions may contain no free variables.

Syntax

We assume known the notions of sort assignment (metavariable X) and terms over Σ and X, denoted by $T_\Sigma(X)$; a generic term will be denoted by t; by $T_\Sigma(X)_{s_1...s_n}$ we denote the set of tuples of terms of sorts s_1, ..., s_n respectively. A finite sort assignment can be written in the form $\{x_1 : s_1, ..., x_n : s_n\}$; $X[s/x]$ denotes the sort assignment which gives s on x, is equal to X elsewhere.

Def. 3.7 The method expressions over $D\Sigma$ are inductively defined in **Fig.3.1**, where X ranges over sort assignments:

- me is a *(non-constant) method expression over $D\Sigma$ and X of sort s (resp. of null sort)* iff $X \vdash^s me$ (resp. $X \vdash me$);

1. $$\overline{X \vdash^{[s]} dop(t_1, \ldots, t_n)} \qquad dop: s_1 \ldots s_n \Rightarrow [s],\ t_1, \ldots, t_n \in T_\Sigma(X)_{s_1 \ldots s_n}$$

2. $$\overline{X \vdash^s t} \qquad t \in T_\Sigma(X)_s$$

3. $$\overline{\vdash^{[s]} dop} \qquad dop: [s]$$

4. $$\frac{X \vdash^{s_1} me_1 \qquad X[s_1/x] \vdash^{[s_2]} me_2}{X \vdash^{[s_2]} \text{let } x = me_1 \text{ in } me_2 \text{ endlet}}$$

5. $$\frac{X \vdash me_1 \qquad X \vdash^{[s_2]} me_2}{X \vdash^{[s_2]} \text{let } me_1 \text{ in } me_2 \text{ endlet}}$$

6. $$\frac{\vdash^{s_1} me_1 \qquad \{x: s_1\} \vdash^{[s_2]} me_2}{\vdash^{[s_2]} \text{let } x = me_1 \text{ in } me_2 \text{ endlet}}$$

7. $$\frac{\vdash me_1 \qquad \emptyset \vdash^{[s_2]} me_2}{\vdash^{[s_2]} \text{let } me_1 \text{ in } me_2 \text{ endlet}}$$

8. $$\overline{X \vdash dop(t_1, \ldots, t_n)} \qquad dop: s_1 \ldots s_n \Rightarrow s,\ t_1, \ldots, t_n \in T_\Sigma(X)_{s_1 \ldots s_n}$$

9. $$\overline{\vdash dop} \qquad dop: s$$

Figure 1: **Syntax**

- me is a *constant method expression over $D\Sigma$ of sort s (resp. of null sort)* iff $\vdash^s me$ (resp. $\vdash me$).

We denote by $ME_{D\Sigma}(X)$ the $[S]$-family of the method expressions over $D\Sigma$ and X and by $ME_{D\Sigma}$ the $[S]$-family of the constant method expressions over $D\Sigma$. $\qquad\qquad\qquad\qquad\qquad\qquad\qquad\qquad\qquad\qquad\qquad\qquad\qquad \Box$

Remarks In metarule 1, the notation $[s]$ means that, if $dop: s_1 \ldots s_n \Rightarrow s$, then $X \vdash^s dop(t_1, \ldots, t_n)$; if dop has null sort, then $X \vdash dop(t_1, \ldots, t_n)$; in the following we assume analogous conventions.

Instead of writing **let** me_1 **in** me_2 **endlet**, we will more often use the notation $me_1; me_2$. The last two metarules express the fact that from a dynamic operation which returns a value we can get a dynamic operation of null sort just "forgetting" the result. Note that X may be the empty family and that $\emptyset \vdash me$ indicates that me is a method expression without free variables but is not a constant method expression (i.e. $\emptyset \vdash me$ should not be confused with $\vdash me$).

Semantics

We assume known the concept of (homomorphic) evaluation of terms into an algebra A, for a valuation r, denoted by $eval^{A,r}$; as usual we write also $t^{A,r}$ for $eval^{A,r}(t)$ and $<t_1,\ldots,t_n>^{A,r}$ for $<t_1^{A,r},\ldots,t_n^{A,r}>$.

Def. 3.8 Let $\mathcal{D} = (D, \{dop^{\mathcal{D}}\}_{dop \in DOP})$ be a d-oid over $D\Sigma$. A *valuation of a sort assignment* Y *in* $\mathcal{D}$ is a S-family of functions

$$r_s: Y_s \to A_s, \text{ for some } A \in D.$$

For every method expression me over X such that $X \vdash^{[s]} me$, and every valuation r of X in $\mathcal{D}$, say $r: X \to A$, the *evaluation of* me w.r.t. $\mathcal{D}$ *and* r , denoted by $\llbracket me \rrbracket^{\mathcal{D},r}$, consists of a transformation of A, say $f: A \Rightarrow B$, and, if s is non-null, of a value $b \in B_s$. The definition adopts the usual big-step inductive (SOS) semantics style (see [3]); we assume $\mathcal{D}$ fixed and write

$$me \underset{r}{\to}{}^{[s]} <f: A \Rightarrow B[,b]>$$

for

$$\llbracket me \rrbracket^{\mathcal{D},r} = <f: A \Rightarrow B[,b]>, \text{ [with } b \in B_s].$$

For every method expression me such that $\vdash^{[s]} me$, the *evaluation of* me w.r.t. $\mathcal{D}$, denoted by $\llbracket me \rrbracket^{\mathcal{D}}$, is a constant method over $\mathcal{D}$ of sort s (of null sort if $\vdash me$), i.e. it consists of a Σ-algebra B, and, if s is non-null, of a value $b \in B_s$; we assume $\mathcal{D}$ fixed and write

$$me \to^{[s]} <B[,b]>$$

for

$$\llbracket me \rrbracket^{\mathcal{D}} = <B[,b]>, \text{ [with } b \in B_s].$$

The evaluation of method expressions is inductively defined in **Fig.3.1**. $\square$

3.2 Towards a kernel language

Like terms in the static case, method expressions can be used as the starting point for building a language for defining methods. In this subsection we show, as an example of construct which can be introduced in the language, a *conditional* (assuming that the underlying data structure includes booleans, i.e. formally every instant algebra has the algebra of booleans as subalgebra) whose semantics is as follows (we show the case of non-constant method expressions, the other is analogous).

$$\frac{me \underset{r}{\to}{}^{bool} <f: A \Rightarrow B, true> \qquad me_1 \underset{r'}{\to}{}^{[s]} <g: B \Rightarrow C[,c]>}{\text{if } me \text{ then } me_1 \text{ else } me_2 \text{ endif} \underset{r}{\to}{}^{[s]} <g \cdot f: A \Rightarrow C[,c]>}$$

1.
$$\overline{dop(t_1,\ldots,t_n) \underset{r}{\to}^{[s]} dop^{\mathcal{D}}{}_{<A,a_1,\ldots,a_n>}}$$

$r\colon X \to A$, $dop\colon s_1 \ldots s_n \Rightarrow [s]$,
$t_1,\ldots,t_n \in T_\Sigma(X)_{s_1\ldots s_n}$, $<t_1,\ldots,t_n>^{A,r} = <a_1,\ldots,a_n>$

2. $\overline{t \underset{r}{\to}^s <id_A\colon A \Rightarrow A, a>}$ $r\colon X \to A$, $t \in T_\Sigma(X)_s$, $t^{A,r} = a$

3. $\overline{dop \to^{[s]} dop^{\mathcal{D}}}$ $dop\colon [s]$

4. $$\frac{me_1 \underset{r}{\to}^{s_1} <f\colon A \Rightarrow B, b> \qquad me_2 \underset{r'}{\to}^{[s_2]} <g\colon B \Rightarrow C[, c]>}{\text{let } x = me_1 \text{ in } me_2 \text{ endlet} \underset{r}{\to}^{[s_2]} <g \cdot f\colon A \Rightarrow C[, c]>}$$

$r\colon X \to A$, $r'\colon X[s_1/x] \to B$, $r'(y) = f(r(y))$, for $y \neq x$, $r'(x) = b$

5. $$\frac{me_1 \underset{r}{\to} f\colon A \Rightarrow B \qquad me_2 \underset{r'}{\to}^{[s_2]} <g\colon B \Rightarrow C[, c]>}{\text{let } me_1 \text{ in } me_2 \text{ endlet} \underset{r}{\to}^{[s_2]} <g \cdot f\colon A \Rightarrow C[, c]>}$$

$r\colon X \to A$, $r'\colon X \to B$, $r'(y) = f(r(y))$;

6. $$\frac{me_1 \to^{s_1} <B[, b]> \qquad me_2 \underset{r}{\to}^{[s_2]} <g\colon B \Rightarrow C[, c]>}{\text{let } x = me_1 \text{ in } me_2 \text{ endlet} \to^{[s_2]} <C[, c]>}$$

$r\colon \{x\colon s_1\} \to B$, $r(x) = b$

7. $$\frac{me_1 \to B \qquad me_2 \underset{r}{\to}^{[s_2]} <g\colon B \Rightarrow C[, c]>}{\text{let } me_1 \text{ in } me_2 \text{ endlet} \to^{[s_2]} <C[, c]>}$$ $r\colon \emptyset \to B$

8. $$\overline{dop(t_1,\ldots,t_n) \underset{r}{\to} f\colon A \Rightarrow B}$$

$r\colon X \to A$, $dop\colon s_1 \ldots s_n \Rightarrow s$, $t_1,\ldots,t_n \in T_\Sigma(X)_{s_1\ldots s_n}$,
$<t_1,\ldots,t_n>^{A,r} = <a_1,\ldots,a_n>$, $dop^{\mathcal{D}}{}_{<A,a_1,\ldots,a_n>} = <f\colon A \Rightarrow B, b>$

9. $\overline{dop \to B}$ $dop\colon s$, $dop^{\mathcal{D}} = <B, b>$

Figure 2: **Semantics**

$r\colon X \to A,\ r'\colon X \to B,\ r'(x) = f(r(x)).$

$$\frac{me \underset{r}{\to}^{bool} <f\colon A \Rightarrow B, false> \qquad me_2 \underset{r'}{\to}^{[s]} <g\colon B \Rightarrow C[,c]>}{\textbf{if } me \textbf{ then } me_1 \textbf{ else } me_2 \textbf{ endif} \underset{r}{\to}^{[s]} <g \cdot f\colon A \Rightarrow C[,c]>}$$

$r\colon X \to A,\ r'\colon X \to B,\ r'(x) = f(r(x)).$

For what concerns *recursive definitions*, it is easy to handle them following the style of inductive semantics (see [1], [3], [9]). We add method variables to the signature (generic element mid) and consider recursive declarations (we show here a single declaration for simplicity) of the form

$$mid(x_1, \ldots, x_n) = me \qquad x_1\colon s_1, \ldots, x_n\colon s_n$$

where in the method expression me only mid may appear of the method variables. Then its semantics in $\mathcal{D}$ is (we show the case of non-constant method expressions, the other is analogous):

$$\frac{me \underset{r'}{\to}^{[s]} <f\colon A \Rightarrow B[,b]>}{mid(t_1, \ldots, t_n) \underset{r}{\to}^{[s]} <f\colon A \Rightarrow B[,b]>}$$

$r\colon X \to A,\ <t_1, \ldots, t_n>^{A,r} = <a_1, \ldots, a_n>,$
$r'\colon \{x_1\colon s_1, \ldots, x_n\colon s_n\} \to A,\ r'(x_1) = a_1, \ldots, r'(x_n) = a_n.$

Finally, it is convenient to allow in the kernel language *compound method expressions*, defined by (e.g. in the constant case)

$$\frac{\vdash^{s_1} me_1, \ldots, \vdash^{s_n} me_n}{\vdash^{[s]} dop(me_1, \ldots, me_n)} \qquad dop\colon s_1 \ldots s_n \Rightarrow [s]$$

which is an abbreviation for

let $x_1 = me_1$ **in**
   let $x_2 = me_2$ **in**
       $\ldots$
      let $x_n = me_n$ **in** $dop(x_1, \ldots, x_n)$ **endlet**
       $\ldots$
  endlet
endlet

4   Towards modelling classes and inheritance

Here we give some hints towards the use of d-oids for modelling object oriented features like semantics of classes (object types) and inheritance; for a paper focused on this issue, see [2].

Consider the following object type, which defines a person as a legal entity in which a third information has been added, using the inheritance mechanism:

```
object type PERSON subtypeOf LEGAL_ENTITY is
instance variables
     SSNo: NUMBER;
operations
     getSSNo () : NUMBER { return SSNo };
     putSSNo (n : NUMBER) { SSNo := n };
end PERSON
```

It is easy to see that the dynamic signature corresponding to this class, say $D\Sigma_{\mathcal{P}}$, can be obtained from the preceding dynamic signature $D\Sigma_{\mathcal{LE}}$ replacing the sort $legEnt$ by the sort $person$ and adding a static operation $(SSNo)$ and two dynamic operations $(getSSNo$ and $putSSNo)$. That is modelled in a natural way by the notion of morphism of dynamic signatures.

Def. 4.9 Let $D\Sigma = (\Sigma, DOP)$, $D\Sigma' = (\Sigma', DOP')$ be two dynamic signatures; a *dynamic signature morphism* σ *from* $D\Sigma$ *into* $D\Sigma'$, written $\sigma: D\Sigma \to D\Sigma'$, is a couple $\sigma = <\sigma^I, \sigma^D>$ where:

- $\sigma^I: \Sigma \to \Sigma'$ is a signature morphism (I stands for "instant");

- $\sigma^D: DOP \to DOP'$ (D stands for "dynamic") is such that

$$\sigma^D(dop: s_1 \dots s_n \Rightarrow [s]): \sigma^I(s_1) \dots \sigma^I(s_n) \Rightarrow [\sigma^I(s)],$$
$$\sigma^D(dop: [s]): [\sigma^I(s)]. \quad \Box$$

We will often write simply σ for σ^I, σ^D.

Dynamic signatures and their morphisms form a category, that we call **DynSig**.

From the semantic point of view, the relation between the "parent" d-oid $\mathcal{LE}$ and the "heir" d-oid $\mathcal{P}$ modelling a universe of systems of persons is more involved. We assume, in what follows, that $\mathcal{LE}$ is the particular version of the d-oid defined in sect.2 where we choose the "pure identities" representation for legal entities, and that $\mathcal{P}$ is an analogous d-oid for persons. That choice allows a simpler formal counterpart of the parent-heir relation; for a more general version see [2].

First of all, note that with this choice a configuration of a system of persons can be obtained from a configuration of a system of legal entities adding, for every existing legal entity, the SSNo information; formally, adding to an instant algebra on $\Sigma_{\mathcal{LE}}$, the interpretation of the static operation $SSNo$. Moreover it is possible, given a system of persons, to "go back", obtaining a system of legal entities, just "forgetting" the third dimension. Intuitively, a system of legal entities gives a particular *view* of a system of persons. That is modelled in a natural way by the notion of *reduct* in the static algebraic framework, formally given below.

Def. 4.10 If $\sigma: \Sigma \to \Sigma'$ is a signature morphism, A' an algebra over Σ', then the *reduct of A' w.r.t. σ, written $A'_{|\sigma}$*, is the algebra A over Σ defined as follows:

- for each $s \in S$, $A_s = A'_{\sigma(s)}$;

- for each $op: s_1 \ldots s_n \to s$ in Σ, $a_1 \in A_{s_1}, \ldots, a_n \in A_{s_n}$,

$$op^A(a_1, \ldots, a_n) = \sigma(op)^{A'}(a_1, \ldots, a_n).$$

In particular, if $\iota: \Sigma \to \Sigma'$ is the embedding, then we write also $A'_{|\Sigma}$ instead of $A'_{|\iota}$. □

We consider now dynamic operations in the parent and heir d-oid. In the example, it seems from an intuitive point of view that the heir class preserves the "behaviour" of the parent class, since no methods are redefined. That is an example of what we call "consistent inheritance".

Formally, the interpretation of *putTelNo* in $\mathcal{P}$ cannot be exactly the old one (since it acts now on algebras on an extended signature), but must be an "extension" of the old one; the intuitive idea is that the method has exactly the old effect on the "old part" (in this case the telephone number and name), and has no effect at all on the "new part" (in this case, it does not change SSNo).

However this property of consistency with the old version may hold also when the method is redefined; for example, if we redefine putTelNo in PERSON as follows:

```
putTelNo (n : NUMBER) { TelNo: = n; SSNo := n }
```

while it does not hold obviously for this redefinition, which is non-consistent:

```
(*) putTelNo (n : NUMBER) { TelNo: = 0 }
```

In all these cases it is possible, given a method on persons, to "go back", obtaining a method on legal entities, just "forgetting" the effect of the method on the SSNo. That is modelled in a natural way by the notion of *reduct* of a method w.r.t. a given dynamic signature morphism, as given below. In the case of consistent inheritance, we get exactly as reduct of the redefined method the old version; but this is not always true in the non-consistent case. For example in the case of (*) the reduct turns out to be a method on legal entities which sets the telephone number to zero, hence different from the old version.

Moreover, the reduct of a method is not always defined; consider for example the following redefinition

```
(**)putTelNo (n : NUMBER) { TelNo: = SSNo }
```

In this case not only the redefinition is not consistent, but it is also impossible to get from this method on persons a method on legal entities; intuitively, the effect of this method on the legal entity view of a person cannot be deduced from the legal entity view alone. In other words, after being reduced, the method is not well-defined. That can be formally expressed by a *regularity condition* on methods, whose informal version is:

if we apply $dop^{\mathcal{P}}$ to two instant tuples in $\mathcal{P}$ which have the same correspondent in $\mathcal{LE}$ (formally, the same image via the σ-reduct operation), then we get two instant couples in $\mathcal{P}$ which still have the same correspondent in $\mathcal{LE}$.

For example, in the case of the definition of *putTelNo* in (*), the regularity condition is satisfied. Indeed if two instant tuples $<A'_1, p_1, n_1>$, $<A'_2, p_2, n_2>$

have the same image via the σ-reduct operation, then A'_1 and A'_2 have the same σ-reduct, p_1 and p_2 must be the same, n_1 and n_2 must be the same. Thus, since the effect of *putTelNo* is local, i.e. a change of the argument person, then the results in the two cases are two configurations still with the same legal entity view, and the two changed persons have still the same legal entity part.

Notice, on the contrary, that the definition (**) of *putTelNo* clearly does not meet this regularity condition.

Formally we have the following definition.

Def. 4.11 Let $D\Sigma = (\Sigma, DOP)$, $D\Sigma' = (\Sigma', DOP')$ be two dynamic signatures, $\sigma: D\Sigma \rightarrow D\Sigma'$, $\mathcal{D}' = (D', \{dop^{\mathcal{D}'}\}_{dop \in DOP})$ a d-oid over $D\Sigma'$; set $D'_{|\sigma} = \{A'_{|\sigma} \mid A' \in D'\}$.

Let $dop: [s]$ be a constant dynamic operation symbol in $D\Sigma$; then the method
$$dop^{\mathcal{D}'|_\sigma}: (D'_{|\sigma})_{[s]}$$

is defined as follows

if $\sigma(dop)^{\mathcal{D}'} = <B'[, b']>$, then $dop^{\mathcal{D}'|_\sigma} = <B'_{|\sigma}[, b']>$.

Let $dop: s_1 \ldots s_n \Rightarrow [s]$ dynamic operation symbol in $D\Sigma$, and assume that the following *regularity condition* holds:

(*) for every A', $B' \in D'$ s.t.
$$A'_{|\sigma} = B'_{|\sigma}, \; a'_1 \in A'_{\sigma(s_1)}(= B'_{\sigma(s_1)}), \; \ldots, \; a'_n \in A'_{\sigma(s_n)}(= B'_{\sigma(s_n)}),$$
if
$$\sigma(dop)^{\mathcal{D}'}_{<A', a'_1, \ldots, a'_n>} = <f: A' \Rightarrow C'[, c']>$$
$$\sigma(dop)^{\mathcal{D}'}_{<B', a'_1, \ldots, a'_n>} = <g: B' \Rightarrow E'[, e']>$$
then
$$C'_{|\sigma} = E'_{|\sigma},$$
$$f(a') = g(a'), \text{ for every } a' \in A'_{|\sigma}(= B'_{|\sigma}),$$
$$[c' = e'].$$

Then the method
$$dop^{\mathcal{D}'|_\sigma}: (D'_{|\sigma})_{s_1 \ldots s_n} \Rightarrow (D'_{|\sigma})_{[s]}$$

is defined as follows:

(**) for every $A'_{|\sigma} \in D'_{|\sigma}$, $a'_1 \in (A'_{|\sigma})_{s_1}, \ldots, a'_n \in (A'_{|\sigma})_{s_n}$,
if
$$\sigma(dop)^{\mathcal{D}'}_{<A', a'_1, \ldots, a'_n>} = <f: A' \Rightarrow C'[, c']>$$
then
$$dop^{\mathcal{D}'|_\sigma}_{<A'_{|\sigma}, a'_1, \ldots, a'_n>} = <f_{|\sigma}: A'_{|\sigma} \Rightarrow C'_{|\sigma}[, c']>,$$
where, for every $a' \in A'_{|\sigma}$, $f_{|\sigma}(a') = f(a')$.

If the condition (*) does not hold, then $dop^{\mathcal{D}'|_\sigma}$ is undefined. $\square$

Def. 4.12 Let $D\Sigma = (\Sigma, DOP)$, $D\Sigma' = (\Sigma', DOP')$ be two dynamic signatures, $\sigma: D\Sigma \to D\Sigma'$, $\mathcal{D}' = (D', \{dop^{\mathcal{D}'}\}_{dop \in DOP})$ a d-oid over $D\Sigma'$, and assume that, for every $dop: s_1 \ldots s_n \Rightarrow [s]$ in $D\Sigma$, the condition (*) holds; then the σ-*reduct of* $\mathcal{D}'$, written $\mathcal{D}'|_\sigma$, is the d-oid over $D\Sigma$ defined as follows:

$$\mathcal{D}'|_\sigma = (D'|_\sigma, \{dop^{\mathcal{D}'|_\sigma}\}_{dop \in DOP}). \quad \Box$$

Hence the reduct is only defined for methods which satisfy the regularity condition, of which consistent inheritance is a particular case.

Referring to the preceding examples, let $\iota: D\Sigma_{\mathcal{L}\mathcal{E}} \to D\Sigma_{\mathcal{P}}$ be the dynamic signature morphism defined by $\iota^{St}(legEnt) = person$, ι is the embedding elsewhere. Then it is easy to see that $\mathcal{L}\mathcal{E}$ turns out to be the reduct of $\mathcal{P}$ w.r.t. ι.

5 Conclusion

We have presented a model for dynamic systems of objects which should be, in our view, the correspondent of algebras, the classical model for static data types. Our model presents many novel features, compared to what is known in the literature, as we are going to discuss briefly. The idea of modelling every configuration as an algebra is not new: it has been used in the COLD language (see [14], part II), for long time within the structural inductive semantics (see [3]) and also much emphasized in the evolving algebra approach (see e.g. [12]). The novelty of the proposed approach is twofold. First we embody the dynamics (the evolution) into the structure: a d-oid is an overall structure which covers both static and dynamic aspects in a uniform way, extending the usual data type concept. The second novelty lies in the way we formalize methods as transformations with the notion of tracking map, which plays a fundamental role in the definition of semantics. The tracking map is also essential in the application to object oriented systems (a subject only touched here); for example a partial tracking map corresponds to allow object disappearance, non-surjectivity corresponds to object creation, non-injectivity to discover that two object are the same ("the murder is the butler") and so on. In [2] we give an attempt at modelling by d-oids different inheritance relations.

In [10] approaches for dealing with objects and their specifications are classified into ADT-based and process-based. Our work is in some sense in an intermediate position between the abstract data type based approach to objects (a recent and extensive analysis in this direction can be found in [5], and algebraic techniques have been used for giving the semantics of a class of object oriented languages eg in [6]) and process-based approaches where the evolution is described using typical models of the concurrency theory like traces. Indeed we go outside of the usual algebraic framework, but do not consider objects as processes, and model their evolution by dynamic operations which are analogous to the static ones, but at a different formal level.

As it should be clear from the presentation we do not deal with concurrency issues. Our semantic model could be the basis for the semantics of languages like C++, Smalltalk and Eiffel. A most interesting topic would be to relate it to process-based models of objects (see [10]) both for an approach based on this idea and references). On the other hand our approach clearly departs from a purelu applicative setting, like the one presented in [8]; we consider objects as data with state.

What we do here is in the spirit of the "languages for data directed design", discussed in [13]; from this viewpoint, classes are a way of defining data and inheritance is a tool for building classes incrementally. Semantics of incremental definition of classes is outside of the scope of this paper and will be the subject of a forthcoming one.

We are currently using d-oids for extending to the dynamic case the theory of abstract data types. A theory has been developed which shows that d-oids constitute the model part of specification formalisms for dynamic systems (institutions, in the sense of Burstall and Goguen [7]).

There is some ground to believe that the semantic model presented here may be used for extending the nice algebraic framework for database query languages of Beeri [4] to deal with update languages. Also, though we have not room for showing it here, it seems possible to use our model as semantic model for the language by Gottlob at al. in [11].

Acknowledgements. We gratefully acnowledge the extremely careful reading and detailed report of an anonymous referee, who helped us to improve the presentation and avoid, we hope, various misunderstanding.

We also thank our colleagues of ISCORE WG for some lively and useful discussions on the subject.

References

[1] P. Aczel. An introduction to inductive definitions. In J. Barwise, editor, *Handbook of Mathematical logic*, Amsterdam, 1977. North-Holland.

[2] D. Ancona, E. Astesiano, and E. Zucca. Towards a classification of inheritance relations. Technical report, Dipartimento di Informatica e Scienze dell'Informazione, Università di Genova, December 1992. Submitted for publication.

[3] E. Astesiano. Inductive and operational semantics. In E. J. Neuhold and M. Paul, editors, *Formal description of programming concepts*, Berlin, 1990. Springer Verlag.

[4] C. Beeri. Theoretical foundations for oodb's - a personal perspective. *Database Engineering*, 1991. To appear.

[5] R. Breu. *Algebraic specification techniques in object oriented programming environment*. PhD thesis, Universität Passau - TU München, Berlin, 1991.

[6] R. Breu and E. Zucca. An algebraic compositional semantics of an object oriented notation with concurrency. In C.E. Veni Madhavan, editor, *Proc. 9th Conference on Foundations of Software Technology and Theoretical Computer Science*, number 405 in Lecture Notes in Computer Science, pages 131–142, Berlin, 1989. Springer Verlag.

[7] R. M. Burstall and J. A. Goguen. Introducing institutions. In E. Clarke and D. Kozen, editors, *Logics of Programming Workshop*, number 164 in Lecture Notes in Computer Science, pages 221–254, Berlin, 1992. Springer Verlag.

[8] W. Cook. *A denotational semantics of inheritance.* PhD thesis, Brown University, 1989.

[9] P. Cousot and R. Cousot. Inductive definitions, semantics and abstract interpretation. In *Proc. POPL '92*, pages 83–94, 1992.

[10] H. D. Ehrich, M. Gogolla, and A. Sernadas. Objects and their specification. In M. Bidoit and C. Choppy, editors, *Recent Trends in Data Type Specification*, number 655 in Lecture Notes in Computer Science, Berlin, 1992. Springer Verlag.

[11] G. Gottlob, G. Kappel, and M. Schrefl. Semantics of object oriented data models-the evolving algebra approach. In J. W. Schmidt, editor, *International Workshop on Information Systems for the 90's*, Lecture Notes in Computer Science, Berlin, 1991. Springer Verlag.

[12] Y. Gurevich. Evolving algebras, a tutorial introduction. *Bulletin of the EATCS*, (43):264–284, 1991.

[13] E. G. Wagner. Some mathematical thoughts on languages for data directed design. Technical Report RC 16686 (73950), IBM Research Division, 1991.

[14] M. Wirsing and J. A. Bergstra, editors. *Algebraic Methods: Theory, Tools and Applications.* Number 394 in Lecture Notes in Computer Science. Springer Verlag, Berlin, 1987.

An Order-sorted Approach to Active Objects

Georg Reichwein

Departamento de Matemática, IST, and
Grupo de Engenharia em Lógica, INESC
Apartado 10105, P-1017 Lisboa Codex, Portugal
ger@inesc.pt

Abstract

Order-sorted conditional equational logic is proposed as a framework for the specification and verification of active objects. One single algebra can be used to cover both data and process aspects of active objects, with pure data objects, e.g. integer numbers, on one end of the spectrum, and pure behaviour, e.g. automata, on the other. The order-sorted approach is presented in a categorial setting which provides a formalization of object interaction and reification through suitable morphisms in a way such that reification distributes over parallel composition.

1 Introduction

There is still a quest for adequate formalisms which capture the essence of active objects in a way that makes specification and verification of behavioural properties feasible, even (and in particular) for large-scale Information Systems. While for passive objects a theory of (abstract) data types has matured (cf. [1] and [2]), active objects have as yet resisted their satisfactory integration into this framework. This paper suggests a unifying algebraic view which integrates abstract data types on one end of the spectrum and general automata on the other.

Objects themselves are a unifying notion whose dimensions (active vs. passive, transient vs. persistent) cover all types of entities which are found in Information Systems. An *object* is usually considered to be a collection of attributes (state dependent variables local to the object) and events. An event of an object Ob can be the answering of another object's query about the state of Ob (leaving the state of Ob unchanged), and/or an action which alters the state of Ob. An object is said to be *active* if it may perform (some of) its events by its own initiative (i.e. if it requires CPU resources). Interacting objects may share certain events, i.e. they synchronize their (otherwise independent) behaviour at these events.

Order-sorted conditional equational logic is used in Abstract Data Type specifications to avoid the problems raised by partial functions (like asking for the top of an empty stack, cf. [3]). Object-oriented conceptual modelling assumes attribute values and event parameters to be of some data type - which can be an abstract one, specified by an order-sorted theory. On the other hand, data stores are conveniently modelled as passive objects of types (classes) like stack, queue,... It is therefore a natural approach to fit active objects into the same framework. The idea is to introduce additional sorts which stand for classes of states, and to model state transitions as functions between these sorts (this is similar to the introduction of a sort "non-empty-stack" in the above ADT example). Terms built from these functions denote object behaviour, and attributes are functions from state sorts into data sorts.

Following [4], one main group of related work on algebraic specification of active objects is that on Entity Algebras. Such algebras distinguish between static and dynamic sorts, where the elements of dynamic sorts are states of objects (in contrast to the approach proposed herein where the states are themselves represented as sorts). Work in this direction is e.g. [5], [6], and [7]. Recently [8] proposed a kind of evolving algebras, called d-oids, as a semantic domain for dynamic systems.

Other approaches define abstract data types for the processes which constitute the behaviour of objects, like in [9]. The research reported herein has been triggered by [10] who introduced equational specification of dynamic objects by specifying the structural aspects of objects, i.e. their data parts, as an abstract data type, and using process algebra to specify the possible behaviour of the objects. Process algebra as a means to specify object behaviour has also been investigated by [11] and [12]. This paper improves the above mentioned approaches by using only one (surprisingly simple) algebra to cover both data and process aspects of active objects. Such objects are composed into systems of concurrently interacting objects using techniques from category theory, namely computing limits of categorial diagrams (see [13] for an introduction to category theory directed to computer scientists). We show how reification fits into this framework, showing that the parallel composition of two reifications is a reification of the composition.

The most similar framework to the one proposed herein is perhaps FOOPS ([14]). It however distinguishes two kinds of conceptual entities, namely functional modules, which are abstract data type definitions, and object modules which define persistent but changing entities. Like FOOPS the approach presented in this paper is based on conditional equational logic, but we prefer to view data and active objects as two extreme cases of the same concept. The proposed order-sorted approach to active objects groups states into situations, where a *situation* is characterized by the set of events which lead to and/or leave from it. Each situation becomes a sort symbol in an algebraic specification of the object, and events are then functions between those sorts. Possible behaviours of the object correspond to possible terms built from the event symbols. This "factors out" the automata part of object behaviour, in a way similar to the behaviour diagrams of OBLOG, as shown in [15]. Attributes, as expected, are functions on the state of the object, and hence have situations as their domains. Among the situation sorts we indicate one topmost sort, to solve the technical difficulty of making the attributes applicable to every possible state, regardless of the grouping into situations. The topmost sort cannot be in the domain of any event, we consider it to correspond to some post-mortem situation. Birth events, on the other hand, are functions having a situation in their codomain, but none in their domain.

In [15] we use order-sorted conditional equational theories to define an algebraic semantics of OBLOG, a graphical design language for large-scale information systems, also addressing the reasoning about behavioural properties of active objects. This paper stresses object interaction and reification. A differ-

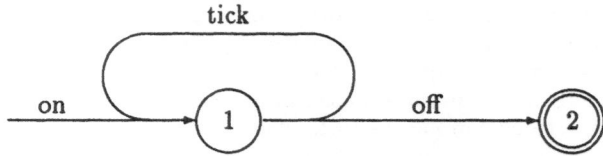

Figure 1: CLOCK

ent approach to equational reasoning about active objects is followed in [16], where equational logic is used to implement a dynamic logic. Temporal logic specification of database dynamics is addressed in [17].

2 Regular Behaviour

A most simple class of active objects are finite automata. Having no internal memory apart from their finite number of states (and hence no attributes), they allow us to specify "pure behaviour", without any data aspects, just like e.g. the Peano axioms specify "pure data" without any process aspects. Consider for example the automaton depicted in figure 1. Its behaviour is described by the regular expression

$$\text{on} \cdot \text{tick}^* \cdot \text{off}$$

which defines a language over the alphabet {on, tick, off}.

We now give an order-sorted specification of CLOCK, using the notation of OBJ3 ([18], [19]). OBJ3 implements order-sorted conditional equational logic, a powerful formalism of which we shall take advantage in the following sections. For the easy case of finite automata, however, all we need are sorted signatures. The regular behaviour exhibited by finite automata is simple enough to be described as the freely generated terms over a sorted signature, without the need to introduce any axioms.

```
obj CLOCK is
  sorts C1 C2 .
  subsort C1 < C2 .
  op on : -> C1 .
  op tick : C1 -> C1 .
  op off : C1 -> C2 .
endo
```

Formally, we define object signatures as a special case of order-sorted equational signatures:

Definition 1 (object signature) *An object signature is a triple* $\Sigma = (S, \leq, F)$ *where*

- $S = \mathsf{S} \cup \{\mathsf{t}\} \cup \mathsf{D}$
  is a set of sort symbols, where D are symbols for data sorts and S are symbols for situation sorts with the distinguished symbol t standing for the topmost situation sort.

- $F = \{F_{u,s}\}_{u \in S^*, s \in S}$
  is an $S^* \times S$-indexed family of function (or operation) symbols whose members are of one of the following forms:

  - $u \in \mathsf{D}^*$ and $s \in \mathsf{D}$ (datatype operations)
  - $u \in \mathsf{tD}^*$ and $s \in \mathsf{D}$ (attributes)
  - $u \in \mathsf{D}^*$ and $s \in \mathsf{S}$ (birth events)
  - $u \in \mathsf{SD}^*$ and $s \in \mathsf{S}\text{-}\{\mathsf{t}\}$ (events)
  - $u \in \mathsf{SD}^*$ and $s = \mathsf{t}$ (death events)

  Moreover, F contains trivial events $skip \in F_{s D*,s}$ for every situation sort $s \in \mathsf{S}$

- $(S, \leq)$ is a partial order satisfying the following conditions:

  - $f \in F_{u,s} \cap F_{u',s'}$ and $u \leq u'$ implies $s \leq s'$ (monotonicity)
    where $s_{1 \dots n} \leq s'_1 \dots s'_n$ iff $s_i \leq s'_i$ for $1 \leq i \leq n$
  - $s \in \mathsf{S}$ implies $s \leq \mathsf{t}$ (topmost situation sort)

The technical reason to distinguish a topmost situation sort symbol t is to have a unique domain for attributes which can be evaluated in every situation. As a convention we shall identify the topmost situation with the final post-mortem state. This makes sense because after a death event nothing else can happen to the object, i.e. there is no applicable event.

In the above example, $\mathsf{S} = \{\mathsf{C1}, \mathsf{C2}\}$ with $\mathsf{t} = \mathsf{C2}$, and $F_{C1} = \{\mathsf{on}, \mathsf{skip}_{C1}\}$, $F_{C2} = \{\mathsf{skip}_{C2}\}$, $F_{C1C1} = \{\mathsf{tick}\}$, $F_{C1C2} = \{\mathsf{off}\}$. There are no data sorts in this simple example. In general events can have parameters of data sorts $s \in \mathsf{D}$, they model data transfer between objects, or provide initializations at birth events. We have no object-valued attributes in our approach. They can be either modelled as attributes which evaluate to object identities which are data values, i.e. key values which serve as pointers to the actual objects, or using aggregation to incorporate the attributes as parts into the object. Such techniques are discussed in section 4.

Object signatures as defined above are signatures of single objects, or, more precisely, single object templates. Systems of composed and interacting objects are intended to be modelled through morphisms between objects, where the system is again viewed as a single object. To achieve this formally we need the trivial events, they represent events from a lower level of abstraction which are "hidden" from the present one. Several objects in one specification would correspond to a partitioning of the state sorts. We achieve this automatically through the computation of categorial limits (details of this construction are defered to section 4 of the paper).

Definition 2 (terms) Given an object signature $\Sigma = (S, \leq, F)$, a set of variables X and a function $\Xi: X \rightarrow S$, the S-indexed set $T(\Sigma)$ of terms over Σ is defined inductively as follows:

- *if $\Xi(v) = s$, then $v \in T(\Sigma)_s$*

- *if $f \in F_{s_1...s_n,s}$ and $t_i \in T(\Sigma)_{r_i}$ such that $r_i \leq s_i$, then $f(t_1,...,t_n) \in T(\Sigma)_s$*

While signatures provide *syntax*, for the specification of computational objects we are also interested in the *semantics* of the expressions built with the syntax, i.e., we need particular entities of the given sorts, and particular functions to interpret the operation symbols.

Definition 3 (order-sorted Σ-algebra) *For an object signature $\Sigma = (S,\leq,F)$, an order-sorted Σ-algebra $\mathbf{A} = (A,\mathsf{A})$ consists of*

- *an S-indexed family A of non-empty carrier sets $\{A_s\}_{s \in S}$ such that $s \leq s'$ implies $A_s \subseteq A_{s'}$*

- *an $S^* \times S$-indexed family A of functions $\mathsf{A}_{u,s}: F_{u,s} \to [A_u \to A_s]$ assigning a function to each function symbol $f \in F_{u,s}$ such that $f \in F_{u,s} \cap F_{u',s'}$ and $u \leq u'$ implies $\mathsf{A}_{u,s}(f) = \mathsf{A}_{u',s'}(f)|_{A_u}$ where $A_{s_1...s_n} = A_{s_1} \times ... \times A_{s_n}$ and $[A \to B]$ denotes the set of all functions from A to B, and $\phi|_A$ is the restriction of ϕ to arguments from A.*

Notice that in the algebras there is one single function (denotation, semantic object) for each polymorphic function symbol in the signature. This is to say that the interpretation of functions on subsorts is the same as the interpretation of the corresponding function on the supersort (which is, because of the type restriction, never applied to non-appropriate arguments). A particularly interesting algebra for the CLOCK signature is (A,A) with

$$A(C1) = \{on\} \cdot \{tick\}^* \qquad \mathsf{A}(on) = on$$
$$A(C2) = \{on\} \cdot \{tick\}^* \cdot off \qquad \mathsf{A}(tick) = \lambda s.s \cdot tick$$
$$\mathsf{A}(off) = \lambda s.s \cdot off$$

Under this interpretation terms denote possible behaviours of CLOCK. The interpretation of terms by a Σ-algebra is formally defined as follows:

Definition 4 (interpretation) *Let $\mathbf{A} = (A,\mathsf{A})$ be a Σ-algebra and $\alpha: X \to A$ an assignment of values in A to the variables in X. Then the interpretation in $\mathbf{A}$ of terms in $T(\Sigma)$ with respect to α is defined as:*

- $[\![v]\!]^{\mathbf{A},\alpha} = \alpha(v)$

- $[\![f(t_1,...,t_n)]\!]^{\mathbf{A},\alpha} = \mathsf{A}(f) \, ([\![t_1]\!]^{\mathbf{A},\alpha},...,[\![t_n]\!]^{\mathbf{A},\alpha})$

3 Non-regular Behaviour

Active objects, of course, are more than finite automata: their behaviour is too complex to be described as a regular language. In particular there may be an infinite number of states, and consequently also an infinite number of transitions. *Attributes* are a way to finitely describe an infinite set of states which is partitioned into a finite number of equivalence classes called *situations*. Transitions between situations are called *events*, and may be parameterized to identify the underlying state transition. (Note the analogy to register machines being finite automata equipped with infinite memory.) Figure 2 shows the

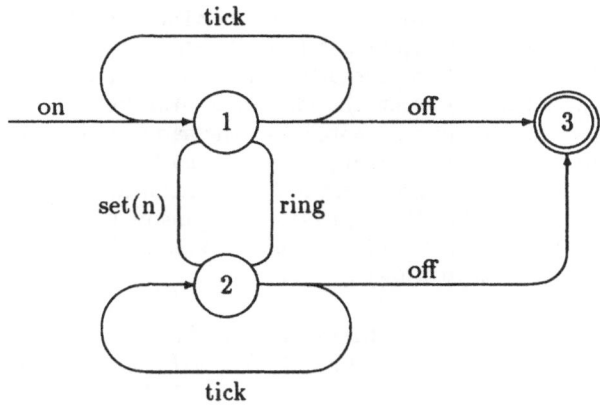

Figure 2: ALARMCLOCK

transition diagram of an alarmclock, which is a clock that can be programmed to ring after a certain number of ticks. Notice that the circles now denote situations, and that the arrows denote events, i.e., classes of state transitions. It is not possible using only finite automata to specify that an alarmclock rings after exactly the elapsed time specified by the parameter of the most recent set(n) event. This behaviour of ALARMCLOCK is described by the non-regular language

$$\text{on} \cdot \text{tick}^* \cdot \{\text{set(n)} \cdot \text{tick}^n \cdot \text{ring} | n \in N_o\}^*$$
$$\cdot (\text{tick}^* \cup \{\text{set(n)} \cdot \text{tick}^m | n,m \in N_o,\, m \leq n\}) \cdot \text{off}$$

The signature of such an object is given below. It has still to be augmented with axioms specifying the effects of the events on the attributes **alarm**, **elapsed**, and **set?**. Notice the use of ordered sorts to allow the application of the access functions (i.e., the attributes) to every reachable state.

```
obj ALARMCLOCK is
  sorts A1 A2 A3 .
  subsort A1 < A3 .
  subsort A2 < A3 .
  ops alarm elapsed : A3 -> Nat .
  op set? : A3 -> Bool .
  op on : -> A1 .
  op tick : A1 -> A1 .
  op tick : A2 -> A2 .
  op set : A1 Nat -> A2 .
  op ring : A2 -> A1 .
  op off : A1 -> A3 .
  op off : A2 -> A3 .
endo
```

Notice the overloading of the event symbols **tick** and **off**. Comparing the graphs reveals an obvious morphism h from ALARMCLOCK to CLOCK, identifying the situations 1 and 2 and forgetting (i.e., mapping to $skip_{C1}$) the transitions **set(n)** and **ring** between the identified situations. Overloaded event symbols with the same name are mapped to the same symbol in CLOCK, in a way that is consistent with the mapping of the sorts. Formally, CLOCK is a quotient of ALARMCLOCK with respect to h, which characterizes ALARMCLOCK as a *superposition* of CLOCK. Superposition morphisms between active objects can be captured by theory morphisms, as is explained below (cf. [20] for a categorial theory of superposition).

Definition 5 (signature morphism) *A morphism* $\phi : \Sigma_1 \to \Sigma_2$ *of object signatures from* $\Sigma_1 = (S_1, \leq_1, F_1)$ *to* $\Sigma_2 = (S_2, \leq_2, F_2)$ *is a pair* (ϕ_s, ϕ_f) *with*

- $\phi_s \colon S_1 \to S_2$ *a map of sorts (a total function) such that* $\phi_s(\mathsf{S}_1) \subseteq \mathsf{S}_2$, $\phi_s(\mathsf{t}_1) = \mathsf{t}_2$, $\phi_s(\mathsf{D}_1) \subseteq \mathsf{D}_2$, *and if* $s \leq_1 s'$ *then* $\phi_s(s) \leq_2 \phi_s(s')$

- $\phi_f \colon F_1 \to F_2$ *an* $S_1^* \times S_1$-*indexed family of total functions* $(\phi_f)_{u,s} \colon F_{1_{u,s}} \to F_{2_{\phi_s^*(u),\phi_s(s)}}$ *such that* $\phi_f(skip_u) = skip_{\phi_s^*(u)}$

where $\phi_s^* \colon S_1^* \to S_2^*$ *is the extension of* ϕ *to strings defined by* $\phi_s^*(\Lambda) = \Lambda$, *where* Λ *denotes the empty string, and* $\phi_s^*(vs) = \phi_s^*(v)\phi_s(s)$ *for* v *in* S_1^* *and* s *in* S_1.

A signature morphism hence maps a state sort to a state sort and a data sort to a data sort while preserving the ordering relation. The functionality of the function symbols is also preserved, and if an event is mapped to **skip**, then the situation sorts in its domain and in its codomain are mapped to the same sort symbol. We shall see below how such morphisms can be used to formalize object interaction and reification, exploiting the fact that object signatures and their morphisms form a finitely complete category.

Proposition 6 (category OBSIG) *Object signatures and their morphisms form a category OBSIG, which is a subcategory of the category of order-sorted conditional equational signatures. OBSIG is finitely complete.*

Signature morphisms compose in an associative way, and for every object signature Σ there is an identity morphism $1_\Sigma \colon \Sigma \to \Sigma$, hence OBSIG is in fact a category. It has a terminal object $\mathsf{T} = (\{\mathsf{t}\}, \{(\mathsf{t}, \mathsf{t})\}, \{skip_t\})$, i.e. for each signature Σ there is a unique morphism $! \colon \Sigma \to \mathsf{T}$. Pullbacks in OBSIG are similar to those of ordinary order-sorted signatures, with some care taken with respect to the state sorts (figure 3 below gives an example of a pullback). Finite completeness of OBSIG thus follows from a general result of category theory.

The semantic notion corresponding to signature morphisms are Σ-homomorphisms, i.e. mappings between Σ-algebras. Syntax and semantics are connected via a *satisfaction condition* stating that when a signature is changed (via a morphism), then the models change consistently (though in the opposite direction). These relationships have been formalized in the theory of institutions ([21]). We shall now show how objects can be formalized as theories in the equational institution, i.e., how non-regular behavioural constraints are expressed in terms of conditional equations.

Definition 7 (equations) *Given an object signature* $\Sigma = (S,\leq,F)$ *and a set of variables* X *with a function* $\Xi\colon X{\rightarrow}S$, *let* $T(\Sigma)$ *be the set of terms over* Σ. *The set* $E(\Sigma)$ *of conditional* Σ-*equations is defined as follows:*

- *if* $t_{i_1}, t_{i_2} \in T(\Sigma)_{r_i}$ *and* $t_1, t_2 \in T(\Sigma)_s$ *for* $r_i, s \in S$, $1 \leq i \leq n$, *and* $Y \subseteq X$, *then* $\langle \forall Y\colon t_1 = t_2 \leftarrow t_{1_1} = t_{1_2}, ..., t_{n_1} = t_{n_2} \rangle \in E(\Sigma)$

Of course the list of conditions may be empty (i.e. n=0); for such unconditional equations we use the simplified notation $\langle \forall Y\colon t_1 = t_2 \rangle$. A most typical example of such an equation is the axiom which specifies the FIFO discipline of access to the data stored in a stack object:

```
eq pop(push(Stack,Elem)) = Stack
```

Definition 8 (satisfaction) *A* Σ-*algebra* **A** *satisfies a conditional equation* $e = \langle \forall Y\colon t_1 = t_2 \leftarrow t_{1_1} = t_{1_2}, ..., t_{n_1} = t_{n_2} \rangle$, *written* $\mathbf{A} \models_\Sigma e$, *iff for all assignments* $\alpha\colon X{\rightarrow}A$

- $[\![t_{1_1}]\!]^{\mathbf{A},\alpha} = [\![t_{1_2}]\!]^{\mathbf{A},\alpha}$ *and ... and* $[\![t_{n_1}]\!]^{\mathbf{A},\alpha} = [\![t_{n_2}]\!]^{\mathbf{A},\alpha}$
  implies $[\![t_1]\!]^{\mathbf{A},\alpha} = [\![t_2]\!]^{\mathbf{A},\alpha}$

For example, every STACK-algebra should satisfy the conditional equation:

```
cq top(push(pop(Stack),Elem)) = Elem
   if empty(Stack) = false .
```

This is to say that if `Elem` is of sort E and `Stack` is of sort stack-of-E, then, for any assignment of elements of the respective carrier sets to these variables: if the interpretation of `empty(Stack)` equals the interpretation of `false`, then the interpretation of `top(push(pop(Stack),Elem))` equals the element assigned to `Elem`.

Definition 9 (object and object specification) *An object specification is a pair* (Σ, E) *where* Σ *is an object signature und* E *is a sufficiently complete finite set of conditional* Σ-*equations, containing an axiom* $\langle \forall \{t\}\colon skip_s(t) = t \rangle$ *for each trivial event* $skip_s$. *A* Σ-*algebra* **A** *is called a model of an object specification* (Σ, E) *if* **A** *satisfies each equation in* E.
Denote by $E^\bullet$ *the set of all equations over* Σ *that are satisfied by every model of* (Σ, E). *Then* $(\Sigma, E^\bullet)$ *is the object specified by* (Σ, E).

Such specifications admit initial semantics, i.e. for each theory (Σ, E) there is a prototypical model **A** (the initial algebra) such that any other model can be obtained as a homomorphic image of **A** (cf. [22], [2]). From the initial algebra we can obtain a labeled transition system which provides an operational semantics for the process aspects of active objects. This construction will be subject of a forthcoming paper.

An important concept from the theory of Abstract Data Types is sufficient completeness. A specification is *sufficiently complete* if it has an equation for each possible application of attributes to terms built from event symbols, i.e. for each combination of an attribute symbol with an event symbol ([23]). The practical benefit of sufficient completeness for the specification of active objects is that the attributes can be evaluated at every situation.

To reach at the sufficiently complete specification of our example we have to augment obj ALARMCLOCK with axioms that constrain the behaviour. To this end we introduce attributes which are operators that have the topmost sort as their domain (and are hence applicable to all situations), and a data sort as their codomain:

```
ops alarm elapsed : A3 -> Nat .
op set? : A3 -> Bool .
```

OBJ3 provides means to include (abstract) data types like Nat and Bool as modules into other specifications. Here we include them in a way such that they are "protected", i.e., the module into which they are included cannot add any new axioms which change the properties of the included data types. Having included (protecting) Nat and Bool the following axioms specify the effects of the events on the attributes:

```
eq alarm(on) = 0 .
eq elapsed(on) = 0 .
var S1 : A1 .
var N : Nat .
eq alarm(set(S1,N)) = N .
eq elapsed(set(S1,N)) = 0 .
var S2 : A2 .
eq elapsed(tick(S2)) = elapsed(S2) + 1 .
var S : A3 .
eq set?(S1) = false .
eq set?(S2) = true .
eq (alarm(S) >= elapsed(S)) = true .
cq alarm(S) = elapsed(S) if set? = false .
```

The last two equations specify an *invariant* (or *safety* condition, [24]) that has to be satisfied by every possible computation. It enforces the non-regular condition on the behaviour of ALARMCLOCK.

Adapting the characterization in [23] a set of axioms is sufficiently complete if all selectors are applied to all constructors. In the case of object specifications, selectors correspond to attributes and constructors correspond to events. Sufficient completeness can be achieved automatically by a completion procedure which implements the *frame rule* that if an event is not explicitly specified to change the value of an attribute, then it leaves the attribute unchanged. Completion thus introduces axioms like

```
eq alarm(tick(S1)) = alarm(S1) .
```

The object ALARMCLOCK is hence composed of the signature and the set of equations given above, plus the additional equations introduced by the completion procedure.

Definition and Proposition 10 (category OBJ) *Given two objects (Σ_1, E_1) and (Σ_2, E_2), an object morphism is a signature morphism $\phi: \Sigma_1 \rightarrow \Sigma_2$ such that $\phi(e) \in E_2$ for each $e \in E_1$. Objects and object morphisms form a finitely complete category OBJ.*

The finite completeness of OBJ follows from the finite completeness of OB-SIG by general properties of the institutional framework. Notice that if we had used specifications instead of objects, the resulting category would not have been finitely complete.

4 Parallel Composition with Interaction

The category OBJ should be finitely complete for the important application to define systems of interacting objects as limits of categorial diagrams, a technique that dates back as far as [25]. Object Ob1 interacts with another object Ob2 by an event e1 of Ob1 calling an event e2 of Ob2. Operationally this means that e1 cannot occur without e2 also occuring, i.e. Ob1 and Ob2 synchronize their behaviour. Parameterized events provide the means to exchange data between the synchronized objects while their attributes remain completely encapsulated.

To illustrate the corresponding categorial construction (deeply studied by [26] for processes) we show the connection of a producer to a consumer via a transmission line that has no buffering capacity, i.e. the **deliver** event of the producer has to be synchronized with the **take** event of the consumer. This is expressed by the **LINK** having a **transmit** event that effects a transition from a situation before the transmission to a distinct situation after the transmission. The composed object **PRODUCER_CONSUMER** and the morphisms from it to its components are computed as a pullback of the triangle given by **PRODUCER**, **CONSUMER**, and **LINK**. Every operator whose mapping is not explicitly indicated in figure 3 is mapped to a suitable **skip** event (for brevity we omit the **skip** events).

The above described technique is intended to capture the interaction (synchronization with possible data transfer) of otherwise independently acting objects. One important application is the incorporation of objects as parts into bigger ones where the parts may interact. Imagine for example modelling a company as the aggregation of its departments, where the departments interact by exchanging files. The way how the parts communicate is specified by the middle object of the pullback which establishes the synchronization; the common communication protocol is incorporated into both objects. Our framework thus favors interaction via shared events over interaction via shared data. In the following we use the notation $ob1|_{ob}ob2$ to denote the parallel composition of objects $ob1$ and $ob2$ with interaction through the common shared subobject ob.

5 Reification

This final section shows how reification (or implementation) of objects over other objects is formalized in the above outlined algebraic framework. We define reification as a special kind of object morphism, and show that it is "well-behaved" when the reified object is put into the context of a composed system. Recall that situations are represented as sorts, and transitions between them as operators. Hence computations, i.e. sequences of event occurrences, correspond to functions obtained as the composition of the basic (one-step)

```
                    obj LINK is
                      sorts L1 L2 .
                      subsort L1 < L2 .
                      op transmit : L1 -> L2 .
                    endo
```

```
sort P1 to L1 .                          sort C1 to L1 .
sort P2 to L2 .                          sort C2 to L2 .
op deliver to transmit                   op take to transmit .
op start to skipL2 .                     op start to skipL1 .
```

```
    obj PRODUCER is                      obj CONSUMER is
      sorts P1 P2 .                        sorts C1 C2 .
      subsort P1 < P2 .                    subsort C1 < C2 .
      op deliver : P1 -> P2 .              op take : C1 -> C2 .
      op produce : P2 -> P1 .              op consume : C2 -> C1 .
      op start : -> P2 .                   op start : -> C1 .
    endo                                 endo
```

```
sort P1xP2 to P1 .                       sort P1xC1 to C1 .
sort P1xC2 to P1 .                       sort P2xC1 to C1 .
sort P2xC1 to P2 .                       sort P1xC2 to C2 .
sort P2xC2 to P2 .                       sort P2xC2 to C2 .
op transmit to deliver .                 op transmit to take .
op produce1 to produce .                 op consume1 to consume .
op produce2 to produce .                 op consume2 to consume .
op start to start .                      opstart to start .
```

```
            obj PRODUCER_CONSUMER is
              sorts P1xC1 P2xC1 P1xC2 P2xC2 .
              subsort P1xC1 < P2xC2 .
              op transmit : P2xC2 -> P1xC1 .
              op produce1 : P1xC1 -> P2xC1 .
              op produce2 : P1xC2 -> P2xC2 .
              op consume1 : P2xC1 -> P1xC2 .
              op consume2 : P2xC1 -> P2xC2 .
              op start : -> P2xC1 .
            endo
```

Figure 3: Parallel composition

operators.

Definition 11 (computational closure) *Given an object signature* $\Sigma = (S, \leq, F)$, *the computational closure* F^* *of* F *is defined inductively as follows:*

- $\{\ f|_s \ | \ f \in F_{su}, \ s \in S \ \} \subseteq F^*$

- *if* $f\colon s \longrightarrow s' \in F^*$ *and* $g\colon s' \longrightarrow s" \in F^*$, *then* $f;g\colon s \longrightarrow s" \in F^*$

The notation $h\colon s \longrightarrow s'$ *is used to distinguish the derived operators in* F^* *from the basic operators in* F.

Notice that we work with restrictions of events to their first parameter, i.e., the situation in which they may occur, thus disregarding data parameters in the definition of the computational closure. This turning of sequences of events into atomic "transactions" has a counterpart in the process categories of [27].

Definition 12 (reification) *Let* $Ob_1 = (\Sigma_1, T_1)$ *and* $Ob_2 = (\Sigma_2, T_2)$ *be objects.* Ob_2 *is a reification of* Ob_1 *if there is an object morphism* $m\colon \Sigma_2 \to \Sigma_1$ *such that for each* $g\colon s_1 \to s_1'$ *in* F_1 *there is a* $h\colon s_2 \to s_2'$ *in* $F_2{}^*$ *such that* $m(s_2)=s_1$ *and* $m(s_2')=s_1'$.

The object morphism m as a signature morphism ensures that every computation (term) in Ob_2 transforms into a computation in Ob_1 of length no greater than the original:

$$y = g(x) \text{ implies } m(y)=m(x) \text{ or } m(y)=m(g)(m(x))$$

where m also denotes its extension to terms. The additional condition ensures that for every transition (one-step computation) in Ob_1 there is at least one computation in Ob_2 which transforms to it. Since the computational closure does not consider data, m really has to be an object morphism to ensure the compatibility of behaviour. We shall use a double headed arrow $\longrightarrow\!\!\!\!\rightarrow$ to indicate that a morphism is a reification. Notice the similarity of this definition with the notion of *micro space* as introduced in [28]. There is however a difference to the usual notions of implementation: in a typical implementation there might be operations on the lower level which have nothing to do with the implemented higher level object, and hence there is no need for a total mapping. A reification as introduced above requires m to be an object morphism, i.e., a total mapping. This corresponds to a top-down strategy of stepwise refinements, in contrast to a bottom-up implementation which builds on an existing lower level.

As a first (though not very typical) example of a reification you may consider ALARMCLOCK to be a reification of CLOCK, through the simple observation that nobody is obliged to ever use the additional alarm feature (cf. [29]). More typical examples are those where the reifying object is a composed one.

The following proposition states that it is possible to reify the components of a composed object separately, such that the composition of the reifica tions of the components is a reification of the composition. This property is crucial for any stepwise refinement approach to software development.

Proposition 13 (reification distributes over composition) *The composition of two reified components is a reification of the composition, i.e., given reification morphisms* ob1 $\longrightarrow\!\!\!\!\rightarrow$ ob1 *and* ob2 $\longrightarrow\!\!\!\!\rightarrow$ ob2, *the following diagram commutes:*

Proof. First consider the pullback which describes the composition ob1|ob2 in the lower right corner of the above diagram (for simplicity we drop the index ob of the composition operator):

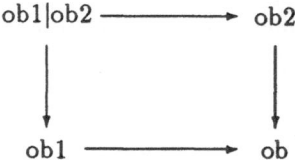

The pullbacks describing the compositions in the lower left and upper right corners are obtained by inserting the respective reification into the diagram of the "non-reified" pullback:

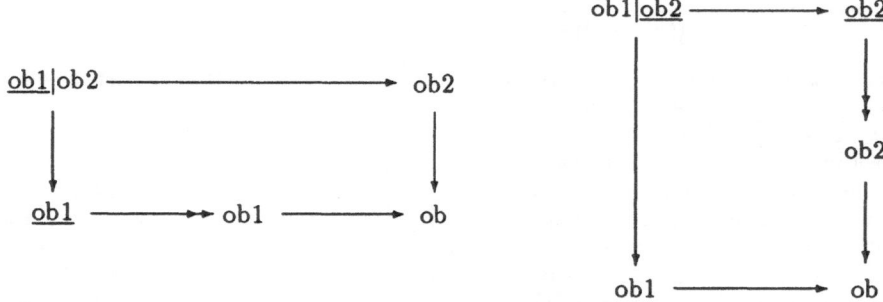

Reification is a special kind of object morphism, so these two diagrams are indeed pullbacks in the category OBJ, due to its finite completeness. Putting them together gives the upper left corner of the diagram in the statement of the proposition:

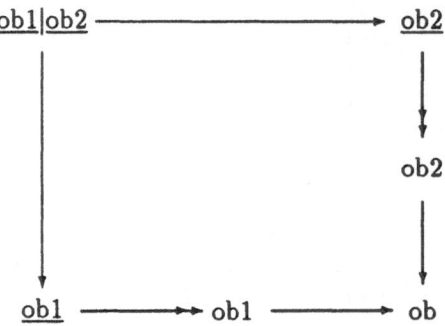

Put together the above yields the following diagram:

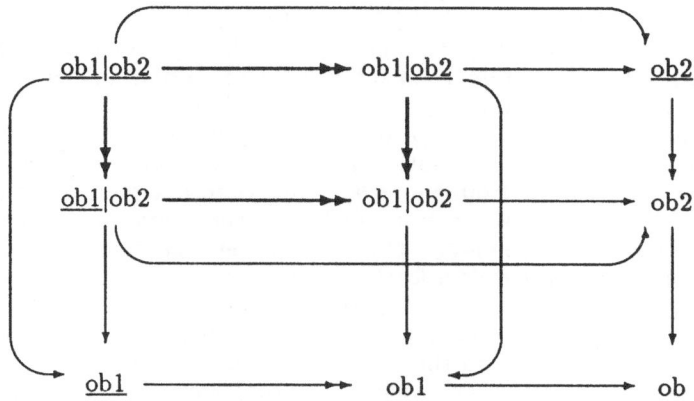

The reifications <u>ob1</u> —▸ ob1 and <u>ob2</u> —▸ ob2 do not "interfere", so the boldface arrows can be filled in as parts of suitable pullbacks.

End of Proof

6 Conclusions

The approach presented in this paper improves on related approaches by using the same algebra to cover both data and process aspects of active objects. The data aspects are specified in the usual order-sorted way, and to cover the process aspects there are additional sorts which stand for classes of states. State transitions are modeled as functions between these sorts, and terms built from these functions denote object behaviour. Non-regular behavioural constraints are expressed as axioms of the equational specification of the active object. Attributes are functions from state sorts into data sorts, where the order-sorted approach allows to define a unique argument sort for all attributes (by convention, this sort corresponds to the post-mortem state of the object). This is important because attributes in principle have values at every state. Using a more elaborated subsort hierarchy it is also possible to make attributes partial, i.e., to make them applicable only in certain situations. For example we could restrict the definedness of the attribute **elapsed** of ALARMCLOCK to the situation where an alarm is set, i.e. to **A2**, by defining

```
op elapsed : A2 -> Nat .
```

instead of

```
op elapsed : A3 -> Nat .
```

In the paper we only used flat sort hierarchies with respect to situations, with only one topmost sort above all the others. However, due to the generality of the order-sorted framework, all construction shown work with more complicated partial orders as well.

Order-sorted specifications of active objects permit initial semantics, i.e., every specification has a unique, prototypical model, viz. the initial one, which can be regarded as the specified object. In the initial model all terms (data and behaviour) which are not distinguished by the equations are identified. The dual concept is that of final semantics, where in a final model everything is distinct which is not identified by the equations. At first sight final semantics seems to be more attractive, since we are specifying classes of objects, but initial semantics has a stronger computational flavour. Besides computing normal forms for data expressions, from an initial model (a term algebra) it is possible to construct a labeled transition system which is the operational semantics of the object viewed as an automaton. This link between algebraic and operational semantics will be the subject of a forthcoming paper.

Active objects can be composed into communities of interacting objects, where the composed object that represents the community is obtained as the limit of the categorial diagram that desribes the interconnection of the components. The same operation also yields the morphisms which incorporate the components as parts into the community. Objects hence interact through sharing events (the transition functions which have a common image in the link object), i.e. their behaviour has to synchronize at the shared events.

The presentation deliberately ignores the distinction between objects and classes, and calls an object what strictly speaking is the template of a homogeneous class of objects. An object, as an instance of its class, has a unique identification attached to its template. This relates interaction and inheritance (cf. [4]): Both are captured by object morphisms, where a morphism between two templates with the same identification describes inheritance, and a morphism between two templates with different identifications describes the incorporation of the target into the source. As shown in section 4, incorporation morphisms are the basic means to describe interaction through shared events. Moreover, on the "data side", they are used to incorporate abstract data types into other ones, consider for example the following specification in OBJ3:

```
obj LIST-OF-INT is protecting INT .
    ...
```

This imports the integers as a parameter into a specification of lists of integers. Here again we have the same concepts applicable for the data aspect on the one side and the process aspect on the other. Notice, however, that it does not make much sense to attribute unique identifications to instances of integer numbers, whereas it makes sense to do so for instances of e.g. stacks or alarmclocks.

Acknowledgement

The author wishes to thank Elena Zucca for many helpful comments on a previous version of this paper.

References

[1] H. Ehrig and B. Mahr: *Fundamentals of Algebraic Specification 1: Equations and Initial Semantics.* Springer Verlag 1985

[2] M. Wirsing: Algebraic Specification. in L. van Leeuwen (ed.): *Formal Models and Semantics*, Handbook of Theoretical Computer Science, Vol. B, Elsevier 1990, pp. 675-788

[3] J. Goguen and J. Meseguer: Order-sorted Algebra Solves the Constructor-Selector, Multiple Representation and Coercion Problem. in *Proc. 2nd Symp. on Logic in Computer Science*, IEEE Computer Soc. Press, 1987, pp. 18-29

[4] H.-D. Ehrich, M. Gogolla and A. Sernadas: Objects and their Specification. in M. Bidoit and C. Choppy (eds.): *Specification of Abstract Data Types*, Springer Verlag, in print

[5] G. Reggio: Entities: Institutions for Dynamic Systems. in H. Ehrig, K.P. Jantke, F. Orejas and H. Reichel (eds.): *Specification of Abstract Data Types*, LNCS 534, Springer Verlag 1991

[6] E. Astesiano, A. Giovini, G. Reggio, E. Zucca: An Integrated Algebraic Approach to the Specification of Data Types, Processes, and Objects. in *Algebraic Methods - Tools and Applications*, LNCS 394, Springer Verlag 1989, pp. 91-116

[7] R. Breu: *Algebraic Specification Techniques in Object-Oriented Programming Environments.* LNCS, Springer Verlag 1991

[8] E. Astesiano, E. Zucca: A Semantic Model for Dynamic Systems. this volume

[9] H. Ehrig, F. Parisi-Presicce, P. Boehm, C. Rieckhoff, Ch. Dimitrovici, M. Grosse-Rhode: Combining Data Type Specification and Recursive Process Specifications using Projection Algebras. *Theoretical Computer Science* 71 (1990), pp. 347-380

[10] R. Wieringa: Equational Specification of Dynamic Objects. in R. Meersman, W. Kent and S. Khosla (eds.): *Object Oriented Databases: Analysis, Design and Construction*, North Holland 1991, pp. 415-438

[11] A. Sernadas, H.-D. Ehrich and F. Costa: From Processes to Objects. *The INESC Journal of Research and Development* 1 (1990), pp. 7-27

[12] A. Sernadas and H.-D. Ehrich: What is an Object, After All? in R. Meersman, W. Kent and S. Khosla (eds.): *Object Oriented Databases: Analysis, Design and Construction*, North Holland 1991, pp. 39-70

[13] M. Barr and C. Wells: *Category Theory for Computing Science.* Prentice-Hall 1990

[14] J. Goguen and D. Wolfram: On Types and FOOPS. in R. Meersman and W. Kent (eds.): *Proc. IFIP 2.6 Working Conf. DS-4*, North Holland, 1990

[15] G. Reichwein and C. Sernadas: Algebraic Semantics of Active Objects. Technical Report, INESC, Lisbon 1992

[16] C. Sernadas, P. Gouveia and G. Reichwein: Temporal Equational Reasoning about Object Specifications. Technical Report, INESC, Lisbon 1992 (to be submitted)

[17] G. Saake and U. Lipeck: Using Finite-Linear Temporal Logic for Specifying Database Dynamics. in E. Börger, H. Kleine Büning and M. Richter (eds.): *Proc. 2nd Workshop Computer Science Logic*, LNCS 385, Springer Verlag 1989, pp. 288-300

[18] J. Goguen, T. Winkler, J. Meseguer, K. Futatsugi and J.-P. Jouannaud: Introducing OBJ. in J. Goguen, D. Coleman and R. Gallimore (eds.): *Applications of Algebraic Specification Using OBJ*, Cambridge University Press, 1992

[19] J.-P. Jouannaud, C. Kirchner, H. Kirchner and A. Mégrelis: Programming with Equalities, Subsorts, Overloading, and Parametrization in OBJ. *Journal of Logic Programming* 12 (1992), pp. 257-279

[20] J. Fiadeiro and G. Reichwein: A Categorial Theory of Superposition. Technical Report, INESC, Lisbon 1992 (submitted)

[21] J. Goguen and R. Burstall: Institutions: Abstract Model Theory for Specification and Programming. *Journal of the ACM* 39 (1992), pp. 95-146

[22] G. Smolka, W. Nutt, J. Goguen and J. Meseguer: Order-sorted Equational Computation. in H. Ait and M. Nivat (eds.): *Resolution of Equations in Algebraic Structures, Vol. 2*, Academic Press 1989, pp. 289-367

[23] J. Guttag: Abstract Data Types and the Development of Data Structures. *Communications of the ACM* 20 (1977), pp. 396-404

[24] L. Lamport: Proving the Correctness of Multiprocess Programs. *IEEE Transactions on Software Engineering* 3 (1977), pp. 125-143

[25] J. Goguen and S. Ginali: A Categorical Approach to General Systems Theory. in G. Klir (ed.): *Applied General Systems Research,* Plenum 1978, pp. 257-270

[26] J.-F. Costa, A. Sernadas, C. Sernadas and H.-D. Ehrich: Object Interaction. to appear in *Proc. Mathematical Foundations of Computer Science '92*

[27] J.-F. Costa and A. Sernadas: Algebraic Theory of Transition Systems Implementation. private communication

[28] A.B. Cremers and T.N. Hibbard: Axioms for Concurrent Processes. in H. Maurer (ed.): *New Results and New Trends in Computer Science*, LNCS 555, Springer Verlag 1991, pp. 54-68

[29] G. Reichwein: Objects and their Data Spaces. *The INESC Journal of Research and Development* 2 (1991), pp. 72-91

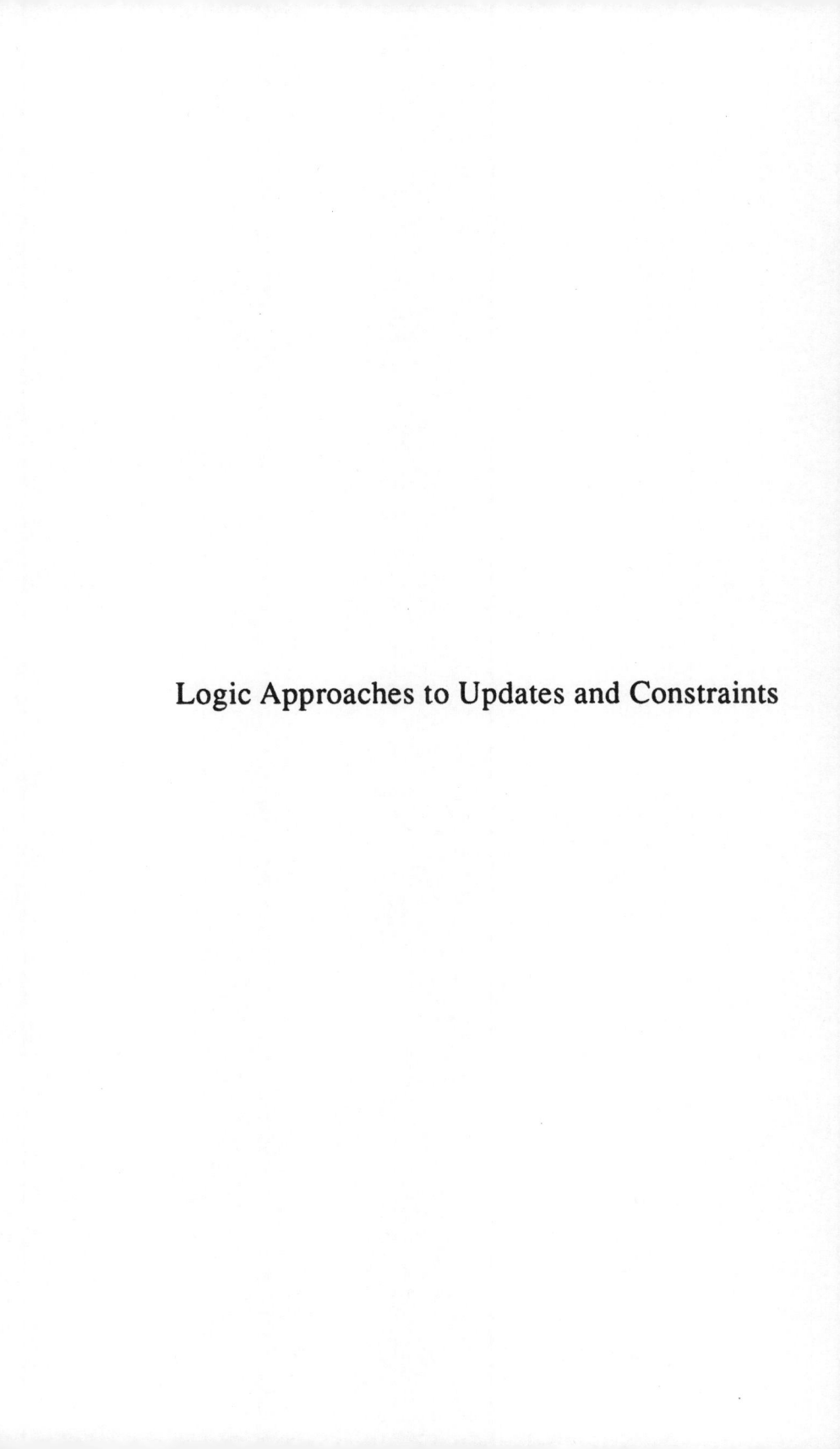

Logic Approaches to Updates and Constraints

Dynamic Database Logic: the First-order Case

Paul Spruit   Roel Wieringa   John-Jules Meyer

Department of Mathematics and Computer Science, Vrije Universiteit

Amsterdam, The Netherlands

Abstract

We present Dynamic Database Logic (DDL), a language designed to reason about database updates. DDL is based on dynamic logic. We give a declarative semantics and a sound proof system for DDL (for a restricted case, we also have a completeness result). We show with a detailed example, how the proof system of DDL can be used to prove correctness of an update program given some specification for the update program. The update language part of DDL is shown to be update complete and specification complete (in the sense of Abiteboul & Vianu).

1   Introduction

In previous work [16, 18] we defined propositional dynamic database logic, a logic designed to reason about database updates. As its name suggests, PDDL is based on PDL (propositional dynamic logic). We use dynamic logic as our starting point, because using dynamic logic is a logic for reasoning about postconditions of terminating programs, which is exactly what we want for database updates. PDDL contains the database updates as part of the logic. Therefore, database updates have a formal semantics within the logic, and reasoning about database updates can be done within the logic. This contrasts most existing approaches that use (some restricted version of) first-order logic to study database updates. First-order logic can be used to specify a database state as well as state transitions; but because state transitions have their own logic it is more appropriate to formalize this in the specification language.

This paper extends our propositional approach of PDDL to the first-order case. We first list the main properties and results we achieved for PDDL. PDDL contains both active updates (that trigger derivation rules) and passive updates (that do not trigger derivation rules). Passive and active updates are the atomic actions in the update language, these are combined by a regular language (containing sequential composition, choice and iteration, as is common in dynamic logic) to update programs. The declarative semantics of PDDL is based on Kripke structures. A proof system that is complete with respect to all structures is hard to construct (the problem is the axiomatization of the the the existence of successor worlds). But we do have a proof system for PDDL that is sound and complete with respect to the full structures: structures such that for all "valuations" a world with that valuation exists. Finally we have given a Plotkin style operational semantics [14] for PDDL, that is equivalent to the declarative semantics.

Not everything we have for PDDL has been achieved for DDL yet (see also the planned future work in section 9). However, we did consider two extra problems that do not apply to the propositional case: object creation and parallel updates to a relation with a set of tuples.

In section 2, we define the syntax of dynamic database logic (DDL). In section 3 we give the declarative semantics for DDL. We then look at object existence in section 4. In section 5 we give a sound axiomatization for DDL (with respect to the full structures). We show by an example how DDL can be used to reason about the correctness an update programs with respect to a specification in section 6. In section 7 we look at the notion of update completeness as defined by Abiteboul & Vianu [2, 3], we show that the update language of DDL is update complete. In section 8 we compare DDL with some other approaches that use modal logic to specify database updates. Section 9 ends the paper with some conclusions and future work.

2 Syntax of DDL

We consider a very simple first-order language: unsorted, without function symbols (but with equality). So we assume Var a set of variables (such as $x, y, \ldots$), Con a set of constant symbols (such as $c, d, \ldots$) and $Pred$ a set of predicate symbols (such as $p, q, \ldots$) with their arities: $ar : Pred \rightarrow \{0, 1, \ldots\}$.

The atomic updates in our propositional update language PDDL are very simple: just make an atom true or false. We could do the same in DDL: just have very simple updates to insert or delete a single tuple at a time. However, we usually want to insert/delete/update a whole range of tuples, specified by a query. We therefore introduce atomic update actions of the form $\&x_1, \ldots, x_n \mathcal{I} p(t_1, \ldots, t_m)$ **where** ϕ, with the intuitive meaning: for all variable interpretations of $x_1, \ldots, x_n$ that make ϕ true, simultaneously insert the tuple $(t_1, \ldots, t_m)$ in the relation p. Of course, we have a similar construction for delete. (We do not have a similar construction for update, see section 9 for some remarks on this choice.)

We make one more generalization with respect to the propositional case: next to the binary choice, we allow a conditional choice. This construction is easily defined and intuitively simple, and we will show that it allows a simple solution to object creation.

Definition 1 *A* **term** *is a constant or a variable. We use $t, \ldots$ for terms.*

We define the sets of update programs and formulas by mutual induction:

Update programs:

1. $\&X \mathcal{I} p T$ **where** ϕ and $\&X \mathcal{D} p T$ **where** ϕ are update programs, for any m-ary predicate symbol p, m-tuple of terms T, finite set of variables X, and formula ϕ.

2. $+X\ \alpha$ **where** ϕ is an update program, for any finite set of variables X, formula ϕ and update program α.

3. $\alpha; \beta, \alpha + \beta$ and α^* are update programs, for any update programs α and β.

4. ϕ? is an update program, for any formula ϕ.

5. The only update programs are those given by 1, 2, 3 and 4.

Formulas:

1. pT is a formula, for any m-ary predicate symbol p and m-tuple of terms T.

2. $\phi\vee\psi$, $\neg\phi$ and $[\alpha]\phi$ are formulas, for any two formula ϕ and ψ and update program α.

3. $\exists x\phi$ is a formula, for any variable x and formula ϕ.

4. $t = t'$ is a formula, for any two terms t and t'.

5. The only formulas are those given by 1, 2, 3 and 4.

The update program $\&X\mathcal{I}pT$ **where** ϕ is called **conditional insertion** (of tuples T in p under condition ϕ). The intended meaning of $\&X\,\mathcal{I}p\,T$ **where** ϕ is to insert the tuples T in relation p, for all values for the variables in X that make the formula ϕ true. The insertions are simultaneous. The **conditional deletion** $\&X\,\mathcal{D}p\,T$ **where** ϕ has a similar meaning. The conditional insertion and deletion are the atomic updates in our language.

The update program $+X\ \alpha$ **where** ϕ is called **conditional choice**. Its intended meaning is to execute α for one of the possible value assignments to all variables in X that makes ϕ true. The update program connectives ;, +, * and ? are the standard dynamic logic constructions, they are called **sequential composition**, **choice**, **iteration** and **test** respectively.

For formulas, $\vee$ and $\neg$ are the standard propositional connectives, called **disjunction** and **negation**, $\exists$ is the standard first-order **existential quantifier** and $[\alpha]$ is the **modal necessity**, the formula $[\alpha]\phi$ is read as: after every (terminating) execution of α, formula ϕ holds. We assume the common propositional constants and connectives $true$, $false$, $\wedge$, $\rightarrow$ and $\leftrightarrow$ are defined in the standard way in terms of $\vee$ and $\neg$ and that the **universal quantification** $\forall x\phi$ is an abbreviation for $\neg\exists x\neg\phi$. Furthermore, the **modal possibility** $\langle\alpha\rangle\phi$ is defined as $\neg[\alpha]\neg\phi$. The formula $\langle\alpha\rangle\phi$ states that there exists a terminating execution of α, after which ϕ holds.

For notational convenience, when an atomic update has an empty set of variables, we omit $\&\emptyset$ and when the condition part of an atomic update or conditional choice is the formula $true$, we omit **where** $true$. We use $\exists X$ and $\forall X$ (for $X = \{x_1, \ldots, x_n\}$ a finite set of variables) in formulas, as a shorthand for $\exists x_1 \cdots \exists x_n$ and $\forall x_1 \cdots \forall x_n$ respectively. (For $X = \emptyset$, $\exists X\phi$ and $\forall X\phi$ just stand for ϕ.) Finally, if we have two m-tuples T and T' (say $T = (t_1, \ldots, t_m)$ and $T' = (t'_1 \ldots, t'_m)$) then we write $T = T'$ for $(t_1 = t'_1)\wedge\cdots\wedge(t_m = t'_m)$. (If $m = 0$, then $T = T'$ is equal to the formula $true$.)

Example 2 Suppose we have a database that stores information about persons and we have the binary predicate symbols p and gp, for the parent and grandparent relations respectively. Then the update program

$$\&\{x,y\}\mathcal{D}gp(x,y) \ ; \ \&\{x,y,z\}\,\mathcal{I}gp(x,z) \ \textbf{where} \ p(x,y)\wedge p(y,z)$$

computes the grandparent relation from the parent relation (by first making the grandparent relation empty, and then filling it with all pairs of persons for which there is someone that is a child of the first and a parent of the second person).

3 Declarative semantics of DDL

We use a standard Kripke semantics for DDL. We make two assumptions that are very common in first-order modal logic: all worlds in the Kripke structure have the same domain of interpretation, and constants are interpreted the same in all possible worlds. We refer to Gamut [8, chapter 3] for a discussion on other possible choices and their consequences.

Definition 3 *1. A* **closed term model** *M is a pair (D, I_C) of a set D called the* **domain** *(of M) and a function $I_C : Con \to D$.*

> *2. A* **possible world** *on a closed term model model $M = (D, I_C)$ is a function $w : Pred \to \bigcup_{i=0}^{\infty} \mathcal{P}(D^i)$, such that for all $p \in Pred$, $w(p) \subseteq D^{ar(p)}$.*

> *3. A* **structure** *S on a closed term model M is a set of possible worlds on M.*

The common modal logic definition of a structure assumes some set of worlds, and assigns an interpretation for the predicate symbols to every world. In the above definition, a possible world *is* an interpretation of the predicate symbols. Therefore, we cannot have two different worlds with the same valuation in our structures.

Definition 4 *A* **variable interpretation** *on a closed term model $M = (D, I_C)$ is a function $I_V : Var \to D$.*

For convenience, we will also use I_V on constants: $I_V(c) = I_C(c)$. This way, I_V is well-defined on all terms. We also extend I_V to tuples of terms $T = (t_1, \ldots, t_n)$: $I_V(T) = (I_V(t_1), \ldots, I_V(t_n))$.

Definition 5 (variants of variable interpretations) *Let I_V be a variable interpretation on $M = (D, I_C)$, let $x \in Var$ and let $d \in D$. The* **variant** *of I_V which maps x to d, $I_V\{x \mapsto d\}$, is defined as*

$$I_V\{x \mapsto d\}(y) = \begin{cases} d & \text{if } y = x \\ I_V(y) & \text{otherwise} \end{cases}$$

Definition 6 (function restriction) *For a function $f : A \to B$ and $A' \subseteq A$, the* **restriction** *of f to A': $f{\restriction}_{A'} : A' \to B$ is defined for $a \in A'$ as: $f{\restriction}_{A'}(a) = f(a)$.*

Definitions 5 and 6 are of course closely related. For some set of variables $X = \{x_1, \ldots, x_n\}$ we have $\exists d_1, \ldots, d_n$ such that $I'_V = I_V\{x_1 \mapsto d_1, \ldots, x_n \mapsto d_n\}$ iff $I'_V{\restriction}_{Var \setminus X} = I_V{\restriction}_{Var \setminus X}$.

We now give the truth-definition for formulas: we write $S, w, I_V \models \phi$ if formula ϕ is true in world w of structure S under variable interpretation I_V. To give a semantics to $[\alpha]\phi$, we also must define the interpretation of an update program, as a relation on possible worlds. We do this by defining a function m for update programs. (Actually, we should write m_S, as m depends on the structure S.) An update program may contain free variables, therefore the function m also takes a variable interpretation as parameter. As formulas can occur in update programs (as test or within the condition of an atomic update or conditional choice) and update programs can occur in formulas (within a modality), we define the interpretation of formulas and update programs by mutual induction.

Definition 7 *We define m and $\models$ by (mutual) structural induction:*

$$m(\&X\,\mathcal{I}p\,T \textbf{ where } \phi)(I_V) = \{(w, w') \in S^2 \mid \forall q \neq p \in Pred : w'(q) = w(q)$$
$$\text{and } w'(p) = w(p) \cup \{I'_V(T) \mid I'_V\lceil_{Var\setminus X} = I_V\lceil_{Var\setminus X} \text{ and } S, w, I'_V \models \phi\}\}$$

$$m(\&X\,\mathcal{D}p\,T \textbf{ where } \phi)(I_V) = \{(w, w') \in S^2 \mid \forall q \neq p \in Pred : w'(q) = w(q)$$
$$\text{and } w'(p) = w(p) \setminus \{I'_V(T) \mid I'_V\lceil_{Var\setminus X} = I_V\lceil_{Var\setminus X} \text{ and } S, w, I'_V \models \phi\}\}$$

$$m(+X\,\alpha \textbf{ where } \phi)(I_V) = \{(w, w') \in S^2 \mid \exists I'_V : I'_V\lceil_{Var\setminus X} = I_V\lceil_{Var\setminus X}$$
$$\text{and } S, w, I'_V \models \phi \text{ and } (w, w') \in m(\alpha)(I'_V)\}$$

$$m(\alpha; \beta)(I_V) = \{(w, w') \in S^2 \mid \exists v \in S : (w, v) \in m(\alpha)(I_V) \text{ and}$$
$$(v, w') \in m(\beta)(I_V)\}$$

$$m(\alpha + \beta)(I_V) = m(\alpha)(I_V) \cup m(\beta)(I_V)$$

$$m(\alpha^*)(I_V) = \{(w, w') \in S^2 \mid \exists n \geq 1, w_1, \ldots, w_n \in S : w_1 = w \text{ and}$$
$$w_n = w' \text{ and } \forall i, 1 \leq i \leq n - 1 : (w_i, w_{i+1}) \in m(\alpha)(I_V)\}$$

$$m(\phi?)(I_V) = \{(w, w) \in S^2 \mid S, w, I_V \models \phi\}$$

$$\begin{aligned}
S, w, I_V &\models pT &&\Leftrightarrow\; I_V(T) \in w(p) \\
S, w, I_V &\models \phi_1 \vee \phi_2 &&\Leftrightarrow\; S, w, I_V \models \phi_1 \text{ or } S, w, I_V \models \phi_2 \\
S, w, I_V &\models \neg\phi &&\Leftrightarrow\; S, w, I_V \not\models \phi \\
S, w, I_V &\models [\alpha]\phi &&\Leftrightarrow\; \forall w' \in S \text{ with } (w, w') \in m(\alpha)(I_V) : S, w', I_V \models \phi \\
S, w, I_V &\models \exists x \phi &&\Leftrightarrow\; \exists d \in D : S, w, I_V\{x \mapsto d\} \models \phi \\
S, w, I_V &\models t = t' &&\Leftrightarrow\; I_V(t) = I_V(t')
\end{aligned}$$

We write $S, w \models \phi$ if for all I_V, $S, w, I_V \models \phi$, $S \models \phi$ if for all $w \in S$: $S, w \models \phi$ and $\models \phi$ (ϕ is valid) if for all structures S, $S \models \phi$. If it is not the case that $S, w, \mathcal{I}_V \models \phi$, then we write $S, w, I_V \not\models \phi$, analogous definitions hold for $S, w \not\models \phi$, $S \not\models \phi$ and $\not\models \phi$.

As mentioned before, the intended meaning of $\&X\,\mathcal{I}p\,T \textbf{ where } \phi$ is to insert the tuples T in relation p, for all values for the variables in X that make the formula ϕ true. This is reflected in the formal semantics (case 1 of definition 7) as follows:

- The condition $w'(p) = w(p) \cup \{I'_V(T) \mid I'_V\lceil_{Var\setminus X} = I_V\lceil_{Var\setminus X}$ and $S, w, I'_V \models \phi\}$ states that the the interpretation of p after the update (in world w') contains all tuples present before the update (in world w) together with all tuples $I'_V(T)$ for I'_V a variable interpretation that interprets the variables in X in some way that makes ϕ true.

- The condition $\forall q \neq p \in Pred : w'(q) = w(q)$ is the frame assumption: the interpretation of all predicate symbols that are not currently updated, remains the same.

The formal semantics of the conditional delete can be understood in a similar way. The interpretation of the test, sequential composition, choice and iteration are the same as in dynamic logic. As mentioned before, the intended meaning of $+X\ \alpha$ **where** ϕ is to execute α for one of the possible variable assignments to variables in X that makes ϕ true. The formal semantics reflects this intended meaning: we can reach every world that results from executing α for some variable interpretation for X that makes ϕ true. The semantics of formulas is standard.

Discussion. If we compare definition 3 with the corresponding dynamic logic definitions of a domain of computation and a state [11], then two main differences are immediately clear:

- Possible worlds in DL are variable assignments, but they are interpretations of predicate symbols in DDL.

- The interpretation of predicate symbols is fixed throughout all possible worlds in DL, in DDL they are different in different possible worlds.

These differences are easily understood if we realize that DL is used for reasoning about imperative programming languages where predicates (like $\leq$ on integers) do not change, whereas DDL is used for reasoning about database updates which are updates of predicates. So in fact although the syntax of DDL is very similar to the syntax of DL, the semantics of DDL is very similar to the semantics of first-order modal logic. **End of discussion.**

4 Existence of objects

In our semantics we have chosen a single domain for the interpretation of the constants. So we assume all objects of interest that will ever exist are present in the domain. (Of course, one can raise philosophical objections against this choice, but assuming different domains for different possible worlds leads to many technical difficulties [8, chapter 3].) When we have different domains for the different possible worlds, then each domain just contains the objects that exist in that world. When we take a single domain for all possible worlds, we need an extra mechanism to be able to talk about the existence of objects in worlds. We adopt the solution from Gamut [8, chapter 3] and assume a (unary) existence predicate E. Note that there is one important difference between the use of the existence predicate in database logic and the use of the existence predicate in philosophical logic: in philosophical logic, $E(a)$ asserts existence of the object a is the "real world", in database logic $E(a)$ asserts the existence of a *in the database*. (In database logic we may for want to instance create the parent of a person, something we never want to do in philosophical logic.)

Example 8 Suppose we have a database containing only the binary predicate p for the parent relation. We now want to enter in the database the information that a is a grandparent of b, but none of the parents of b is present in database (the parents of b do not exist in the database). We must then create an object in the database that represents the parent of b. The update program

$$+\{x\}\ (\mathcal{I}E(x)\ ;\ \mathcal{I}p(a,x)\ ;\ \mathcal{I}p(x,b))\ \textbf{where}\ \neg E(x)$$

does what we want.

5 Axiomatization of DDL

We construct a proof system for DDL by extending a proof system for first-order modal logic with axioms for the PDL program operators (;, + and *) and with axioms for the DDL atomic updates and the DDL conditional choice construction. In the propositional update logic PDDL, we argued that there are several problems when we try to axiomatize truth in *all* structures. These problems concern axiomatizing the existence of successor worlds of atomic updates. The same problems are also present in DDL, we therefore adopt the same solution for DDL as we used for PDDL: we axiomatize truth in the *full* structures. A full structure on a closed term model M is the set of *all* possible worlds on M (cf. definition 3).

Before we can give the axioms, we need four definitions.

Definition 9 *We define the* **free variables** *of terms, tuples of terms, formulas and update programs (by mutual structural induction):*

$$
\begin{aligned}
FV(c) &= \emptyset \\
FV(x) &= \{x\} \\
FV((t_1,\ldots,t_m)) &= FV(t_1) \cup \cdots \cup FV(t_n) \\
FV(pT) &= FV(T) \\
FV(\phi \vee \psi) &= FV(\phi) \cup FV(\psi) \\
FV(\neg \phi) &= FV(\phi) \\
FV([\alpha]\phi) &= FV(\alpha) \cup FV(\phi) \\
FV(\exists x \phi) &= FV(\phi) \setminus \{x\} \\
FV(t = t') &= FV(t) \cup FV(t') \\
FV(\&X\ \mathcal{I}p\,T \text{ where } \phi) &= (FV(T) \cup FV(\phi)) \setminus X \\
FV(\&X\ \mathcal{D}p\,T \text{ where } \phi) &= (FV(T) \cup FV(\phi)) \setminus X \\
FV(\alpha; \beta) &= FV(\alpha) \cup FV(\beta) \\
FV(\alpha + \beta) &= FV(\alpha) \cup FV(\beta) \\
FV(\alpha^*) &= FV(\alpha) \\
FV(+X\ \alpha \text{ where } \phi) &= (FV(\phi) \cup FV(\alpha)) \setminus X \\
FV(\phi?) &= FV(\phi)
\end{aligned}
$$

Definition 10 *An occurrence of a variable x in a formula ϕ is called* **bound** *iff there is a subformula of ϕ of the form $\forall x \psi$ and the occurrence of x is within this subformula. If an occurrence of a variable in a formula is not bound, then it is called* **free**. *For convenience, we also call any occurrence of any constant in a formula free (so that we can talk about the occurrence of a term being free or not in a formula).*

Definition 11 *A term t is* **free** *for a variable y in ϕ iff there is no free occurrence of t within some subformula of ϕ of the form $\exists y \psi$. For convenience, we also call any term free for any constant (so that we can speak of a term being free for another term in a formula).*

Definition 12 *The* **substitution** *of a term t_1 for a term t_2 in a formula ϕ, denoted $\phi[t_1/t_2]$, is the formula ϕ with all free occurrences of t_2 in ϕ replaced by t_1.*

Axioms for DDL:

(1) all substitution instances of propositional tautologies

(2) $\forall x\phi \to \phi[t/x]$, with x free for t in ϕ instantiation

(3) $t = t$ identity

(4) $t = t' \to (\phi \to \phi[t'/t])$, with t free for t' in ϕ substitution

(5) $[\alpha](\phi \to \psi) \to ([\alpha]\phi \to [\alpha]\psi)$ K axiom

(6) $\forall x[\alpha]\phi \to [\alpha]\forall x\phi$, for $x \notin FV(\alpha)$ shrinking domains

(7) $[\alpha + \beta]\phi \leftrightarrow [\alpha]\phi \wedge [\beta]\phi$ + axiom

(8) $[\alpha\,;\beta]\phi \leftrightarrow [\alpha][\beta]\phi$; axiom

(9) $[\phi?]\psi \leftrightarrow (\phi \to \psi)$? axiom

(10) $[\alpha^*]\phi \to (\phi \wedge [\alpha][\alpha^*]\phi)$ * axiom

(11) $(\phi \wedge [\alpha^*](\phi \to [\alpha]\phi)) \to [\alpha^*]\phi$ induction axiom

(12) $[+X\ \alpha\ \textbf{where}\ \phi]\psi \ \leftrightarrow\ \forall X(\phi \to [\alpha]\psi)$,
     for $FV(\psi) \cap X = \emptyset$ conditional choice axiom

(13) $pT' \vee \exists X(\phi \wedge T=T')\ \to\ [\&X\ \mathcal{I}p\,T\ \textbf{where}\ \phi]pT'$
     for $FV(T') \cap X = \emptyset$

(14) $\neg(pT' \vee \exists X(\phi \wedge T=T'))\ \to\ [\&X\ \mathcal{I}p\,T\ \textbf{where}\ \phi]\neg pT'$
     for $FV(T') \cap X = \emptyset$ insertion axioms

(15) $pT' \wedge \neg\exists X(\phi \wedge T=T')\ \to\ [\&X\ \mathcal{D}p\,T\ \textbf{where}\ \phi]pT'$
     for $FV(T') \cap X = \emptyset$

(16) $\neg(pT' \wedge \neg\exists X(\phi \wedge T=T'))\ \to\ [\&X\ \mathcal{D}p\,T\ \textbf{where}\ \phi]\neg pT'$
     for $FV(T') \cap X = \emptyset$ deletion axioms

(17) $q\,T' \to [\&X\ \mathcal{I}p\,T\ \textbf{where}\ \phi]q\,T'$, for $q \neq p$ frame assumption

(18) $q\,T' \to [\&X\ \mathcal{D}p\,T\ \textbf{where}\ \phi]q\,T'$, for $q \neq p$ frame assumption

(19) $\neg q\,T' \to [\&X\ \mathcal{I}p\,T\ \textbf{where}\ \phi]\neg q\,T'$, for $q \neq p$ frame assumption

(20) $\neg q\,T' \to [\&X\ \mathcal{D}p\,T\ \textbf{where}\ \phi]\neg q\,T'$, for $q \neq p$ frame assumption

(21) $\langle\&X\ \mathcal{I}p\,T\ \textbf{where}\ \phi\rangle true$ insert successor existence

(22) $\langle\&X\ \mathcal{D}p\,T\ \textbf{where}\ \phi\rangle true$ delete successor existence

Inference rules for DDL:

(1) $\dfrac{\phi \to \psi,\ \phi}{\psi}$ modus ponens

(2) $\dfrac{\phi}{[\alpha]\phi}$ modal generalization

(3) $\dfrac{\phi \to \psi}{\phi \to \forall x\psi}$, for $x \notin FV(\phi)$ universal generalization

Some remarks on the axioms:

1-4 With rule (3), these axioms form a standard axiomatization of first-order logic with equality (without function symbols).

5,6 Standard axioms for a normal modal logic with constant domains. Axiom (6) is commonly called the Barcan formula. If we have a semantics that allows different worlds to have different domains, then axiom (6) states that worlds reachable via α must not have a larger domain than the current world. As we have constant domains, we would also expect an axiom which specifies that worlds reachable via α must not have a smaller domain than the current world. This can be enforced by the axiom $\exists x[\alpha]\phi \rightarrow [\alpha]\exists x\phi$ (for $x \notin FV(\alpha)$) [8, chapter 3]. But this formula is already derivable using the other axioms and rules, so the proof system indeed enforces constant domains. We give a short proof sketch of the "growing domains formula". By first-order logic, $\vdash \phi \rightarrow \exists x\phi$. Monotonicity of [ ] (a derivable inference rule, see also section 6) gives $\vdash [\alpha]\phi \rightarrow [\alpha]\exists x\phi$. Propositional reasoning (take the contraposition) gives $\vdash \neg[\alpha]\exists x\phi \rightarrow \neg[\alpha]\phi$ and as $x \notin FV(\neg[\alpha]\exists x\phi)$, inference rule (3) gives $\vdash \neg[\alpha]\exists x\phi \rightarrow \forall x\neg[\alpha]\phi$. By propositional reasoning (contraposition) and the definition of $\forall$ in terms of $\exists$ and $\neg$, we get $\vdash \exists x[\alpha]\phi \rightarrow [\alpha]\exists x\phi$.

7-11 Standard dynamic logic axioms that axiomatize the behavior of the program constructors.

12 The conditional choice axiom states that all ways of executing the program $+X\ \alpha$ **where** ϕ lead to ψ iff for all values for the variables in X that make ϕ true, any execution of α makes ψ true. If ψ would contain free variables that occur in X, then left of the $\leftrightarrow$, these free variables would not be bound by $+X$, but right of the $\leftrightarrow$, they would be bound by $\forall X$. It would then be easy to construct a counterexample to the axiom, therefore we have the requirement $FV(\psi) \cap X = \emptyset$.

13-16 Axiom (13) states that if pT' holds before the insertion or if tuple T' is inserted, then pT' holds after the insertion. Axiom (14) states that if pT' does not hold before the the insertion and pT' is is not inserted, then pT' does not hold after the insertion. Note that we cannot replace (13) and (14) by the single axiom (13') $pT'\vee\exists X(\phi \wedge T=T') \leftrightarrow [\&X\ \mathcal{I}p\ T$ **where** $\phi]pT'$, because we then cannot derive axiom (14). However, if use axiom (13') in combination with the determinism axiom $\langle\&X\ \mathcal{I}p\ T$ **where** $\phi\rangle pT' \rightarrow [\&X\ \mathcal{I}p\ T$ **where** $\phi]pT'$, then we can derive axiom (14). Axioms (15) and (16) have the same function for delete as axioms (13) and (14) have for insert.

17-20 The frame axioms that axiomatize that all predicates different from the updated predicate remain unchanged.

21,22 These axioms state that atomic updates always succeed. These axioms are sound, because we axiomatize truth in the full structures, they are of course not sound in all structures.

Definition 13 *A* **proof** *of a formula ϕ is a finite sequence of formulas such that*

- *The formula ϕ is the last formula in the sequence, and*

- *each formula in the sequence is an axiom or follows by one of the inference rules from previous formulas in the sequence.*

If there exists a proof of ϕ, then we call ϕ a **theorem** *and we write $\vdash \phi$.*

Proposition 14 *The proof system for DDL is sound for full structures, that is all formulas that are derivable in the proof system, are valid in all full structures (if $\vdash \phi$ then $S \models \phi$, for any full structure S).*

PROOF: We must prove that all axioms are true in all full structures and that if the premises of an inference rule are true in all full structures, then the conclusion of the inference rule is true in all full structures. The proof requires a lot of detail, but is not very difficult. It has been omitted here, but it is given in the full report [17].

□

Of course, we also would like to have completeness of the proof system, this has however not been proven yet. But we do have a proof of completeness under two extra assumptions: Reiters domain closure and unique naming assumptions for logic databases [15]. These assumptions are formulated as extra axioms in the proof system. To be able to formulate them in a finitary logic, we must assume the set of constants is finite (so actually, we have a third assumption here). The axioms are then:

(23) $\forall x \bigvee_{c \in Con} x = c$ domain closure
(24) $\bigwedge_{c,c' \in Con, c \neq c'} \neg(c = c')$ unique naming

For this extended proof system, we can define a proof just as in definition 13. If ϕ is derivable in the extended proof system, we write $\vdash_{ud} \phi$. (It is clear that if $\vdash \phi$, then also $\vdash_{ud} \phi$, but not the other way around.)

Semantically, we must assume that the domain of a closed term model contains a unique element for every constant. We make the simpler (but equivalent) assumption that the domain of interpretation *is* the set of constants (the interpretation function for constants is then the identity). Structures that are based on such a closed term model are called standard.

Proposition 15 *The axiomatization of DDL is sound and complete under the domain closure and unique naming assumptions. So $\vdash_{ud} \phi$ iff for all full, standard structures S: $S \models \phi$.*

Proving soundness is fairly straightforward and omitted. Here, we give a sketch of the completeness proof, which is based on a completeness proof for PDDL [18]. The full soundness and completeness proofs are given in [17].

We use the notion of *complete information formulas* (cifs). A cif is a formula that completely determines the interpretation of some finite subset of the predicate symbols and variables. Formally, given finite $P \subseteq Pred$ and $X \subseteq Var$, a cif *over P and X* is a formula of the form

$$\bigwedge_{x \in X} x = c_x \ \land \ \bigwedge_{p \in P} \bigwedge_{T \in Con^{ar(p)}} l_p T$$

where for each $x \in X$, $c_x \in Con$ and for each $p \in P$ and $T \in Con^{ar(p)}$, $l_p T$ is either pT or $\neg pT$. If γ is a cif over P and X, and ϕ is a formula which only contains predicate symbols in P and for which $FV(\phi) \subseteq X$, then we say that γ is a cif *over ϕ*. Cifs have three important properties:

1. Given a cif γ over formula ϕ, we have either $\vdash_{ud} \gamma \to \phi$ or $\vdash_{ud} \gamma \to \neg\phi$. So a cif over a formula is like a possible world; it contains enough information to "evaluate" the formula as true or false.

2. If for some $P \subseteq Pred$ and $X \subseteq Var$ we can derive for all cifs γ over P and X that $\vdash_{ud} \gamma \to \phi$, then $\vdash_{ud} \phi$. Again we see that a cif is the "syntactic counterpart" of a possible world; if a formula is implied by all cifs (true in all possible worlds) then it is derivable (valid).

3. For every full, standard structure S and every cif γ, there is a world $w \in S$ and variable interpretation I_V such that $S, w, I_V \models \gamma$. (So every cif is satisfyable in every full, standard structure.)

Of these three properties of cifs, the second and third are easily proven, but the first one requires some work. We give a very short description of the proof of this property.

First, we prove by induction on the structure of formulas that property 1 holds for formulas that do not contain modalities. We then show that an atomic update transforms a cif to another cif and we use this to prove that property 1 holds for formulas of the form $[\alpha]\phi$, with α a conditional insert or delete and ϕ a formula that doesn't contain modalities. We then prove by induction on the structure of formulas that property 1 holds for all formulas that do not contain the $*$ operator (and in order to make the induction proof work, we simultaneously prove a related property for $*$-free update programs). Using this last result, we can then prove completeness of the proof system for $*$-free formulas (just as we do below for the whole proof system). Using the completeness result for $*$-free formulas, we show with a semantic argument that we can "eliminate" the $*$-operator, and we get that property 1 holds for any formula.

Using the three properties of cifs, completeness is easily proven as follows. Let ϕ be some formula and suppose that for all full, standard structures S, we have $S \models \phi$, we then must prove $\vdash_{ud} \phi$. Let P be the set of predicate symbols in ϕ and let $X = FV(\phi)$. By property 2, it is sufficient to prove for all cifs γ over P and X that $\vdash_{ud} \gamma \to \phi$. So let γ be some cif over P and X. By property 1, we have $\vdash_{ud} \gamma \to \phi$ or $\vdash_{ud} \gamma \to \neg\phi$. To finish the completeness proof, we show that the second case cannot occur. Assume $\vdash_{ud} \gamma \to \neg\phi$. By property 3, there is a world $w \in S$ and variable interpretation I_V such that $S, w, I_V \models \gamma$. As the proof system is sound for full, standard structures, we have $S, w, I_V \models \gamma \to \neg\phi$. With the definition of the semantics we then easily derive $S, w, I_V \not\models \phi$, but as $S \models \phi$, this leads to a contradiction. $\square$

Note that in the above proof method it is essential that the number of constants is finite, so it cannot be used to prove completeness of DDL in the more general case.

6 Specification and implementation of update programs

In this section we give a detailed example, showing how we can use the proof system of the previous section, to prove correctness of an implementation of an update program, given a specification for it.

Consider a "copy" update program, which copies the extension of the unary predicate symbol q to p. The specification of the copy program α consists of two formulas:

1. $\forall y(q(y) \leftrightarrow [\alpha]q(y))$, the extension of q remains unchanged under the update.

2. $[\alpha]\forall y(p(y) \leftrightarrow q(y))$, after the update, p has the same extension as q.

(Note that we assume that the first-order language only contains the predicate symbols p and q, otherwise we should also specify that none of the other predicate symbols is changed by the update.) We prove that the following implementation of the update program satisfies the specification:

$$\alpha = \&\{x\}\, \mathcal{D}p(x) \ ; \ \&\{x\}\, \mathcal{I}p(x) \ \textbf{where}\ q(x)$$

We must prove $\vdash \forall y(q(y) \leftrightarrow [\alpha]q(y))$ and $\vdash [\alpha]\forall y(p(y) \leftrightarrow q(y))$. Proving this using only the axioms and derivation rules given in the proof system of section 5 is extremely tedious. We therefore use a number of abbreviations in constructing the proofs:

- When we need a first-order theorem, we just write it down without proof. (In fact, to give a proof, we need some axiom base for first-order logic, which we left unspecified in section 5.) When we can derive a formula from another formula in a few steps, using only first-order properties of $\exists$ and $\forall$, then we do not give all steps of the derivation, but we just say the second formula follows from the first by "first-order reasoning".

- When we can derive a formula from another formula in a few steps, only using the properties of the propositional connectives $\neg$, $\vee$, $\wedge$, $\rightarrow$ and $\leftrightarrow$, then we do not give all steps involved in this derivation, but we just say the second formula follows from the first by "propositional reasoning". For some specific cases of propositional reasoning, we use special names. Below, we use: transitivity of $\leftrightarrow$, symmetry of $\leftrightarrow$, transitivity of $\rightarrow$, definition of $\rightarrow$ (in terms of $\neg$ and $\vee$) and definition of $\leftrightarrow$ (in terms of $\rightarrow$ and $\wedge$).

- When we can derive a formula from another formula, using only standard properties of (propositional) modal logic (so using the K axiom and modal generalization), then we do not give all steps of the derivation, but we just say the second formula follows from the first by "modal reasoning". One special case of modal reasoning is the derivation rule monotonicity of $[\,]$ (from $\vdash \phi \rightarrow \psi$ derive $\vdash [\beta]\phi \rightarrow [\beta]\psi$ and from $\vdash \phi \leftrightarrow \psi$ derive $\vdash [\beta]\phi \leftrightarrow [\beta]\psi$).

- When we can derive a formula from another formula in a few steps, using one of the specific dynamic logic axioms (7)-(11), then we say the second formula follows from the first by "dynamic reasoning (nr. of axiom)". Dynamic logic reasoning is usually used to replace a (sub)formula by an equivalent formula, for one of the equivalence axioms (7)-(9). We also use one specific inference rule, called the sequential composition rule (from $\vdash \phi \rightarrow [\beta_1]\phi'$ and $\vdash \phi' \rightarrow [\beta_2]\phi''$ derive $\vdash \phi \rightarrow [\beta_1;\beta_2]\phi''$ with as special case for $\phi = true$: from $\vdash [\beta_1]\phi'$ and $\vdash \phi' \rightarrow [\beta_2]\phi''$ derive $\vdash [\beta_1;\beta_2]\phi''$).

- From the frame axioms, it is easy to derive the frame theorems, which are the same as the axioms, only having bi-implications instead of implications (so $q\,T' \leftrightarrow [\&X\,\mathcal{I}p\,T\ \textbf{where}\ \phi]q\,T'$, etc.).

There are of course many other interesting derivable inference rules and theorems than the ones listed above, we have only given the rules and theorems that we will use in the proof below. Note that we do not prove the derivable rules and theorems here, they are proven in the full report [17].

We now prove that the implementation of α satisfies the specification. In the proof, we use $\alpha_1 = \&\{x\}\,\mathcal{D}p(x)$ and $\alpha_2 = \&\{x\}\,\mathcal{I}p(x)\ \textbf{where}\ q(x)$ as abbreviations (so $\alpha = \alpha_1; \alpha_2$).

First, we prove $\vdash \forall y(q(y) \leftrightarrow [\alpha_1; \alpha_2]q(y))$.

1. $q(y) \leftrightarrow [\alpha_2]q(y)$	frame theorem
2. $[\alpha_1]q(y) \leftrightarrow [\alpha_1][\alpha_2]q(y)$	monotonicity of $[\,]$, 1
3. $q(y) \leftrightarrow [\alpha_1]q(y)$	frame theorem
4. $q(y) \leftrightarrow [\alpha_1][\alpha_2]q(y)$	transitivity of $\leftrightarrow$, 3, 2
5. $q(y) \leftrightarrow [\alpha_1; \alpha_2]q(y)$	dynamic reasoning (8), 4
6. $\forall y(q(y) \leftrightarrow [\alpha_1; \alpha_2]q(y))$	universal generalization, 5

Next, we prove $\vdash [\alpha_1; \alpha_2]\forall y(p(y) \leftrightarrow q(y))$.

1. $\neg(p(y)\wedge\neg\exists x(true\wedge x{=}y)) \rightarrow [\alpha_1]\neg p(y)$	axiom (16)
2. $\neg(p(y)\wedge\neg\exists x(true\wedge x{=}y))$	first-order theorem
3. $[\alpha_1]\neg p(y)$	modus ponens, 1, 2
4. $\forall y[\alpha_1]\neg p(y)$	universal generalization, 3
5. $\forall y[\alpha_1]\neg p(y) \rightarrow [\alpha_1]\forall y\neg p(y)$	axiom (6)
6. $[\alpha_1]\forall y\neg p(y)$	modus ponens, 5, 4

7. $p(y)\vee\exists x(q(x)\wedge x{=}y) \rightarrow [\alpha_2]p(y)$	axiom (13)
8. $q(y) \leftrightarrow \exists x(q(x)\wedge x{=}y)$	first-order theorem
9. $p(y)\vee q(y) \rightarrow [\alpha_2]p(y)$	replace equivalents, 7, 8
10. $\neg p(y) \rightarrow (\neg q(y)\vee[\alpha_2]p(y))$	propositional reasoning, 9
11. $\neg q(y) \leftrightarrow [\alpha_2]\neg q(y)$	frame theorem
12. $\neg p(y) \rightarrow ([\alpha_2]\neg q(y)\vee[\alpha_2]p(y))$	replace equivalents, 10, 11
13. $\neg p(y) \rightarrow [\alpha_2](\neg q(y)\vee p(y))$	modal reasoning, 12
14. $\neg p(y) \rightarrow [\alpha_2](q(y) \rightarrow p(y))$	definition of $\rightarrow$, 13

15. $\neg(p(y)\vee\exists x(q(x)\wedge x{=}y)) \rightarrow [\alpha_2]\neg p(y)$	axiom (14)
$\dots$	(similar to 8-13)
22. $\neg p(y) \rightarrow [\alpha_2](p(y) \rightarrow q(y))$	definition of $\rightarrow$, 21

23. $\neg p(y) \rightarrow [\alpha_2]((q(y) \rightarrow p(y))\wedge(p(y) \rightarrow q(y)))$	modal reasoning, 14, 22
24. $\neg p(y) \rightarrow [\alpha_2](p(y) \leftrightarrow q(y))$	definition of $\leftrightarrow$, 23
25. $\forall y(\neg p(y) \rightarrow [\alpha_2](p(y) \leftrightarrow q(y)))$	universal generalization, 24
26. $\forall y\neg p(y) \rightarrow \forall y[\alpha_2](p(y) \leftrightarrow q(y))$	first-order reasoning, 25
27. $\forall y[\alpha_2](p(y) \leftrightarrow q(y)) \rightarrow [\alpha_2]\forall y(p(y) \leftrightarrow q(y))$	axiom (6)
28. $\forall y\neg p(y) \rightarrow [\alpha_2]\forall y(p(y) \leftrightarrow q(y))$	transitivity of $\rightarrow$, 26, 27

29. $[\alpha_1; \alpha_2]\forall y(p(y) \leftrightarrow q(y))$	seq. composition rule, 6, 28

This concludes the proof that the update program α satisfies the specification of a "copy" update program.

7 Update completeness of DDL

If we have a language to update databases, then a natural question to ask is what the expressive power of this language is. Ideally, we would like some completeness result: every "reasonable" function from database states to database states can be expressed in the update language. Abiteboul and Vianu [2, 3] define such a notion of completeness of update languages for *relational* databases and show that the specific update language TL is update complete. As a relational database is a special case of a logic database, it is not too difficult to translate their definitions of database schema and instance to DDL. This section contains such a translation. (Note that as this section is mainly concerned with relational databases, we will frequently use the word "relation" instead of the word "predicate".) The basic result of this section is that the update language of DDL is (relational) update complete.

For the translation, we restrict the semantics to one special structure $\mathcal{R}$, the *relational structure*. This structure is based on the closed term model (Con, id_{Con}) and has as worlds all functions that interpret all predicate symbols as a *finite* sets of tuples (of constants). (Note that we do not consider the problem of axiomatizing this logic here, but some infinitary axiomatization seems to be the most natural.)

Definition 16 *A **database schema** is a finite subset of the predicate symbols. An **instance** of a relational database schema S is the restriction of some element of $\mathcal{R}$ to S (note that elements of $\mathcal{R}$ are indeed functions with as domain the predicate symbols). The set of instances of a database schema S is denoted $Inst(S)$.*

The notion of update completeness is based on the notion of C-genericity. Intuitively, a function on instances is C-generic, if it treats all constants "uniformly", except maybe for the constants of C (the constants that occur in the update).

Definition 17 *Let S and T be database schemas. Let $C \subseteq Con$ be a finite set of constants. A function r from $Inst(S)$ to $Inst(T)$ is C-**generic** iff for every bijective function ρ on Con which is the identity on elements of C, we have that $r \circ \rho = \rho \circ r$. (Here, we use ρ as a function on instances: just change all the constants in the instance in the way indicated by ρ.)*

Definition 18 *Let S and T be database schemas. A **database mapping** is a function from $Inst(S)$ to $Inst(T)$ which is computable and C-generic, for some finite set of constants C.*

In general, database updates may need relations to store temporary results. As such relations are not important in the final result, we have the notion of i-o schemas (S, T) (where S and T are database schemas). An update over an i-o schema (S, T) uses the relations of S to compute the relations of T and may also use relations not in S or T to store temporary results. All relations used in the update that are not in S are assumed to be initially empty, all relations not in T do not count in the final result.

Definition 19 *An update language is* **update complete**, *if for every database mapping from $Inst(S)$ to $Inst(R)$, there is an update over the i-o schema (R, S) such that the semantics of this update is exactly the database mapping.*

Abiteboul & Vianu [2] give a specific language called TL (Transaction Language) that is update complete. This language contains:

- atomic insert and delete actions: $i_P(r)$ and $d_P(r)$, for P a relation and r a tuple;

- sequential composition: if t and t' are TL expressions, then $t; t'$ is a TL expression;

- a while construction: if Q is a conjunction of literals (including possibly the $=$ predicate) and t is a TL expression, then **while** Q **do** t is a TL expression.

Intuitively, atomic inserts and deletes just insert/delete one tuple (or do nothing if the tuple is already (not) present), sequential composition just executes the two updates, one after the other, and **while** Q **do** t repeatedly picks values for the variables in Q that make Q true and executes t with these values, until there exists no value-assignment to the variables of Q that makes Q true.

The formal semantics of a TL expression is given (just as for DDL update programs) as a relation on the possible worlds of $\mathcal{R}$. The easiest way of defining the formal semantics of TL expressions, is by giving equivalent DDL update programs for the TL expressions: $i_P(r) = \mathcal{I}P(r)$, $d_P(r) = \mathcal{D}P(r)$, $t; t' = t; t'$ and **while** Q **do** $t = (+FV(Q)\ t$ **where** $Q)^*; (\neg \exists FV(Q)Q)?$. As we are able to define the semantics of TL expressions in terms of DDL update programs, we immediately get from the update completeness of TL, that the DDL update language is update complete.

Discussion. In general, updates need temporary relations to make sure that TL is update complete. As the update language of DDL contains more constructs than TL, it may be possible to prove that any TL expression over i-o schema (R, S) which uses temporary relations, can be expressed in DDL without the use of temporary relations. In this section, we only looked at update completeness for *relational* databases and for this purpose, we have used a restricted version of DDL (the main restriction is in the notion of database state). If we use the notion of database state as a general first-order formula (that may contain disjunctive information), we may be able to define a more general notion of update completeness for *logic* databases. We can then again ask the question if DDL is update complete for this more general notion. As we would then need a general construction to introduce disjunctive information, we expect TL not to be update complete for logic databases (as TL lacks a general choice operator). We intend to look at both these matters in the future. **End of discussion.**

8 Comparison with other approaches

Many approaches to database updates attack the more difficult cases like view updates (e.g. [19]) and updates with incomplete information (e.g. [4, 5, 6, 7, 20, 21]). The work on view updates is as yet incomparable to our work, as we have only studied base updates. Updates with incomplete information are commonly established by allowing the insertion of a disjunction. Such an update can, however, be interpreted in various ways, see the list of references above. In DDL, we can use the choice operation to insert indefinite knowledge. The exact relation between the DDL choice and updates with disjunctive formulas has yet to be established.

Golshani et al. [9] and Khosla et al. [10] use modal logic with multiple modalities; they assume a modal operator $[u]$ for every update action u. However, the interpretation of the update action is not fixed (as it is in our semantics) but must be specified by giving some defining axioms. Furthermore, they do not allow update actions to be combined into update programs.

Manchanda and Warren [12] also use modal logic with multiple modalities. Just like we do, they assume for every base atom an insert and a delete action with a fixed interpretation. They combine such atomic updates into programs by means of *update rules* of the form $\langle E \rangle \leftarrow C_1 \wedge \langle E_1 \rangle (C_2 \wedge \langle E_2 \rangle (\ldots))$ (the update E is defined in terms of updates E_i, every C_i is a conjunction of atoms). In contrast, we combine atomic updates into programs by the standard dynamic logic operators.

9 Conclusions and future work

We have defined DDL, a language designed to reason about database updates (in particular, reasoning about correctness of an update program with respect to a specification). We have given a model based declarative semantics and a sound axiomatization for DDL.

Future work includes first of all the incorporation of various ideas in the present first-order language, which have already been worked out in detail for the propositional case [18]. For instance, we want to include derivation rules. Just as in the propositional case, we can then distinguish between *active* updates (which trigger the derivation rules to compute changes in derived predicates) and *passive* updates (which are just the updates we defined in this paper). We also want to give an operational semantics to DDL.

Second, we want to study the "expressiveness" of our update language and we want to compare our update language with other update languages [1, 12, 13]. DDL is based on dynamic logic, which was designed to reason about (imperative) programming languages. We therefore may need some extra/other (update) language primitives that are particularly useful in the context of updating databases. (In fact, next to the insert and delete actions, we have already introduced one such primitive: the conditional choice). One problem in this respect is the updating of tuples in some relation. Updating a single tuple is easily established in our language: just delete the tuple and insert the updated version. But we also want conditional updates (like the conditional insert and delete we introduced as atomic updates). Simulating conditional updates with conditional deletes and inserts is possible but cumbersome (we need extra predicate symbols to hold intermediate results). It may therefore be convenient to introduce conditional updates as an extra atomic action in our language.

Research that is planned for a more distant future includes negative actions (which we first intend to study in our simpler propositional framework) and the extension of DDL with function symbols and equations (abstract datatypes).

Acknowledgements. We would like to thank the Volkse participants for the useful discussions we had. Especially, we thank Catriel Beeri for stressing the relevance of the work of Abiteboul and Vianu on update completeness (see section 7) and we thank Marcelo Finger for a proof sketch of the "increasing domains formula" (see section 5).

References

[1] S. Abiteboul. Updates, a new frontier. In J. Paredaens and D. Van Gught, editors, *International Conference on Database Theory*, pages 1–18. Springer, 1988. Lecture Notes in Computer Science 326.

[2] S. Abiteboul and V. Vianu. A transaction language complete for database update and specification. In *6th ACM SIGACT-SIGMOD symposium on the principles of database systems*, pages 260–268, San Diego, Cal., March 23-25 1987.

[3] S. Abiteboul and V. Vianu. Procedural and declarative database update languages. In *7th ACM SIGACT-SIGMOD symposium on the principles of database systems*, pages 240–250, Austin, Texas, March 21-23 1988.

[4] L. Cholvy. Update semantics under the domain closure assumption. In M. Gyssens, J. Paredaens, and D. van Gucht, editors, *International Conference on Database Theory*, pages 123–140. Springer, 1988. Lecture Notes in Computer Science 326.

[5] Jürgen Cronau. Update semantics for deductive databases. Technical Report 322, FB Informatik, University of Dortmund, Dortmund, 1990.

[6] M. Dalal. Investigations into a theory of knowledge base revision: Preliminary report. In *Proceedings AAAI, volume 2*, pages 475–479, 1988.

[7] F. Dignum and R.P. van de Riet. Addition and removal of information for a knowledge base with incomplete information. *Data and Knowledge Engineering*, 8(4):293–307, August 1992.

[8] L. T. F. Gamut. *Logic, Language, and Meaning.* The University of Chicago Press, 1991. Volume 2: Intensional Logic and Logical Grammar.

[9] F. Golshani, T.S.E. Maibaum, and M.R. Sadler. A modal system of algebras for database specification and query/update support. In *Proceedings of the Nineth International Conference on Very Large Databases*, pages 331–359, 1983.

[10] S. Khosla, T.S.E. Maibaum, and M. Sadler. Database specification. In T.B. Jr. Steel and R. Meersman, editors, *Database Semantics (DS-1)*, pages 141–158. North-Holland, 1986.

[11] D. Kozen and J. Tiuryn. Logics of programs. In J. van Leeuwen, editor, *Handbook of Theoretical Computer Science*, pages 789–840. Elsevier Science Publishers, 1990.

[12] S. Manchanda and D.S. Warren. A logic-based language for database updates. In J. Minker, editor, *Foundations of Deductive Databases and Logic Programming*, pages 363–394. Morgan Kaufmann, 1988.

[13] S. Naqvi and S. Tsur. *A Logical Language for Data and Knowledge Bases*. Computer Science Press, 1989.

[14] G. D. Plotkin. A structural approach to operational semantics. Technical Report DAIMI FN-19, Computer Science Department, Aarhus University, 1981. reprinted 1991.

[15] R. Reiter. Towards a logical reconstruction of relational database theory. In M.L. Brodie, J. Mylopoulos, and J.W. Schmidt, editors, *On Conceptual Modelling*, pages 191–233. Springer, 1984.

[16] P.A. Spruit, J.-J.Ch. Meyer, and R.J. Wieringa. Declarative semantics of passive and active updates in logic databases. In *Proceedings, 3rd International Workshop on Foundations of Models and Languages for Data and Objects*, pages 37–46, Aigen, Austria, September 1991.

[17] P.A. Spruit, R. J. Wieringa, and J.-J. Ch. Meyer. Dynamic database logic. Technical report, Department of Mathematics and Computer Science, Vrije Universiteit, Amsterdam. in preparation.

[18] P.A. Spruit, R.J. Wieringa, and J.-J.Ch. Meyer. Axiomatization, declarative semantics and operational semantics of passive and active updates in logic databases. Technical Report IR-294, Department of Mathematics and Computer Science, Vrije Universiteit, Amsterdam, June 1992.

[19] R. Torlone and P. Atzeni. Updating deductive databases with functional dependencies. In C. Delobel, M. Kifer, and Y. Masunaga, editors, *Proceedings of the Second International Conference on Deductive and Object-Oriented Databases*, pages 278–292. Springer Verlag, 1991. Lecture Notes in Computer Science 566.

[20] A. Weber. Updating propositional formulas. In *First International Conference on Expert Database systems*, pages 373–386, 1986.

[21] M. Winslett. *Updating Logical Databases*. Cambridge University Press, 1990.

Modelling Database Updates with Constraint Logic Programming

Elisa Bertino, Maurizio Martelli

Dipartimento di Informatica e Scienze dell'Informazione,
Università di Genova
Via Benedetto XV 3, 16132 Genova, Italia
{bertino,martelli}@cisi.unige.it

Danilo Montesi

Dipartimento di Informatica, Università di Pisa
Corso Italia 40, 56125 Pisa, Italia
montesi@di.unipi.it

Abstract

This paper addresses the problem of integrating the update language into
a declarative query language. Elementary updates are expressed in a
declarative style by means of a constraint language. The constraint logic
programming framework is used to provide a declarative query-update
language. Its semantics is defined in two steps. In such framework an
update query behaves as a transaction. A transactional behaviour of
update queries is provided.

1 Introduction

The need for including dynamic aspects into database design and specification
has been recognized [7, 2]. Several rule-based languages have been designed to
support queries and updates (DL [2], RDL1 [21], DLL [22], DatalogA [23], $\mathcal{LDL}$
[24], Hypothetical Datalog [6], Glue-Nail [10], Starburst [25]). The declarative
languages are based on logic languages and the procedural ones are based on
production rule languages. Some of the above languages are declarative (DL,
DLL, and Hypothetical Datalog) and some are procedural (Starburst). The
others have some components expressed in a declarative language and other
components are expressed in a procedural language. Queries and updates can
be expressed by means of declarative and/or procedural languages. Declarative
languages have been investigated in the database context as query languages.
For example relational calculus [4] and Datalog [8] are powerful database languages. The advantage of a declarative language over a procedural one does
not need comments. The tendency of new generations of rule based databases
is to merge updates into a declarative query language. The updates can be
expressed in a procedural language as in Glue-Nail or in a declarative language
such as DatalogA, $\mathcal{LDL}$, DL, DLL, and Hypothetical Datalog. This is achieved
by introducing some control features trying to maintain a declarative semantics.

The various proposals of integrating updates into a declarative query language such as Glue-Nail, DatalogA and $\mathcal{LDL}$ approached the update problem introducing updates in the language whose semantics was either lacking or given in a different formalism such as dynamic logic [14, 22]. Other proposals such as DL [3] and Hypothetical Datalog [6] have no explicit mechanism for deletion.

All the above approaches to the update problem are based on the immediate updates semantics. Under such semantics, updates are executed as soon as they are evaluated. For example, considering updates in rule bodies, such as in $\mathcal{LDL}$, a single query can be evaluated on different states. Starting from the current database state s_1, the query fires the rules of the database. During the course of satisfying the rules the current database state s_1 becomes $s_2, s_3 \ldots$ ending in the final state s_n. Such a process leads to complex semantics. Similarly, considering updates in rule heads, such as in DL, the computation start from a database state and goes through a sequence of states. Considering immediate update semantics the problem of the transactional behaviour has not been addressed in Glue-Nail, DatalogA, $\mathcal{LDL}$, Hypothetical Datalog and DL due to complex semantics and/or of lack of formal definition of transactions. The fundamental reason is that immediate update semantics is related to non-monotonic reasoning. Indeed, all the above approaches are based on the monotonicity of a fixpoint operator. Note that one of the difficulties of modelling updates is due to its non-monotonicity which does not fit with the fixpoint construction of rule based languages.

In this paper we take a different approach, that is, updates are not immediately executed as soon as they are evaluated. That is, they have a non-immediate update semantics. Therefore, considering updates in rule bodies, a single query is evaluated in the same state, that is the current state, namely on the state prior to any change. Only after successful completion of the query such updates are executed. This is close to the "mark and update" phases [26]. In the marking phase the updates are collected and in the update phase they are executed altogether. In addition "updates to a database are expressed as constraints in a constraint language". Roughly speaking, a constraint expresses a relationship existing among some entities [19]. Constraints are not integrity constraints. In our proposal a database state is a set of ground facts, that is the extensional database (EDB). The intensional database (IDB) is a set of rules. Each rule has in the body the constraints to express the updates. Thus, in order to provide a unique language to express a declarative query language and to express updates with a declarative language we have to integrate the logic language and the constraint language. Note that constraint languages are declarative ones.

Our current research work approaches the above problem using constraint logic programming (shortly $CLP(X)$) [16, 17], which is definitely one of the most important extensions of the logic programming paradigm from a theoretical and pragmatic point of view. From a theoretical point of view it has been used to model the combination of the deductive power of logic programming and different kinds of computational aspects (from handling real numbers to concurrency). $CLP(X)$ is a schema which generalizes logic programming by including constraints. Moreover, a nice property such as equivalent model-theoretic, fixpoint and proof-theoretic semantics is maintained. In this schema, various constraint logic programming languages can be accommodated according to the choice of the constraint domain. This integration allows, for example, to tackle problems having a numerical and/or logical character in a declarative way. Some existing proposals of $CLP(X)$ languages are $CLP(\mathcal{R})$ [18], CHIP [11] and Prolog III [9]. Aside from the Herbrand domain, which they share, they have different domains to express constraints. For example, $CLP(\mathcal{R})$ only permits constraints on real terms, Prolog III on linear rational and on boolean terms and CHIP on linear rational, boolean and finite domain terms. ¿From a pragmatic point of view the idea behind $CLP(X)$ is to have an active use of constraints to prune the search space *a priori* by removing combinations of values which cannot appear together in a solution. Search procedure based on consistency techniques are best viewed as the iteration of two steps: 1. propagate the constraints as much as possible, and 2. make assumptions on the values of some variables until the problem is solved [15].

In our approach we instantiate the $CLP(X)$ over a particular constraint domain. Such domain provides an interpretation for the constraint language expressing elementary updates to the extensional database. The semantics is defined as a two step semantics modelling the mark and update phases. The first step is an instance of the $CLP(X)$ semantics. The second step perform the updates modelling the set-oriented feature and the transactional behaviour of a query. Through this paper, we assume the reader is familiar with the basic notions of (constraint) logic programming [16, 20] and deductive databases [13]. Section 2 gives an introduction of the query-update language, Section 3 defines the its semantics.

2 The query-update language

In this section we define the language to query and update the database. The query language can be defined as a stand alone language. For example the classic Datalog language [8]. The update language can be defined either within the query language or in a separate language. In our approach we consider the former case. In the following, however, we introduce the update language as a stand alone language.

2.1 Updates as constraints

Updates in DLL, DatalogA and $\mathcal{LDL}$ are modelled by some specials atoms of the form

$$\pm p(t_1, \ldots, t_n)$$

where p is an n-ary base relation, and $t_1, \ldots, t_n$ are ground terms. Intuitively, the meaning of $+p(\tilde{t})$ is to insert the tuple $\tilde{t}$ into the base relation p. Similarly, the meaning of $-p(\tilde{t})$ is to delete the tuple $\tilde{t}$ from the base relation p. Given an update, say $+p(a)$ on a database state s the desired result of the update is that $p(a)$ belongs to the database state s'. Similarly, the absence of $p(a)$ from the database state s' is the result of the update $-p(a)$. Thus, given the current database state and the updates the new database state can be easily computed. For example, $p(a)$ can be inserted by means of the equation $s' = s \cup \{p(a)\}$ and $p(b)$ can be removed by means of $s' = s \setminus \{p(b)\}$. To insert $p(a)$ and remove $p(b)$ one can consider the equation $s' = s \cup \{p(a)\} \setminus \{p(b)\}$. Note that we do not allow to insert and remove the same atom.

The above equations respectively express the given updates. We could then say that the desired result of the updates $+p(a)$ and $-p(b)$ is achieved by starting from a database state s, adding $p(a)$ and removing $p(b)$ to it to get the database state s'. Note that this is equivalent to remove $p(b)$ first and then add $p(a)$. The equation can also be interpreted as constraints. A program in a constraint language consists of the set of relations between a set of objects. In our constraint program, s and s' are the objects, which in this case are database states, and the equation defines the relationship between these objects. Given a value for s, the constraint-satisfaction system can use the problem-solving rules of the set operators to solve the constraints. In some sense an equation express an assignment. The difference between imperative languages and constraints languages is highlighted by their treatment of equality. Procedural languages require two (or more) different operations for equality and assignment. For example in Pascal the relational operator $=$ returns true or false depending on whether its two arguments are equal, and $:=$ is used to assign the value of an expression to a variable. In a constraints language, equality is used only as a relational operator, equivalent to the corresponding operator in the conventional languages. An assignment operator is unnecessary in a constraints language: the constraint-satisfaction mechanism "assigns" value to variable by finding values for the variable that makes the equality relationship true. For example, in the constraint language statement $X = 3$ the equal sign is used as a relational operator (as in mathematics), but to make this statement true the constraint-satisfaction system will give the value 3 to X. Thus the equal sign acts similarly to an assignment operation. Unlike the imperative assignment operation, however, arbitrary expressions can appear as its left argument. For example, the previous statement could be written in many different but semantically equivalent way: $3 = X, X - 2 = 1, 2X = X - 3$ Also note that, in a constraint language, the equal sign expresses an invariant (a *constraint*) between objects that is permanent during the program's execution. Expressing updates as constraints, if we limit ourselves to updates with ground terms only, the class of updates we can perform is going to be severely restricted. We can relax this restriction integrating the update language with the query language to provide bindings for the variables in the updates. In the following we denote in our language the updates as $+p(X)$ and $-p(X)$ instead of the equations. Moreover, we consider strong updates. Strong updates are updates which can be executed only if the preconditions are satisfied. For example, to remove (insert) $p(a)$, it must (not) be present in EDB.

Example 2.1 *Consider the update query, that is a query with update*

$$? + p(X), q(X, Y)$$

where capitals letters denote variables. In this case only those $X-$tuples are to be added to the current state for which $q(X, Y)$ holds. This is equivalent to saying that $q(X, Y)$ provides a binding for the variable of the constraint.

◇

We now extend our approach from update queries to update rules. In the following we consider the words update query (update rule) and query (rule) synonymous respectively.

Example 2.2 *Assume that* eds *is a base relation giving the salaries and department of employees. Considering s_1 as the current database state we want to transfer all employees from the* shoe *department to the* toy *department.*

$$EDB_1 = \{ \quad \text{eds(bob, shoe, 15K)}$$
$$\text{eds(tom, shoe, 20K)} \quad \}$$

$$IDB = \{ \quad \text{transafer(X)} \leftarrow \quad -\text{eds(X, shoe, Y)},$$
$$+\text{eds(X, toy, Y)},$$
$$\text{eds(X, shoe, Y)} \quad \}$$

The query $?\text{X} = \text{bob}, \text{transfer(X)}$ *evaluated in* $DB_1 = IDB \cup EDB_1$ *is computed in two steps. The first step, that is the marking phase, collects the updates* $-\text{eds(bob, shoe, 15K)}, +\text{eds(bob, toy, 15K)}$. *The bindings for the variables of the equations are provided by* eds(X, shoe, Y). *The second step, that is the update phase, performs the updates altogether. Informally, the new state is* $EDB_2 = \{\text{eds(bob, toy, 15K)}, \text{eds(tom, , shoe, 20K)}\}$.

$\diamond$

The update constraints are collected during the derivation process. The only computation on the update constraints is the solvability checking (see Subsection 3.1), that is, one checks that no complementary updates are collected. The solution is delayed until the derivation successful terminate. Thus, the constraints express hypothetical updates which are computed only in the update phase. The query is evaluated only on the current state, for instance in EDB_1 for the Example 2.2. This correspond to a deterministic language [1]. In addition to constraints expressing updates, one need also to express bindings between the variables of the query and constants. For example the bindings between X and bob in the Example 2.2 is denote as $\text{X} = \text{bob}$. Thus, roughly speaking, rules can have in their bodies variable constraints and update constraints.

2.2 Constrained Datalog

We now define a Constrained Datalog language (CD) to model deductive databases with updates. The name suggest a version of $CLP(X)$ for databases purposes as it was for Datalog. CD inherits the formal setting of $CLP(X)$. A (CD) database with elementary updates is made of IDB and EDB. EDB is a set of base relations (as in Datalog) built over the extensional predicate symbols Π_{EDB}. IDB and a query Q can contain updates. IDB is a set of rules. A rule has the head (H) and the body. The body is made of three parts. The query part $(B_1, \ldots, B_n)$, that is the "traditional" body of a rule in Datalog, the update constraints $(c_1^u, \ldots, c_s^u)$ and the variable constraints $(c_1^v, \ldots, c_k^v)$.

$$H \leftarrow c_1^v, \ldots, c_k^v, c_1^u, \ldots, c_s^u, B_1, \ldots, B_n$$

H and B_i are atoms as in Datalog built over the intensionally defined predicate symbols Π_{IDB} and $\Pi_{IDB} \cup \Pi_{EDB}$ respectively. Note that the query part can also be empty (see Example 2.3). The variable constraints $c_1^v, \ldots, c_k^v$ (shortly c^v) are a set, possibly empty, of equations. For example $X = a, Y = b$. Such equations are called variable constraints to stress the fact that they provide a binding for the variables of a query with the constants of the language. The update constraints $c_1^u, \ldots, c_s^u$ (shortly c^u) is a set, possibly empty, of constraints of the form $\pm p(X)$ (where $p \in \Pi_{EDB}$). We denote a query Q [1] as

$$c^v, c^u, B_1, \ldots, B_n$$

where c^v and/or c^u can be empty. Note that a query can update a database even if it has no updates ($c^u = \emptyset$), since it can trigger constrained rules with updates in their bodies (see Example 2.3). The intuitive meaning of a rule is: "if $B_1, \ldots, B_n$ is true and the constraints c^v, c^u are solvable, then H is true". The notion of solvability is formally given in Subsection 3.1. Intuitively the solvability of the variable constraints is that they express equalities which have a solution. For example the constraints $X = \text{bob}, X = \text{tom}$ are not solvable. The solvability of the update constraints express the fact that if we want to insert (delete) $p(t)$, then $p(t) \notin EDB_i$ ($p(t) \in EDB_i$, respectively).

Example 2.3 *Let us consider the following example where updates to ground base relations are considered. DB_1 is $IDB \cup EDB_1$ (where $\cup$ denotes the union between sets of rules).*

$$EDB_1 = \{q(b)\}$$

$$
\begin{aligned}
IDB = \{ \quad & p(X) \leftarrow -q(X), q(X) \\
& r(X) \leftarrow +t(X), p(X) \\
& k(X) \leftarrow +q(X), t(X) \\
& s(X) \leftarrow t(X) \\
& v(X) \leftarrow +q(X) \quad \}
\end{aligned}
$$

The query $Q_1 = ?r(X)$ evaluated in DB_1 computes the binding $X = b$ and computes the hypothetical updates $-q(b), +t(b)$. Informally, the new extensional database $EDB_2 = \{t(b)\}$ is the result of the application of those updates to EDB_1. The query $Q_2 = ?s(X)$ evaluated in DB_2 computes the binding $X = b$, and does not compute any update and thus the new extensional database is still EDB_2. The query $Q_3 = ?v(X)$ evaluated in DB_2 computes the binding $X = b$ and computes the updates $+q(b)$. Informally, the new extensional database $EDB_3 = \{t(b), q(b)\}$ is the result of the application of this update to EDB_2.

$\diamond$

Note that we assume our database is safe through invocation by a query ensure us that the updates are always ground even if the intensional database contains non-ground rules without body (see the above Example).

---

[1] In the examples, following the tradition, we prefix a query with the symbol "?".

3 Semantics of Constrained Datalog

Constrained Datalog as $CLP(X)$ has the model-theoretic, fixpoint and proof-theoretic semantics. Their definition and equivalence is given in [12]. Therefore, the top-down and bottom-up evaluation methods of Datalog, i.e. Query-Subquery and Naive evaluation [5] can be easily extended to our language. In this way the marking phase can be computed top-down and bottom-up. In the following we only define the proof-theoretic semantics for CD. However, it should be clear that CD has also a fixpoint semantics. The second step semantics, based on the previous one model the update phase, capturing the set-oriented and the transactional behaviour of a query.

Definition 3.1 *(derivation step) Let DB be a CD database. A derivation step of a query $Q = ?c^v, c^u, G_1, \ldots, G_t$ in DB results in a query of the form $?c'^v, c'^u, \tilde{B}_1, \ldots, \tilde{B}_t$, and is denoted by $c^v, c^u, G_1, \ldots, G_t \xrightarrow{\Re} c'^v, c'^u, \tilde{B}_1, \ldots, \tilde{B}_t$ if there exist t variants of rules in DB, $H_j \leftarrow c_j^v, c_j^u, \tilde{B}_j$, $j = 1, \ldots, t$ with no variables in common with Q and with each other, such that c'^v, c'^u is $\Re$-solvable with $c'^v = c^v \cup c_1^v \cup \ldots \cup c_t^v \cup \{H_1 = G_1\} \cup \ldots \cup \{H_t = G_t\}$ and $c'^u = c^u \cup c_1^u \cup \ldots \cup c_t^u$.*

Note that the derivations are given with respect to a fixed solvability notion which is defined over the algebraic structure $\Re$ (see Subsection 3.1).

Definition 3.2 *(derivation) Let DB be a CD database. A derivation of a query Q is a finite or infinite sequence of queries such that every query, apart from Q is obtained from the previous one by means of a derivation step.*

Definition 3.3 *(successful derivation) Let DB be a CD database. A successful derivation of a query Q is a finite sequence whose last element is a query of the form c'^v, c'^u. c'^v, c'^u is the answer constraint of the derivation. All other finite derivations are finitely failed. The successful derivation of a query Q which yields the answer constraint c'^v, c'^u, is denoted by $Q \xmapsto{\Re}{}^* c'^v, c'^u$.*

3.1 The structure $\Re$

The algebraic structure $\Re$ is used to define notion of solvable constraints [16]. Generally speaking a constraint c is *solvable* iff there exists a substitution θ (*solution*) mapping variables to elements of the domain of $\Re$ such that $c\theta$ is true in $\Re$. In the following we define our structure. Note that such structure interprets the updates in a strong way. The constraint domain is $\langle \mathcal{H}, EDB \rangle$ where $\mathcal{H}$ denotes the Herbrand universe and $EDB \subseteq \mathcal{H}B_{EDB}$ is a subset of the Herbrand base built over Π_{EDB} that is the current database state.

Definition 3.4 *A structure $\Re$ is defined over a (finite) one sort alphabet Π and Σ of predicate and constant symbols. $\Re$ consist of*

- *a pair $\langle \mathcal{H}, EDB \rangle$*

- *an assignment which maps each constant symbol $c \in \Sigma$ into itself in $\mathcal{H}$*

- *an assignment to each predicate symbol in Π_c such that*

1. *Variable*, $= \in \Pi_{c^v}$. $=$ *is interpreted as syntactic equality over* $\mathcal{H}$.

2. *Update*, $\forall p \in \Pi_{EDB}$

    (a) $+p(\tilde{t}) = true$ *iff* $p(\tilde{t}) \notin EDB$

    (b) $-p(\tilde{t}) = true$ *iff* $p(\tilde{t}) \in EDB$

An $\Re$-valuation for a (Π, Σ)-expression is a mapping $\theta : V \to \mathcal{H}$ where V is the set of all variables, and $\theta(X) \in \mathcal{H}$.

Note that the above interpretation of updates does not allow to insert (remove) ground atoms that were (not) in EDB, respectively. For example considering the extensional database $EDB = \{p(a)\}$ the update $+p(a)$ is not allowed. If C is a set of atomic constraints, $\Re \models C\theta$ iff $\forall (c^v, c^u) \in C$ $\Re \models (c^v, c^u)\theta$ $((c^v, c^u)\theta$ is $\Re$-equivalent to true) holds.

Definition 3.5 *($\Re$-solvability) A constraint c^v, c^u is $\Re$-solvable iff there exists an $\Re$-valuation θ for c^v such that $\Re \models (c^v, c^u)\theta$, that is, $\Re \models c^v\theta$ and $\Re \models c^u\theta$. θ is called the $\Re$-solution of c^v, c^u.*

Note that the consistency among update constraints is checked at each derivation step by means of the $\Re$-solvability, that is $\Re \models (c^v, c^u)\theta$. Thus complementary updates are not solvable due to the fact that they must belong and must not belong at the same time to the extensional database.

3.2 The first step semantics

We now define the proof-theoretic semantics.

Definition 3.6 *Let $DB = IDB \cup EDB$ be a database. Then we define*

$$\mathcal{O}(DB) = \{p(\tilde{X}) \leftarrow c^v, c^u \in B \mid true, p(\tilde{X}) \overset{\Re}{\longmapsto}{}^* c^v, c^u\}$$

where B denotes a set of constrained atoms [12].

We recall that *tru4* denotes the empty constraints. Let us now show the soundness and completeness results for $\mathcal{O}(DB)$.

Theorem 3.1 *Let DB be a database and $Q = c^v, c^u, G_1, \ldots, G_t$ any query. Then $Q \overset{\Re}{\longmapsto}{}^* c'^v, c'^u$ iff there exists t constrained atoms $H_j \leftarrow c_j^v, c_j^u \in \mathcal{O}(DB)$, $j = 1, \ldots, t$ which share no variables with DB and with each other, such that $c^v \cup c_1^v \cup \ldots \cup c_t^v \cup \{G_1 = H_1\} \cup \ldots \cup \{G_t = H_t\}$ and c'^v have the same solutions for the variables in DB and $c^u \cup c_1^u \cup \ldots \cup c_t^u$ and c'^u are equivalent.*

Example 3.1 *Let us consider the following database. We denote the syntactic domain in "typewriter" style and the semantic domain in "roman" style.*

$$
\begin{array}{ll}
DB = \{ & \\
\quad \texttt{p(X)} \leftarrow \texttt{-q(X),q(X)} & \mathcal{O}(DB) = \{ \quad p(X) \leftarrow X = a, -q(X), \\
\quad \texttt{k(X)} \leftarrow \texttt{+t(X),q(X)} & \qquad\qquad\quad k(X) \leftarrow X = a, +t(X), \\
\quad \texttt{s(X)} \leftarrow \texttt{q(X)} & \qquad\qquad\quad s(X) \leftarrow X = a, \\
\quad \texttt{v(X)} \leftarrow \texttt{-t(X)} & \qquad\qquad\quad v(X) \leftarrow -t(X), \\
\quad \texttt{q(X)} \leftarrow \texttt{X = a} & \qquad\qquad\quad q(X) \leftarrow X = a \quad \}
\end{array}
$$

The query $?k(X), p(X)$ *evaluated in* DB *computes the answer* $X = a$ *and the new database state* $\{t(a)\}$. *The query* $?v(X)$ *evaluated in the new database state computes the answer* $X = a$ *and the empty database state.*

◇

3.3   The second step semantics

The first step semantics does not perform the updates computing the new state and does not consider the set oriented and transactional behaviour of a query. For example, if a query has two or more successful derivations then we need to check the solvability of all the updates collected in all the successful derivations. For example, the query $?p(X)$ evaluated in the following database

$$DB = \{ \quad \begin{aligned} &p(X) \leftarrow -q(X), t(X) \\ &p(X) \leftarrow +q(X), q(X) \\ &s(X) \leftarrow q(X) \\ &q(X) \leftarrow X = a \\ &t(X) \leftarrow X = a \quad \} \end{aligned}$$

must fail due to the complementary updates collected by the query in two different successful derivations. Such behaviour is not captured by the semantics introduced so far. Moreover, the transactional behaviour of a query should be modelled. Before introducing the semantics with respect to a query, note that in order to model the set of answers, we can consider $\mathcal{O}(Q, DB)$ as the set of c_j^v, c_j^u such that $Q \overset{\Re}{\longmapsto}{}^* c_j^v, c_j^u$. In the following we define the semantics of a query Q with respect to the intensional database IDB evaluated in the state EDB_i. The *observable behaviour* of such semantics is: the set of answers, the (possibly) new state and the result of the query which behaves as a transaction and therefore can be either Abort or Commit. Therefore we define a function S, which maps the query, the intensional database and the current state to the set of answers, the new state and the result of the transaction.

Definition 3.7 *Let* $DB_i = IDB \cup EDB_i$ *be the database,* $Q = c^v, c^u, G_1, ..., G_t$ *be a query, Then the semantics is defined by means of* $S : GOALS \times IDBS \times 2^{\mathcal{HB}_{EDB}} \rightarrow 2^{C^*} \times 2^{\mathcal{HB}_{EDB}} \times Result$. $Q \in QUERIES$, $IDB \in IDBS$, $EDB_i \in 2^{\mathcal{HB}_{EDB}}$, $\{c_1^v, ..., c_k^v\} \in 2^{C^*}$ *and* $Result = \{Abort, Commit\}$. S *is defined as follow*

$$S[Q, IDB]_{EDB_i} = \begin{cases} \langle Answers, EDB_{i+1}, Commit \rangle & \text{if } OK \\ \\ \langle \emptyset, EDB_i, Abort \rangle & \text{otherwise} \end{cases}$$

where $Answers = \{c_j^v \mid c_j^v, c_j^u \in \mathcal{O}(Q, DB_i)\}$, EDB_{i+1} *is computed by means of all the updates* $\bar{c}^u$ *with respect to the current database state, and the condition* OK *expresses the fact that the set* $\bar{c}^u = \bigcup_j c_j^u \hat{c}_j^v$ *is consistent, that is, there are not complementary ground updates. By* $c_j^u \hat{c}_j^v$ *we denote the ground updates obtained by substituting the variables in* c_j^u *with the ground terms associated with the variables in* c_j^v.

Note that the definition above provides the set of all possible answers to the query Q and considers all possible updates in order to compute the new database state. This is effectively done only if the set of updates is consistent.

Example 3.2 *Let us consider* $DB_1 = IDB \cup EDB_1$, $EDB_1 = \{q(b), t(a)\}$ *and*

$$IDB = \{ \quad p(X) \leftarrow -q(X), q(X)$$
$$r(X) \leftarrow +t(X), p(X)$$
$$k(X) \leftarrow -t(X)$$
$$s(X) \leftarrow t(X) \quad \}$$

The semantics of $Q_1 = ?r(X)$ *with respect to of* DB_1 *is*

$$S[Q_1, IDB]_{EDB_1} = \langle \{X = b\}, EDB_2, Commit \rangle$$

where $EDB_2 = \{t(a), t(b) \}$. *The semantics of* $Q_2 = ?s(X)$ *with respect to* DB_2 *is*

$$S[Q_2, IDB]_{EDB_2} = \langle \{\{X = a\}; \{X = b\}\}, EDB_2, Commit \rangle$$

The semantics of $Q_3 = ?X = a, p(X)$ *with respect to* DB_2 *is*

$$S[Q_3, IDB]_{EDB_2} = \langle \emptyset, EDB_2, Abort \rangle$$

◇

References

[1] S. Abiteboul, E. Simon, and V. Vianu. Non-Deterministic Languages to Express Deterministic Transformations. In *Proc. of the ACM Symposium on Principles of Database Systems*, pages 218–229. ACM, New York, USA, 1990.

[2] S. Abiteboul and V. Vianu. A Transaction Language Complete for Database Update and Specification. In *Proc. of the ACM Symposium on Principles of Database Systems*, pages 260–268. ACM, New York, USA, 1987.

[3] S. Abiteboul and V. Vianu. Procedural and Declarative Database Update Languages. In *Proc. of the ACM Symposium on Principles of Database Systems*, pages 240–251. ACM, New York, USA, 1988.

[4] P. Atzeni, C. Batini, and V. De Antonellis. *Relational Database Theory: a Comprehensive Introduction*. Benjamin Cummings, 1992. To appear.

[5] F. Bancilhon and R. Ramakrishnan. Performance Evaluation of Data Intensive Logic Programs. In J. Minker, editor, *Foundation of Deductive Databases and Logic Programming*, pages 439–519. Morgan-Kaufmann, 1987.

[6] A. J. Bonner. Hypothetical Datalog: Negation and Linear Recursion. In *Proc. of the ACM Symposium on Principles of Database Systems*, pages 286–300. ACM, New York, USA, 1989.

[7] M. L. Brodie. On Modelling Behavioural Semantics of Databases. In C. Zaniolo and C. Delobel, editors, *Proc. Seventh Int'l Conf. on Very Large Data Bases*, pages 32–42, 1981.

[8] S. Ceri, G. Gottlob, and L. Tanca. What You Always Wanted to Know About Datalog - And Never Dared to Ask. *IEEE Tran. on Knowledge and Data Eng.*, 1(1):146– 164, March 1989.

[9] A. Colmerauer. Opening the Prolog-III universe. BYTE magazine, vol. 12, n. 9, 1987.

[10] M. A. Derr, G. Phipps, and K. A. Ross. Glue-Nail: A Deductive Database System. In *Proc. Int'l Conf. ACM on Management of Data*, pages 308–317, 1991.

[11] M. Dincbas et al. The Constraint Logic Programming Language CHIP. In *Proc. Int'l Conf. on Fifth Generation Computer Systems*. Institute for New Generation Computer Technology, 1988.

[12] M. Gabbrielli and G. Levi. Modeling Answer Constraints in Contraint Logic Programs. In K. Furukawa, editor, *Proc. Eighth Int'l Conf. on Logic Programming*, pages 238–252. The MIT Press, Cambridge, Mass., 1991.

[13] H. Gallaire, J. Minker, and J. M. Nicolas. Logic and database: A deductive approach. *ACM Computing Surveys*, 16(2):153–185, June 1984.

[14] D. Harel. *First-Order Dynamic Logic*, volume 68 of *Lecture Notes in Computer Science*. Springer-Verlag, Berlin, 1979.

[15] P. Van Hentenrych. *Constraint Satisfaction in Logic Programming*. The MIT Press, Cambridge, Mass., 1989.

[16] J. Jaffar and J.-L. Lassez. Constraint Logic Programming. In *Proc. Fourteenth Annual ACM Symp. on Principles of Programming Languages*, pages 111–119. ACM, New York, USA, 1987.

[17] J. Jaffar and J.-L. Lassez. Constraint Logic Programming. Technical report, Department of Computer Science, Monash University, June 1986.

[18] J. Lassez and S. Michaylov. Methodology and Implementation of a CLP system. In J.-L. Lassez, editor, *Proc. Fourth Int'l Conf. on Logic Programming*, pages 196–218. The MIT Press, Cambridge, Mass., 1987.

[19] W. Leler. *Constraint Programming Languages: Their Specification and Generation*. Addison-Wesley, 1988.

[20] J.W. Lloyd. *Foundations of logic programming*. Springer-Verlag, Berlin, 1987. Second edition.

[21] C. Maindreville and E. Simon. Modelling Non Deterministic Queries and Updates In Deductive Databases. In F. Bancilhon and D. J. DeWitt, editors, *Proc. Fourteenth Int'l Conf. on Very Large Data Bases*, pages 395–406, 1988.

[22] S. Manchanda and D. S. Warren. A Logic-based Language for Database Updates. In J. Minker, editor, *Foundation of Deductive Databases and Logic Programming*, pages 363–394. Morgan-Kaufmann, 1987.

[23] S. Naqvi and R. Krishnamurthy. Database Updates in Logic Programming. In *Proc. of the ACM Symposium on Principles of Database Systems*, pages 251–262. ACM, New York, USA, 1988.

[24] S. Naqvi and S. Tsur. *A Logic Language for Data and Knowledge Bases.* Computer Science Press, 1989.

[25] J. Widom. A Denotational Semantics for the Starburst Production Rule Language. Technical Report RJ 8581, IBM, 1992.

[26] M. Zloof. Query-by-example: a Data Base Language. *IBM Systems Journal*, 16(4):324–343, 1977.

A Formalisation of Logic Databases and Integrity Constraints

Nader Azarmi

Intelligent Systems Research Section
BT Labs
Martlesham Heath
Ipswich - U.K. IP5 7RE

ABSTRACT

This paper presents a meta-level/object-level framework (MOF) for the formalisation of logic databases (LDBs). The MOF is based on first order logic and thus benefits and employs many of the properties and results of that logic, eg. rich representation language, well-defined semantics, resolution theorem proving, etc. The meta theory in the MOF provides a sound formalisation environment in which we can tackle many as yet open LDB problems such as capturing the "true intended meaning" of the notion of integrity constraints where they contain subtle presumptions in their natural language statements, formalisation and enforcement of "dynamic" integrity constraints within the same framework as their static counter-parts, declarative representation of concepts of database update operations, query evaluation and optimisation, and control of the reasoning in the underlying LDB theory (i.e. the object theory of the MOF). Finally, from implementation view point, one can implement useful classes of LDBs formalised in the MOF within a suitable logic programming environment such as METAPROLOG or GODEL.

1. Introduction

Recently, many database researchers have been employing formal logic as the underlying formalism for many theoretical studies of databases. There are many reasons for the choice of formal logic, namely:

i) Logic provides an expressive environment for capturing the semantics of a domain.

ii) Logic has a well-defined theory which provides much of the theoretical foundations required for the database systems.

iii) Logic allows declarative expression of databases, and its application to the studies of database concepts such as query answering and maintenance of integrity constraints, has already provided better understanding of these concepts and is resulting in satisfactory solutions to many database problems.

The significant result of these formal studies has been the emergence of a new generation of databases which have deductive capability. These databases are known as logic databases (LDB). They have a sound theoretical foundation and their advantage over traditional databases is their representational and operational uniformity. This is because in LDBs deductive rules, facts, queries and constraints are all represented in the same first order logic language, and that LDB's query evaluation and constraints satisfaction are achieved through the first order theorem proving.

LDB : a Database view

One of the main advantages of the LDBs over traditional databases is their ability to include a set of deductive rules. This has the immediate advantage of not having to store a large amount of factual knowledge since they can be derived on demand through the use of deductive rules. Moreover, the relational databases are a special kind of LDBs. Therefore, many of the results of the research and development in relational databases are also applicable to LDBs.

Current LDBs, however, suffer from major shortcomings. Among these we have identified :

Incomplete formalisation :

In current formal studies of databases, LDBs are viewed as a restricted first order "theory". The rules and facts in the database form the axioms in the "theory". Queries and integrities are also represented as first order formulas. Moreover, the query evaluation and integrity satisfaction are done by theorem proving at the "theory" level. For example, an answer to a query formula is "YES" if only if it is proved to be a theorem of the "theory".

A Database system provides other functionalities than "query answering" and "integrity satisfaction", namely the update operations : "Addition" and "Deletion". In current formalisation of the LDBs, there is a lack of formalisation of the update operations. Furthermore, conceptualisation of the notions of query answering and integrity satisfaction in terms of the proof theory of LDB formalisations, although it is correct in concept, is moving away from the requirement of declarative representation of the database and its operations. We can envisage situations in which answering a query involves more knowledge processing before and after the theory level theorem proving. We therefore, call the present formalisations of the LDBs *incomplete*, in the sense that they only declaratively represent the contents of a database and make no attempt to do the same for the database operations and properties.

Improper view of integrity constraints (IC) :

In current LDB studies, ICs are viewed as first order formulas of the language of database theory. ICs are the particular characteristics of the database theory and they have the role of maintaining the consistency of that theory. Furthermore, in these studies ICs satisfaction is done through some form of theorem proving in the database theory.

Unfortunately, there are two major problems with the traditional perspective of ICs. Firstly, the representation of the ICs as sentences of the language of database theory does not capture the true intended meaning of the ICs (see section 2.3). ICs are statements about and properties of the database theory and its content knowledge (i.e., database formulas), and as such they cannot always be represented correctly as the formulas of the first order language of database theory [1][2]. Secondly, definitions of IC satisfaction in current LDB formalisations are dependent on some of the restrictions imposed on the theory, such as 'Closed World Assumption' restriction. For a LDB to be a useful tool for general application, we do not wish to always impose such restrictions. Hence, the present ICs satisfaction definitions are not general enough.

A further shortcoming with current LDBs is the lack of representation and enforcement of **Dynamic ICs**. Briefly, dynamic ICs are those ICs which represent dynamic properties of the database and control proper transition of the database as a result of an update from one state to the next. Current LDB formalisations consider the current state of a database alone and have no representational or reasoning capabilities to deal with dynamic ICs.

The above discussion demonstrates the need for a much more powerful and flexible logical formalisation of the LDBs. In the rest of this paper we present a formal framework for the formalisation of LDBs. This framework is developed by embedding the epistemic logic concepts into a first order logic via meta-level extension of the latter logic [3]. We shall briefly describe the framework and specify its main characteristics. Furthermore, we present our formalisation of a LDB in this framework and in particular present the database integrity constraints representation and enforcement.

2. A Meta-level/Object-level Framework for LDB Formalisation

In this paper we present a meta-level/object-level framework (MOF) for the formalisation of the LDBs. Broadly speaking, this framework is composed of two non-amalgamated first order theories. The object-level theory represents the LDB theory. The meta-level theory contains as its terms all the objects (i.e.: terms, formulas, etc.) of the object-level theory together with correct representations of relations among those objects namely, "provability", "resolution" (if the object-level database theory has a resolution theorem prover), etc. We have developed a powerful naming mechanism/relation for the correct representation of the object-level language at the meta-level, see [4]. This naming relation (ie., a "ground representation" naming relation) allows us to represent object-level theories as meta-level terms, hence meta formulas can be written which use those terms.

The most important task in our framework is that of representing the provability relation among theorems (i.e. formulas) of the object-level theory and the theory itself. We introduce a meta language binary predicate, namely "provable", to correctly capture the provability relation of the object-level theory. Thus, for all object-level theories "t" and well-formed formulas "s" of the object-level language :

$$t \mid_{obj} s \quad \text{iff} \quad Pr \mid_{meta} \text{provable}(s',t')$$

(From a given set of assumptions "Pr" in the meta theory. Note that "t'" and "s' " are the meta-level representation of "t" and "s" respectively. Note also that "$\mid_{obj}$" and "$\mid_{meta}$" represent derivability in the object-level and meta-level theories respectively).

Based on the ability to represent object-level theories as meta terms and the representation of the object-level provability relation, we are able to formalise, at meta-level, the main database operations, namely "addition", "deletion", "query answering" and "integrity satisfaction". We can also demonstrate techniques which will have important consequences for extension of the knowledge of the object-level LDB at meta-level. Our framework provides some facilities for dealing with modal queries, and more importantly formalisation of query optimisation techniques [4].

The MOF formalisation of LDBs allows the true intended meaning of ICs to be captured and represented. In our view ICs represent the properties of the object-level theory and provide knowledge about the contents of that theory. Hence, they must be viewed as **meta-theoretic** in nature and should be represented as formulas of the meta-level theory. Furthermore, we are able to represent **dynamic constraints** of the database in our formalisation. This is due to the representation of object-level theories as meta terms. Moreover, the uniform representation of all types of ICs has paved the way for a uniform ICs satisfaction definition, which is one of the important advantages of our formalisation over traditional LDB formalisations.

2.1. The Framework

Broadly speaking, the MOF is a non-amalgamated meta-level/object-level framework for the formalisation of a LDB. To create the framework we have combined the first order languages of the object-level and the meta-level (assuming there are tools in these languages to handle recursion). The combination of the two languages is known to provide more expressive power and a greater problem solving capability [5], and all of these can be achieved while remaining within the boundary of the formal semantics of the first order logic [6].

The basic idea behind the creation of such a framework is to define, in the meta-level language, the *Provability* relation of the object-level language. Therefore, the proof procedure of the object-level language is simulated entirely within the meta-level language.

The object-level is the LDB theory, i.e. a (restricted) first order language, an inference apparatus and a set of axioms. The choice of the object-level language is generally application dependent. We choose as the language underlying our object-level theory a function-free, fixed domain first-order logic language with equality and ability to handle recursion. An additional constraint which we impose on object language is the domain closure (DC) assumption. This assumption leads to the decidability of the object-level theory under certain conditions [4]. A general refutation resolution-based theorem-prover (e.g. SL resolution [5]) will be a sufficient inference apparatus for a clausal form of a theory based on the above object-level language.

A meta-level theory is usually a theory in which a particular logical theory is discussed and studied. Ideally, the language of meta-level logic should be the same as the language of object-level logic. The advantage to be gained from this approach is that the tools which we have for dealing with object-level logic can also be used for meta-level logic.

Primarily, a meta theory is concerned with manipulating the linguistic objects of the object-level theory. These are : terms, well-formed formulas (WFFs), theories of object-level language, substitutions and proofs. This requires that meta-level language must have some sort of data structures with which it represents these linguistic objects of object-level language. Mapping of the objects of object-level language to the data structures of meta language is done by the *Naming Relation* (see [4] and Appendix 1). Once naming relation is defined, we can correctly represent important relations among the object-level linguistic objects via meta-level predicates, i.e. provability, resolution, etc. The meta theory also includes the integrity constraints and other definitions which are needed for correct representation of the database query answering and other database operations.

As it is apparent, our meta-theory is based on a first order language (with equality and ability to handle recursion). We have not imposed any restrictions on the language of meta-level theory and expect that in general it will be in non-clausal form. We can however represent the meta-level theory in clausal form and use a general purpose refutation resolution theorem prover (such as SL resolution) for meta-level reasoning.

Feasible implementation of the framework requires taking advantage of certain principles, known as *Reflection Principles*, which delegate much of the inefficient problem solving task of the meta-level to object-level.

2.1.1. Meta-level representation of Object-level Theory

The meta-level theory is a collection of assertions which collectively describe the object-level language, a collection of formulas which define the meta-predicates which correctly represent the corresponding relations on the linguistic objects of the object-level language (e.g. resolution and provability), a collection of formulas which represent the specific knowledge/data stored in the object theory, and a collection of formulas which represent definitions of the properties and database operations of the object-level theories (for example, definitions of integrity constraints or update operations of a LDB).

The full definition of object language at meta-level is given in [4]. We shall now give the meta definition of a *clausal* object theory as follows (based on the definitions of [4]) :

The predicate symbol *theory*, which is true if its argument is the representation of a (possibly empty) theory of the object-level language :

$\forall x$ (theory(x) <->
$\qquad$ {Ey (x=sentence(y))} V
$\qquad$ {Ey Ez (x=and(y,z) & ~(y=Empty V z=Empty) &
$\qquad\qquad$ theory(y) & theory(z))})

The predicate symbol *sentence*, which is true when its argument is the representation of a clausal WFF of the object-level language.
In this paper, we are assuming that our object-level is in a clausal form.
Hence : a "sentence" is equivalent to a "clause" :

$\forall x$ (sentence(x) <->
$\qquad$ {x=Empty} V {literal(x)} V
$\qquad$ {Ey Ez (x=or(y,z) & ~(y=Empty V Z=Empty) &
$\qquad\qquad$ & sentence(y) & sentence(z))})

(Note that we have made the assumption that all free variables in the WFFs of object-level language/theory are universally quantified.)

The described framework allows for each object-level theory to be uniquely represented at the meta-level (i.e., as a meta term). In the domain of databases we usually construct a new theory (or a new database state) by updating the current one. Such progressive construction of theories requires a notion of partial ordering among the meta-level representations of the object-level theories, if we are to represent each one of those theories at meta-level. Moreover, such ordering enables us to (explicitly) identify the successive and preceding theories in relation to any one given theory. This ability is central to correct declarative meta-level representation of the properties and operational behaviour of the object-level LDBs.

We have chosen to attach a conceptual time (or order) number (i.e., a natural number) to each object-level LDB theory. This numbering starts with the initial LDB theory (or LDB state) being stamped as theory/state "1" and subsequent constructed theories/states being numbered "2", "3", ..., etc.

Hence, we extend the definition of the meta predicate 'theory' to include this notion of time stamping :

The meta predicate *time-theory*, which is true when its argument is the representation of time stamped object-level theory :

$$\forall t \ (\text{time-theory}(t) <->$$
$$\text{En Eth} \ (t=[n|th] \& \ \text{time-nb}(n) \ \& \ \text{theory}(th)) \ )$$

Where the meta predicate *time-nb* is defined as follows :

$$\forall n \ (\text{time-nb}(n) <->$$
$$(n=1) \ V \ \text{Ey} \ (n>1 \ \& \ \text{time-nb}(y) \ \& \ n=y+1)) \ )$$

Note that in the rest of this paper we assume that an object-level theory, say "t", is represented by a meta term (ie, a list) "[n|th]", and that we can access "n" via meta-level function call "th-nb(t)" and "th" via meta-level function call "obj-th(t)".

The notion of current state of the database is of importance if we are to achieve the formalisation of database update operations, see section 2.2.2.:

The meta predicate *current-theory*, which is true when its argument is the representation of latest/current object-level theory :

$$\forall t \ (\text{current-theory}(t) <->$$
$$\text{time-theory} \ (t) \ \&$$
$$\sim \text{Et'} \ (\text{time-theory}(t') \ \& \ \text{th-nb}(t') > \text{th-nb}(t)) \ )$$

So far our meta-level language has a full description of the language and objects (in the general sense) of the object-level theory. But in order to write useful meta-level formulas about the properties and operational behaviour of our object-level LDB theories, we need to have available meta-level predicates to represent important proof theoretic relations among object-level objects

For the purpose of this paper we are basically interested in representing object-level relations such as *Resolution, and Provability* on the domain of the objects of object-level language. In the following sections we shall present meta representations of these relations.

2.1.2. Resolution Relation

In the majority of cases object-level language is a clausal First Order language with the resolution inference rule as its derivation rule. We can use a three place meta predicate, say "resolve", to represent the resolution relation of the object-level language

resolve(p,q,r) ; where the sentence "r" is the resolvent
of the first two sentences "p" and "q".

As mentioned earlier, we are assuming that the object-level theory is in clausal form, hence each formula of the theory is in clausal form too. Furthermore, meta-level representation of the object-level formulas and theories are in list forms. Note also that a "sentence" is equivalent to a "clause".

Generally, the resolution principle states that, " given two sentences, if $\underline{x}$ is a positive literal of the first sentence and $\underline{\text{not}(y)}$ is a literal of the second sentence ("y" is a positive literal) and there is a most general unifier for "x" and "y", then the resolvent of the two sentences is reached by removing the complementary literals (i.e. "x" and "not(y)"), combining the remaining literals of the two sentences and applying the unifier to this newly formed sentence".

$$\forall x \forall y \forall a \forall b \forall s \forall c \; (\; resolve(a,b,c) <->$$
$$sentence(a) \; \& \; sentence(b) \; \& \; atom(x) \; \& \; atom(y) \; \& $$
$$is\text{-}part\text{-}of(x,a) \; \& \; is\text{-}part\text{-}of(not(y),b) \; \& $$
$$most\text{-}gen\text{-}unifier(x,y,s) \; \& $$
$$c = substitut(combin(remov(x,a), \; remov(not(y),b)) \; ,s) \;)$$

Note that in the above definition, meta functions "remov", "is-part-of", "combin", "most-gen-unifier", "substitut" and "resolve" have been used which are not defined in this paper, see [4].

2.1.3. Provability Relation

The most important task in our framework is that of correctly representing the provability relation between theorems (i.e. derivable formulas) of the object-level theory and the theory itself. We introduce a meta-level language binary predicate, namely "provable", and state that this meta predicate will correctly represents the provability relation of the object language if and only if for all set of formulas "t" (i.e. the object-level theory) and a single formula "s" of the object language :

$$t \; |\text{-}_{obj} \; s \quad iff \quad MT \; |\text{-}_{meta} \; provable(s',t')$$

(From a given set of assumptions in the meta theory "MT" [5].
Note that "t' " and "s' " are the meta-level representation
of "t" and "s" respectively.)

It can be shown that the meta-level provability predicate would be axiomatised through the meta-level representation of the inference rule of the object-level theory. That is to say, given the object-level theory is in clausal form and resolution is the theory's inference rule then we can give the following meta-level definition of provability (based on general refutation resolution) :

$$\forall s' \; \forall t' \; (provable(s',t') <->$$
$$time\text{-}theory(t') \; \& \; \neg(obj\text{-}th(t')=Empty) \; \& $$
$$(\; (sentence(s') \; \& $$
$$(is\text{-}in\text{-}theory(s',obj\text{-}th(t')) \; V$$
$$Ea \; Eb \; (\; provable(a,[th\text{-}nb(t')| \; and(not(s'),obj\text{-}th(t'))]) \; \& $$
$$provable(b,[th\text{-}nb(t')| \; and(not(s'),obj\text{-}th(t'))]) \; \& $$
$$resolve(a,b,Empty) \;)$$
$$) \;)V$$
$$((formula(s') \; \& \; \neg(sentence(s')) \; \& $$
$$(Ex \; Ey \; ((s'=and(x,y) \; \& \; provable(x,t') \; \& \; provable(y,t'))$$
$$V \; (\neg(s'=and(x,y)) \; \& \; provable(clausal(s'),t'))$$
$$)))) \;) \quad)$$

The above resolution-based axiomatisation of the provability relation is very powerful and expressive. This is to say that the meta term "s'" can represent any arbitrary first order WFF "s" of the object-level language (to be precise, these WFFs are in prenex normal form). If "s'" happens to be in clausal form then we can apply the resolution component of the definition to check the provability of "s'" in the theory "t'". If "s'" is not in clausal form we first produce its equivalent clausal form, say "s", and then apply the resolution part of the provability relation. The meta function *clausal* will produce the clausal form of an arbitrary meta-level representation of a first order formula of the object-level language (see [4] for the definition of meta function "clausal").

The above definition of the resolution-based provability relation will enable us to write meta-level representation of arbitrary formula of the object-level language which is natural and essential for concepts such as integrity constraints representation and satisfaction and also for the meta-level extension of the content knowledge of the LDB.

The MOF described so far is capable of a complete formalisation of a LDB. For the purpose of this paper we shall only concentrate on the formalisation of basic database operations (ie., query evaluation and update operations) and integrity constraints and integrity satisfaction. For the formalisation of query optimisation and techniques for extension of object theory knowledge at meta level see [4].

2.2. Formalisation of Database Operations in the MOF

2.2.1. Query Operation :

For reasons of simplicity and without loss of generality we shall define a query operation for closed queries as follows:

Note that in the following definition, We are assuming our object-level theories to be *decidable*, see [4]. Note also that "YES", "NO", and "UNKNOWN" are meta-level constants.

$$\forall s \; \forall t \; \forall Ans \; (\; query(s,t,Ans) <->$$
$$formula(s) \; \& \; time\text{-}theory(t) \; \& \; answer(Ans) \; \&$$
$$\{ \; \{provable(s,t) \; \& \; Ans='YES'\} \; V$$
$$\{provable(not(s),t) \; \& \; Ans='NO'\} \; V$$
$$\{\sim provable(s,t) \; \& \; \sim provable(not(s),t)$$
$$\& \; Ans='UNKNOWN'\}$$
$$\} \quad)$$

Where :
$$\forall a \; (\; answer(a) <-> (a='YES') \; V \; (a='NO') \; V \; (a='UNKNOWN') \;)$$

2.2.2. Update Operations

The LDB will undergo changes by its "update operations" in time. One of the problems of the current LDB paradigms where the database is formalised as a first order theory (i.e. at object-level only), is that the update operations cannot be formalised in these LDBs. This is due to the fact that these operations in effect manipulate and modify the underlying theory of the LDB and consequently they cannot be represented declaratively within the first order theory of the LDB. Hence, there is a need for a meta theory to represent these operations.

Another problem with the update operations is that an updated (theory of) database must satisfy its integrity constraints (NB.: We are making the assumption that the old database theory satisfies the ICs before updating it). If these constraints are not satisfied we either have to abandon the update, or modify the updated database to satisfy the ICs. In this paper we have taken the first option.

We will basically look at two update operations, namely *addition* and *deletion* operations. We shall view the update operations as meta functions which take two arguments: meta terms "s" and "t" which are meta representations of an object formula and an object theory respectively. The result of each of these functions is a meta term "t1" which is the representation of the updated object theory.

Addition Operation

The following definition conceptualises the addition of a WFF to a database theory and construction of a new valid theory (i.e. with respect to satisfaction of ICs):

$$\forall s \forall t \forall t1 \ (\ db\text{-}addition(s,t)=t1 <->$$
$$formula(s) \ \& \ current\text{-}theory(t) \ \&$$
$$(\ (provable(s,t) \ \& \ t1=t \ ) \ V$$
$$(\sim provable(s,t) \ \&$$
$$Es' \ Ett \ (\ s'=clausal(s) \ \&$$
$$tt=[th\text{-}nb(t)+1l \ and(s',obj\text{-}th(t))) \ \&$$
$$(\ (\ integrity\text{-}satis(tt) \ \& \ t1=tt \ )$$
$$V \ (\sim integrity\text{-}satis(tt) \ \& \ t1=t \ )))) \ ) \ )$$

Deletion Operation

The following is the meta-level definition of the deletion of a object-level formula from a LDB theory :

$$\forall s \forall t \forall t' \ (\ db\text{-}deletion(s,t)=t' <->$$
$$current\text{-}theory(t) \ \& \ formula(s) \ \&$$
$$(\ (\sim provable(s,t) \ \& \ t'=t) \ V$$
$$(provable(s,t) \ \&$$
$$Et1 \ Ett \ (\ t1=db\text{-}del\text{-}formula(clausal(s),t) \ \&$$
$$tt=[th\text{-}nb(t1)+1l \ obj\text{-}th(t1)] \ \&$$
$$(\ (\ integrity\text{-}satis(tt) \ \& \ t'= tt \ )$$
$$V \ (\sim integrity\text{-}satis(tt) \ \& \ t'=t \ ) \ ) \ ) \ ) \ ) \ )$$

Note that we are assuming that the object-level formulas are in clausal form :

$$\forall s \forall t \forall t1 \ (\ db\text{-}del\text{-}formula(s,t)=t1 <->$$
$$current\text{-}theory(t) \ \&$$
$$(\ (\ sentence(s) \ \& \ t1=db\text{-}del\text{-}sent(s,t) \ ) \ V$$
$$(\ Ex \ Ey \ (\ s=and(x,y) \ \& \ formula(x) \ \& \ formula(y) \ \&$$
$$t1=db\text{-}del\text{-}for(x,db\text{-}del\text{-}formula(y,t)) \ ) \ ) \ ) \ )$$

The following is the meta-level definition of the deletion of an object-level sentence/clause from a LDB theory :

$$\forall s\ \forall t\ \forall t1\ (\ \text{db-del-sent}(s,t)=t1\ <->$$
$$\text{sentence}(s)\ \&$$
$$(\ (\ \sim\text{provable}(s,t)\ \&\ t1=t\ )\ V$$
$$(\ \text{provable}(s,t)\ \&$$
$$(\ (\ \text{is-in-theory}(s,\text{obj-th}(t))\ \&$$
$$t1=\text{db-del-sent}(s,\text{delete-all}(s,t))\ V$$
$$(\ \sim\text{is-in-theory}(s,\text{obj-th}(t))\ \&$$
$$\text{Ea1 Eb1}\ (\ \text{provable}(a1,t)\ \&$$
$$\text{provable}(b1,t)\ \&\ \text{resolve}(a1,b1,s)\ \&$$
$$t1=\text{db-del-sent}(s,\text{db-del-sent}(a1,t)\ 2))\ )))))$$

2.3. Integrity Constraints in the MOF

Integrity constraints (ICs) are statements about the database, the enforcement of which guarantees validity of all database states in the process of database evolution. Historically, there are two main types of integrity constraints. These are *Static Integrity Constraints* (their enforcement only depends on the current state of the database), and *Dynamic Integrity Constraints* (their enforcement involves more than one state of the database) [4].

The conventional view of LDBs and their ICs is comprised of two parts:

1) a LDB is a set of first order formulas (i.e. statements about the world),
2) ICs are also represented as a set of first order formula.

In this view constraint enforcement is usually done either through the *Theoremhood* method [7] or the *Consistency* method [8]. Such approaches have proved problematic for *general* LDBs (see **Note1) as ICs and their enforcement may not correctly represent their <u>true intented meanings</u>.

Let us illustrate some of these problems by way of an example. Consider the constraint "Every student in the university database must have a definite registration number". This constraint is usually represented as the following first order formula :

$$\text{"}\forall x\ (\text{student}(x)\ ->\ \text{Ey}\ (\text{st-reg-nb}(x,y)))\text{"} \ .$$

Consistency Method Problem :

Now suppose that the LDB contains only a single fact "student(jack)". According to the consistency method, the "LDB + IC" is a consistent theory. However, our intention is to detect a violation of integrity, as there is no knowledge about the registration number of 'jack'. Hence, the consistency method cannot always fully enforce ICs with respect to their intended meanings.

Theoremhood Method Problem :

On the other hand, consider an empty LDB. According to this method we cannot derive the above IC from the LDB theory, hence a violation of the integrity constraints will be reported. This is not acceptable. There is no knowledge about any

---

**Note1 : The term general LDB refers to the LDBs which are less restrictive than Stratified LDBs, Indefinite LDBs and Definite LDBs. For example, general LDBs are not under CW assumption.

student, hence no knowledge about the student's registration number is expected in the LDB.

As it can be seen, none of the two methods are applicable to a general LDB. We must however point out that both of the above methods work satisfactorily for LDBs which are *closed* by either being under the 'closed world (CW) assumption', or being 'completed' in the sense of [9].

The natural conclusion that has to be drawn from the above examples is a need for a more expressive language for IC representation, and a more powerful and general definition for the IC satisfaction. In the following sections we shall present a new approach for representation of integrity constraints. We demonstrate the advantages of this approach over the traditional approaches. We show that, in our meta-level/object-level framework (i.e. MOF), all types of ICs can be represented, and that they all can be enforced via a single and uniform IC satisfaction definition. We further argue that MOF's view of ICs is compatible with their true intended meanings (see **Note2).

2.3.1. Meta-level Integrity Constraints

The representational problem discussed in the previous section, indicates a need for a richer and more powerful language in which integrity constraints can be represented. For example, in the above mentioned constraint, the intention is to state that if we are to prove that "x" is a known student in the database then we must also be able to prove that registration number of "x" is known to the database. In MOF, a very natural way to represent this constraint is as follows :

$$\forall x \ \forall t \ (provable(student'(x),t) \rightarrow Ey \ (provable(st\text{-}reg\text{-}nb'(x,y),t))))$$

The above logical formula truly captures the intended meaning of our constraint. For example, for an empty database, as we can neither prove that "x" is a student nor that his registration number is known, no violation will be detected, which is in fact correct. Also if there was only knowledge in the database about "x" being a student and nothing about registration number of "x", then in this case "student'(x)" is provable in the theory "t" and because of the logical implication in the IC, we must be able to prove in "t" that the registration number of "x" is known and provable. However, this is not possible and the IC violation is detected.

As it was mentioned earlier, the root of the problems mentioned lie with the somewhat improper traditional view of the ICs adopted by the database researchers. That view of ICs has been shown to be useful only for very special cases of LDBs (for example the LDBs under CW assumption).

In this paper we adopt a different view of the ICs. In this view an IC is seen as a statement about the content of the LDB whereas the formulas in the LDB are about the world/UoD that the LDB is representing. The underlying principle behind this view of ICs is the fact that ICs are **meta-theoretic** in nature and should be represented and enforced at the meta-level [1][2][10].

**Note2 : To explain this issue further, we must note that a natural language sentence describing an integrity constraint usually contains many hidden and implied (sometimes commonsense or default) properties. These properties are not always possible to capture in the conventional approaches to integrity constraint representations. In contrast, as it is discussed in the next section, MOF provides machinery to articulate such complex natural language implications and thus capture the true and full intention of the integrity constraints.

Such a meta-theoretic view of ICs allows us to use the full representational power of the meta-level language and in particular the 'provability' relation. This will enbale us to write logical (and more natural) formulas which represent the true intended meaning of the ICs. For example, in our approach we are able to write formulas such as :

"provable(s,t) V provable(p,t)"   and   "provable(or(s,p),t)";
"provable(not(s),t)"   and   "~provable(s,t)";
"provable(s,t) -> provable(p,t)"   and   "provable(if(p,s),t)".

We can differentiate between the above meta-level formulas and use them when they are appropriate for the IC representation task. this is not the case for many of the present IC work which is based on one level formalisation of the LDB. Various examples given in the next two sections will show the representational power of our IC view. One main advantage to be gained from the meta-theoretic view of the ICs, is the ability to represent and enforce **dynamic integrity constraints** [10].

In the next two sections, we shall present the representation of different classes of ICs in the MOF.

2.3.2. MOF Representation of Static Integrity Constraints

Static constraints are those ICs whose enforcement depends on only one state of the database (i.e. always the current state). Almost all of the previous works on IC representation and enforcement have considered these ICs and some promising results have been reported. However, practically all of those approaches have their foundations in Logic Programming paradigm and as a result they lack the ability to represent many kinds of static ICs.

To demonstrate the expressive power of the meta-theoretic ICs representations in MOF, let us present some examples of Static ICs :
(Note that in the following examples 't' represents the meta-level representation of an object- level theory.)

1) "The object-level theory must never be *inconsistent*"

∀t (st-cons1(t) <->
         ∀s (~provable(and(s,not(s)),t)))

(This is a very fundamental constraint which guarantees
the consistency of any object-level LDB.)

2) "Every employee has a salary" (Existential IC)

∀t (st-cons2(t) <->
         (∀e (provable(emp(e),t) ->
                  provable(forsome([MX1'],salary(e,MX1')),t))))

(This IC will be satisfied if the LDB contained disjunctive facts such as
"(salary(jim,20) V salary(jim,30))".)

3) "Every employee must have a definite salary"

∀t (st-cons3(t) <->
        (∀e (provable(emp(e),t) -> Es provable(salary(e,s),t))))

(This IC will be violated if the LDB contained disjunctive facts of the type given in example 2 above.)

4) "A rail-card can only be issued to a youth or a student"

∀t (st-cons4(t) <->
        (∀x (provable(rail-card-holder(x),t) ->
                  provable(or(youth(x),student(x)),t))))

5) "Every person must be assigned to a property of being either a man or a woman" (Domain IC)

∀t (st-cons5(t) <->
        (∀x (provable(person(x),t) ->
              {provable(man(x),t) V provable(woman(x),t)})))

6) "Every student must have only one student-number" (Functional Dependency IC)

∀t (st-cons10(t) <->
        (∀st∀y∀z ({provable(student-nb(st,y),t) &
                provable(student-nb(st,z),t)} ->
                  provable(equal(z,y),t))))

(The following LDB is valid as far as this IC is concerned :
"LDB = { student(jim,20) & student(joe,30) & student(may,20)}".)

Note that example 3 above, shows that a meta-theoretical view of integrity constraints allows us to represent *quantifying-in* integrity constraints which have no analogues in just the traditional views of ICs. Examples 4 and 5 demonstrate the power of the framework to represent different meanings that can be attached to the logical operator "or". Also the ability to use quantification at the object-level as well as at the meta-level is quite notable and useful. For more examples of ICs in MOF see [4]. In the next section we consider the dynamic constraints.

2.3.3. MOF Representation of Dynamic Integrity Constraints

Broadly speaking, dynamic constraints are those ICs the enforcement of which requires access to two or more states of the database. One major problem with many previous approaches to logic database formalisations, which do not use meta-level, is that they cannot explicitly refer to object-level database theories (i.e. database states) and discuss provability in them. Hence for those approaches, dynamic integrity constraints are not logically representable or enforceable.

In our MOF formalisation of a LDB, we have formally represented the database operations (or functions) which control the evolution of the LDB. For example, the meta-level function "db-addition" of section 2.2.2, after a successful addition, constructs a new state (or theory) from the old state and the newly added data. This new theory is then stamped by a distinct number which enables us to access that theory via that number directly. This theory, like any other object-level theory, is represented by a meta term.

This ability to access and represent the object-level theories as the meta terms, will enable us to write meta-level formulas, which contain and quantify over these theories, to correctly represent dynamic constraints.

In the following examples, MOF's representation of dynamic constraints are presented. We should bear in mind that the theory variable indicates the order of the theories. For example, "t2" is the theory/state constructed immediately after "t1", where "t1" is the theory immediately after "t". In addition, in examples 2 and 3 below the "¬provable" conditions are necessary as we are generally assuming that in each state of the database there is only one unique instance of a person's salary or his job status.

1) "A person can only get divorced if he was married before"

$\forall$t1 (dy-cons2(t1) <->
$\qquad$ ($\forall$p Et ({provable(divorced(p),t1) & provable(married(p),t) }
$\qquad\qquad\qquad$ -> (th-nb(t1) > th-nb(t)))))

(We assume that knowledge about person "p" marriage has been deleted before knowledge about his divorced has been asserted).

2) "A promotion to senior lectureship in a university department must be accompanied by an increase in the salary"

$\forall$t1 (dy-cons3(t1) <->
$\qquad$ ($\forall$p $\forall$s1 $\forall$s $\forall$t ({ provable(post(p,'s-lect'),t1) &
$\qquad\qquad$ ¬provable(post(p,'lect'),t1) & provable(post(p,'lect'),t) &
$\qquad\qquad$ (th-nb(t1) > th-nb(t)) & provable(salary(p,s1),t1) &
$\qquad\qquad\qquad$ provable(salary(p,s),t) & ¬provable(salary(p,s),t1)}
$\qquad\qquad\qquad\qquad$ -> (s1>s))))

(We assume that nobody holds more than one post at any one state).

3) "In a university department for a person to be promoted to a professorship, he must have gone through the promotion ladder, i.e. : ("lect" -> "s-lect" -> "prof")."

$\forall$t3 (dy-const4(t3) <->
$\qquad$ ($\forall$p $\forall$t2 $\forall$t1 (
$\qquad$ {provable(post(p,'prof'),t3) &
$\qquad$ ¬provable(post(p,'lect'),t3) & ¬provable(post(p,'s-lect'),t3) &
$\qquad$ provable((post(p,'s-lect'),t2) &
$\qquad$ ¬provable(post(p,'lect'),t2) & ¬provable(post(p,'prof'),t2) &
$\qquad$ provable(post(p,'lect'),t1) &
$\qquad$ ¬provable(post(p,'s-lect'),t1) & ¬provable(post(p,'prof'),t1) &
$\qquad$ (th-nb(t3) >= 3) & (the-nb(t2) >= 2) & (th-nb(t1) >= 1) }
$\qquad\qquad$ -> {((th-nb(t1) < th-nb(t2)) & (th-nb(t2) < th-nb(t3))}))))

The above examples show that dynamic constraints can involve multiple theories at multiple times. Also note that in the examples, "obj-th(t)" need not be a subset of "obj-th(t1)" so long as we have "th-nb(t) < th-nb(t1)". This is because the most recent theory (i.e. "t1") might be obtained after a deletion operation rather than an addition operation.

In example 3 above, we have made the assumption that everybody is initially employed as a lecturer and made use of three database states which follow one another but they are not necessarily <u>successive</u>. We can simplify this IC by writing two ICs which represent constraints on promotion from lectureship to senior lectureship, and senior lectureship to professorship. It is easy to show that these two ICs together are equivalent to the IC of example 3 above.

The simplification suggested for example 3 can be generalised for the representation of dynamic constraints with multiple states (or theories). In general, a dynamic constraint can, by <u>suitable transformation,</u> be reduced to an equivalent transition constraint or a set of transition ICs (see **Note3). The ability to represent both dynamic ICs and static ICs as the formulas of the same language, in the MOF, has an important advantage. That is, both types of ICs will be enforced using one integrity satisfaction method. Such a *uniform representation and enforcement of ICs must be seen as an important justification for our formalisation of LDBs in the MOF*. Next, we discuss the formalisation of object-level IC satisfaction in the MOF

2.3.4. Integrity Constraints Satisfaction : Reasoning about ICs and ICs satisfaction

Broadly speaking, we require some sort of proof theory to reason about the ICs. This is essential as we need to check if ICs are consistent with each other or if they entail one another (which means some ICs may be redundant).

In our framework ICs are formulas of the meta-level theory. As it was mentioned earlier, the meta-level theory is a first order theory and has a refutation resolution theorem prover as its inference procedure which is sound and complete for first order logic. Hence we can say that the meta-level theory and its resolution inference procedure provide an adequate proof theory for the ICs and for reasoning about them.

In the context of such a proof theory, we can define our formal notion of ICs satisfaction :

Definition
We say that a LDB theory "t" satisfies its ICs, where "MT" is the meta-level theory and IC_t is the set of all integrity constraints of "t" at meta-level "MT" :

$$MT \; |-_{meta} IC_t$$

(where IC_t is IC_1 & IC_2 & .. & IC_n).

We use the meta-level language for the representation of our LDB's integrity constraints, and define the integrity satisfaction operation for that LDB based on the above proof-theoretic definition.

Definition

**Note3 : Dynamic constraints which are only considering two consecutive states are known as *transition* integrity constraints.

The following is our proposed definition of the meta-level integrity satisfaction operation :

$$\forall t \ (\text{integrity-satis}(t) <->$$
$$(\text{time-theory}(t) \ \&$$
$$(\text{st-cons1}(t) \ \&...\& \ \text{st-consN}(t) \ \&$$
$$\text{dy-cons1}(t) \ \& ...\& \ \text{dy-consM}(t))))$$

(NB. "st-cons1" represents a static constraint and "dy-cons1" represents a dynamic constraint, see examples in previous sections.)

In the above definition we are assuming that there are "N" static ICs and "M" dynamic ICs in the meta-level theory for the object-level theory. The ICs are named "st-cons1" to "st-consN" and "dy-cons1" to "dy-consM".

2.3.5. Integrity Constraints : A Comparative Discussion

In this paper we presented our view that ICs are statements about the contents of the Object-level database theory, where the database contains knowledge about the world. Hence, ICs are meta-theoretic in nature. Moreover, We showed that based on such a view of ICs, we can uniformly represent and enforce all types of a LDB's integrity constraints, in the MOF. We further defined the ICs satisfaction operation for our LDB formalisation work.

Meta-level interpretation of ICs has also been suggested by Reiter in [2] and Jiang in [11]. However, Reiter and Jiang both define such an interpretation in an autoepistemic logic. Such a logic takes away the well-developed properties of first-order logic. In addition, because there is no multi-theory concept (only an implicit single theory is assumed), the autoepistemic logical approach thus cannot represent dynamic constraints.

An alternative to our non-amalgamated MOF and the above autoepistemic logical system is to employ a self-referential framework for meta-level representation and enforcement of ICs. Such a framework is normally based on a fully first order self-referential language [6]. However, precisely due to its self-referential nature, special care and proof notions need to be defined in order to avoid paradoxes. In contrast, the MOF does not suffer from any such problems.

3. Conclusions

In this paper we have argued for a formalisation of LDBs in a meta-level/object-level framework (MOF). The main technical objective of our work has been to develop the MOF in order to overcome the problems existing in the current formalisation frameworks of LDBs. We have adopted a non-amalgamated meta-level/object-level framework and have formalised integrity constraints and database operations purely at the meta-level and database (i.e., its content knowledge) purely at the object-level. Moreover, in order to demonstrate the applicability and constructive nature of our formalisation approach, we have undertaken a preliminary implementation of a LDB in PROLOG programming language. The results of the implementation verifies the validity of the concepts presented in the MOF formalisation of LDBs (see [4]).

We believe that the MOF has the following important properties :

*) It is **Logically Faithful** :
in the sense that it is developed within the boundary of formal semantics of first

order logic.

*) It is **Formalisationally Complete** :

in the sense that it allows for formalisation of both the knowledge contained within database and database operations which manipulate that knowledge.

*) It is **General for Integrity Constraints** :

in the sense that it uniformly represents both dynamic and static integrity constraints at meta-level and enforces those constraints through one definition.

*) It is **Representationally Rich** :

in the sense that in the MOF the content knowledge of the LDB can be extended at meta-level which possesses much more expressive power than the object-level.

Finally, the MOF provides a powerful specification language for the formalisation of LDBs. Hence, it can be seen as a tool in a formal database design methodology where design options can be made unambiguously with predictable consequences.

ACKNOWLEDGEMENTS

This work was partly supported by BT plc and CEC-RACE under AIM project (R1006). The author wishes to thank M. Azmoodeh and R. Smith (BT) for support and helpful comments, and acknowledges the permission granted by BT plc for the publication of this paper.

REFERENCES

[1] Azarmi N. & Azmoodeh M. 1989, *Logic Databases and Integrity Constraints*, In Proceedings of INFORMATICS 10 Conference, pp 295-302, University of York, U.K., March 1989, ASLIB Publications

[2] Reiter R. 1990, *On Asking What a Database Knows*, In "Proc. of Computational Logic Symposium", Brussels, pp 96-113, November 1990, Springer-Verlag, Berlin.

[3] Jiang Y.J. & Azarmi N. 1988, *Meta Logic Programming for Epistemic Notions*, In Proceedings of the 1st International Workshop on Meta-Programming in Logic Programming (META 88), Bristol University, Bristol, U.K., June 1988, MIT Press

[4] Azarmi N. 1991, *A Formalisation of Logic Databases and Their Integrity Constraints*, Thesis, University of Essex, U.K., Mar 1991.

[5] Kowalski R.A. 1979, *Logic for Problem Solving*, Elsevier, North Holland, New York

[6] Eshghi K. 1986, *Meta-language in Logic Programming*, Thesis, Imperial College, London

[7] Lloyd J.W. & Topor R.W. 1984, *A Basis for Deductive Database System II*, in Jnl. of Logic Programming, Vol. 3, pp 55-67

[8] Sadri F. & Kowalski R. 1988, *A Theorem Proving Approach to Database Integrity Checking*, In 'Foundations of Deductive Databases and Logic Programming', pp 313-362, Morgan & Kaufmann

[9] Clark K.L. 1978, *Negation as Failure*, In Logic and Databases, pp 293-322, Plenum Press, New York

[10] Azarmi N. & Jiang, Y.J. 1990, *Logic Databases and Integrity Constraints: a Meta-level/Object-level Framework*, In Proc. of 4th Int. Symposium on Knowledge Engineering, pp 85-90, Barcelona, Spain, May 1990

[11] Jiang Y.J. 1989, *An autoepistemic logical view of knowledge base*, In 9th Int. Conf. on Foundation of Software Tech. and Theoretical Comp. Sc., India, 1989.

APPENDIX 1: Naming Relation

It is assumed that : the meta-level language has finitely many constants, among which are C's, MX's, Empty, Nil, 0 . It also contains function symbols "successor" and "not" (of arity 1), "and", "or", "if", "iff", "forall", "forsome" (of arity 2). We are also allowing for existence of the standard mathematical functions and mathematical relations in their infix forms. The most widely used of these functions and relations in this paper are "+", "<", "=<", ">", ">=" and "=". The meta language has the capability to represent, construct and handles lists, ie. it contains a function of arity 2, called "cons (a list constructing function which is also denoted as [x|y]", where x is a term and y is a list of terms).

Let us now outline main concepts of the naming relation and :

1) Representation of every constant C, n-ary function symbol F and n-ary predicate symbol P of the object language, is a constant C' , a n-ary function symbol F' and a n-ary function symbol P' respectively, in the meta language.

2) Representation of any variable X_i of the object language, is a meta constant $MX_i{}'$.

3) Representation of an object term $F(t_1,...,t_n)$ is a meta term $F'(t_1{}',...,t_n{}')$, where $t_1{}',...,t_n{}'$ are meta-level representation of object-level terms $t_1,...,t_n$ respectively, and representation of an object atom $P(t_1,...,t_n)$ is a meta term $P'(t_1{}',...,t_n{}')$ in the meta-level language.

4) If the formulas F and S of object language are represented by F' and S', and the variables $X_1,...,X_n$ in the formulas are represented by $MX_1{}',...,MX_n{}'$ respectively, then ¬F, F & S, F V S, F <- S, F <-> S, $\forall X_1,...,\forall X_n(F)$ and $EX_1,...,EX_n(F)$ are represented by not(F'), and(F',S'), or(F',S'), if(F',S'), iff(F',S'), forall([$MX_1{}',...,MX_n{}'$],F'), and forsome([$MX_1{}',...,MX_n{}'$],F'), respectively in the meta language. Finally, assuming that object theory consists of conjunctions of formulas, its meta representation is a meta term and(F', and(S', and(...))). An empty object theory is represented by meta term Empty.

Integrity Enforcement

Automatic Rule Generation for Constraint Enforcement in Active Databases

Piero Fraternali, Stefano Paraboschi, Letizia Tanca

Dipartimento di Elettronica e Informazione, Politecnico di Milano

Milano, Italy

Abstract

In conventional database systems, consistency is preserved either by forbidding operations that violate integrity constraints or by rolling back transactions that produce inconsistent database states. A third way to integrity maintenance is that of post processing faulty transactions, by introducing system-generated compensating actions that lead to a database state which is consistent and as close as possible to that intended by the user. Active databases provide the appropriate technology to implement this paradigm.

We introduce a framework in which constraints are expressed in a logical language and automatically translated into a set of database rules. We stress automatic derivation not only of the triggering conditions of rules but also of the compensating actions, so that the user is presented with the complete set of actions available to repair constraint violations. This approach ensures that if the execution of the rules triggered by a faulty transaction eventually comes to an end, the final state reached is correct with respect to all the declared constraints. Then, we briefly discuss compile-time analysis of termination and present the features of the run-time system needed to cope with conflicts among rules enforcing different constraints or the same constraint in several ways.

1 Introduction

Consistency is the property of an item to be non-contradictory, according to some formal specification of its expected behavior. In the database field, consistency is expressed as a set of integrity constraints, which characterize those configurations of data in the database that are considered legal. So far, research in the field of integrity constraints has favored topics like the design of constraint languages that deal with complex constraints, e.g., based on arbitrary predicates over database states, and the investigation of techniques for the efficient detection of actual or possible violations.

We focus instead on the topic of constraint enforcement, pursuing the way undertaken in [7]. The problem we face has two distinct but related aspects: the translation of constraints into the set of compensating actions that enforce them; the subsequent management of the execution of multiple and possibly conflicting compensating actions. In this paper we focus on the former issue and adopt a logical style for constraints and a rule-based programming style for compensating actions. Thus, constraints are represented as formulas of Domain

Relational Calculus with a restricted pattern, like in [5, 17], and their semantics is such that a database state is consistent with respect to a constraint if and only if it satisfies the formula that expresses that constraint. Compensating actions are encoded as production rules. In the context of database systems, rules can be viewed as specifications of operations on data that are automatically performed whenever specified events or database configurations occur [13, 18]. In this paper, we allow database rules with triggering conditions based only on the state of the database and which perform a single data manipulation operation. As a framework for the proposed approach, we envision an Integrity Maintenance System, which is a complex system integrating the capabilities of a design environment and of a sophisticated run-time system [3]. The former component aids the user in declaring the constraints, deriving automatically the production rules needed to enforce them and analyzing the rule set to guarantee properties like termination and correctness of the computation. On the other hand, the run-time system supports the execution of the production rules derived from the constraints, by implementing conflict resolution strategies that rely both on compile and run-time information.

In the paper, after settling the context of the research in Section 2, we present in some detail the process of rule generation and sketch the work done in the areas of rule analysis and execution control:

- Section 3 and 4 contain preliminary material describing the syntax and semantics of the constraint and rule language.

- Section 5 focuses on the task of rule generation, setting the foundations for the automatic derivation of compensating rules from constraints. In particular, compensating actions are sought that do not require deletion or insertion of tuples, but exploit information in the database to replace appropriate fields of incorrect tuples. The treatment of built-in constraints is also introduced, as part of the rule derivation process.

- Section 6 introduces the architecture of an Integrity Maintenance System. The main issues concerning rule analysis, selection and run-time control are presented. The rationale is to enable integrity maintenance even in presence of multiple constraints and potentially conflicting rules.

Finally, in Section 7 we discuss the planned extensions of the work described.

Some of the topics mentioned in the paper are the main focus of other publications: [3, 9] introduce the general architecture of an Integrity Maintenance System and discuss in greater detail the problem of dealing with cyclic rule sets; [8] contains the formalization of the correctness and termination problem for cyclic rules as an optimization problem, and discusses its complexity and approximate solutions.

2 Related Work

Most results in the field of database integrity constraints are centered on the problem of efficient detection of constraint violations. The focus is either on determining in advance database updating operations that are likely to contravene constraints [7, 14, 17] or on ex-post assessment of a database state to discover violations [5]. The approaches mainly differ in the style adopted to convey constraints—logical [5, 12, 15, 17] or SQL-oriented [7]—and on the kind of constraint analysis performed—static or dynamic. Less has been done in the field of compensating actions. Our work is based on the approach contained in [7], which addresses the problem of translating constraints expressed in an SQL-like declarative language into the set of production rules that enforce them. The process of derivation therein illustrated is limited to yielding rule templates, i.e., rule skeletons whose condition part is supplied automatically and whose action side has to be added by the user. The automatically generated left-hand side includes a *transition predicate*, listing the data manipulations that trigger the rule, and an arbitrary predicate over the database state, which is checked at run-time prior to firing the rule. Rule-set analysis and optimization are also dealt with, to help the user verify system termination and correctness and enhance performance, by reducing the amount of information needed to evaluate a rule's precondition. We also benefit from research in the field of active databases, which addresses the problems of giving database production systems a precise semantics [19] and formally investigates properties like termination, correctness and determinism of the computation [1, 20]. Another related area is that of transaction design systems [14, 17], in which constraints are used to validate the design of database transactions and form the basis of explanation tools providing helpful feedback to transaction designers.

3 The Constraint Language

In this paper constraints are expressed as safe closed formulas of Domain Relational Calculus [16].

In the sequel, we use the vectorial notations $\vec{x}$, $\vec{c}$, to denote generic sets of variables or constant values. We also write $A(\vec{x})$, to indicate that the variables $\vec{x}$ are all the free variables of the (sub)formula A. Lowercase letters p, q, l, m, possibly indexed, will be used to denote generic database literals, i.e., literals whose predicate represents a database relation, while small capital letters stand for the corresponding database relations.

3.1 Syntax

Definition 1: a constraint, in *standard conjunctive form (s.c.f.)*, is a closed formula of Domain Relational Calculus having the following pattern:

$$\forall \vec{x} \, \exists \vec{w} \, \neg(p_1(\vec{x}) \wedge \ldots \wedge p_n(\vec{x}) \wedge \neg q_1(\vec{x}, \vec{w}) \wedge \ldots \wedge \neg q_m(\vec{x}, \vec{w}) \wedge G(\vec{x}))$$

Following [5], we also call this form *denial*[1].

Each p_i, q_j stands for a database literal, while $g(\vec{x})$ stands for an arbitrary quantifier free subformula (called *restriction* subformula) containing only non-database atoms of the form $(t_i \; comp \; t_j)$, where t_i and t_j are either constants or variables and *comp* is a usual comparison operator. Without loss of generality, we require that each p_i and q_j be positive. In addition, we require constraints to be safe formulas [5, 15, 16], so that their satisfaction can be determined considering only the values stored in the relations appearing in them. This also

---

[1]The s.c.f. is a semantically equivalent alias of the more common implicative form $\forall \vec{x} \, (p_1(\vec{x}) \wedge \ldots \wedge p_n(\vec{x}) \Rightarrow \exists \vec{w} \, q_1(\vec{x}, \vec{w}) \vee \ldots \vee q_m(\vec{x}, \vec{w}) \vee G(\vec{x}))$, used in [5, 17]

ensures that the formula expressing the constraint can be evaluated in finite time and yields a finite result, which is a necessary condition for an efficient implementation of run-time constraint checking mechanisms. Due to the pattern imposed on standard conjunctive form formulas, the safety requirements reduce to the fact that universally quantified variables appearing in a literal q_j or in the subformula g must also occur in a literal p_i.

We also assume that existentially quantified variables occurring in different literals are distinct.

3.2 Semantics

The semantics of the constraint language is straightforward: a constraint is satisfied in a database state S if and only if S is a Herbrand model for the formula that represents it [6, 15]. It is then possible to formally denote the set of violations of a constraint occurring in a given database state.

Definition 2: given a constraint $C \stackrel{\text{def}}{=} \forall \vec{x} \exists \vec{w} \, C$, the violation condition of C is $C^\star(\vec{x}) \stackrel{\text{def}}{=} \forall \vec{w} \, \neg C$.

The violation condition of a constraint is simply obtained by negating its s.c.f. and by freeing all the resulting existentially quantified variables. $C^\star$ can be interpreted as a query over the database, that returns all the substitutions for $\vec{x}$ that correspond to database tuples violating the constraint:

Definition 3: given a database state S and a constraint C, a violation of C in S is a substitution θ of $\vec{x}$ such that $C^\star\theta$ is satisfied in S. Given a database state S and a constraint C, we denote by $\Theta_{S,C}$ the set of all violations of C in S.

As to the efficient evaluation of $\Theta_{S,C}$, the conditions imposed for the safety of the s.c.f. of a constraint also assure that the corresponding violation condition is a safe formula. Therefore, in the case of an underlying relational DBMS, it is always possible to translate the violation condition into a relational query yielding the elements of $\Theta_{S,C}$, i.e., all the substitutions violating C in S [16].

Therefore, in our approach, the problem of assessing whether a database state is consistent with respect to a given set of constraint in s.c.f. is decidable and efficiently solvable, provided that one sticks to safe constraint formulas. In particular, all the optimization techniques developed for set-oriented query evaluation in relational databases can be used to efficiently implement the constraint checking mechanism.

3.3 Examples

To illustrate the language, we use examples drawn from a simplified version of a case study (the Power Distribution Design System (PDDS)), introduced in [7]. The case deals with a database describing Power Distribution Networks, where users are connected to plants (possibly via intermediate nodes) by wires contained within tubes.

Integrity constraints on the database include:

- topology constraints (e.g., plants have only outgoing connections)

- power constraints (e.g., the incoming power for each user is no less than the required power)

- constraints on wires and tubes (e.g., no tubeless wires)

- reliability constraints (e.g., each user is connected to at least two plants)

- general database integrity constraints (e.g., referential integrity on wire and tube types).

A simplified database schema contains the following relations:

```
PLANT(plant-id, location, power)
USER(user-id, location, power)
WIRE(wire-id, from, to, wire-type, voltage, power)
WIRE-TYPE(wire-type, max-volt, max-pow, wire-section)
TUBE(tube-id, from, to, tube-type)
TUBE-TYPE(tube-type, protection, tube-section)
```

From conceptual design we also know that tables WIRE-TYPE and TUBE-TYPE are read-only and that fields from, to are an additional key for table TUBE.

When writing formulas based on the running example, we use some short-hands to make them more readable: three dots in the variable list of a literal (as in WIRE(wire-id, ...) stand for all the variables appearing in the definition of the predicate that are not explicitly listed. Since variables in a predicate are always given distinct names, the order in which they are listed in a literal may be different from that used in the definition of the predicate, without ambiguity. The notation $\exists (\forall) * F$, means that the quantification ranges over all the free variables of F.

Constraint 1: high voltage wires connecting two locations must be contained within protected tubes

```
∀* ¬(WIRE(fr, to, voltage, ...) ∧
     TUBE(fr, to, tube-type, ...) ∧
     TUBE-TYPE(tube-type, protection, ...) ∧
     (voltage>5k) ∧ (protection ≠ "protected"))
```

The formula that expresses Constraint 1 is safe, since every universally quantified variable appears in at least one database literal. The restriction subformula is $g \stackrel{\text{def}}{=}$ (voltage>5k) ∧ (protection ≠ "protected").

The violation condition for Constraint 1 is the following:

```
WIRE(wire-id, fr, to, voltage, ...) ∧
TUBE(tube-id, fr, to, tube-type) ∧
TUBE-TYPE(tube-type, protection, ...) ∧
(voltage>5k) ∧ (protection ≠ "protected")
```

Its translation in Relational Algebra is: $\sigma_g(\text{WIRE} \bowtie_{\theta_1} (\text{TUBE} \bowtie_{\theta_2} \text{TUBE-TYPE}))$, where θ_1 is (WIRE.fr = TUBE.fr) ∧ (WIRE.to = TUBE.to), and θ_2 is (TUBE.tube-type = TUBE-TYPE.tube-type).

4 The Rule-Based Language

While constraints require a declarative style, compensating actions are procedural in nature, since they prescribe the data manipulation operations that are to be performed when a constraint is violated. It is widely recognized that active databases, which couple data storing facilities and rule-based programming, provide a good framework for describing compensating actions, as they allow the expression of self-contained code segments that can be executed independently in an event-driven fashion [20]. In this viewpoint, active databases with forward-chaining operational semantics are called Rule Triggering Systems (RTS).

Definition 4: a Rule Triggering System is a triple $< DB, \mathcal{R}, \prec_r >$, where DB is a relational database, $\mathcal{R}$ is a set of production rules and $\prec_r$ is a a total order on $\mathcal{R}$.

4.1 Syntax

Before introducing the syntax of the rule-based language, we need to specify the available database updating operations:

Definition 5: a database updating operation $\mathcal{O}$ is one of the following expressions:

- insert(P $(t_1, \ldots, t_n)$)
- delete(P $(t_1, \ldots, t_n)$)
- replace(P $(t_1, \ldots, t_n, t_k \leftarrow t'_k)$)

where P is a database relation and each term t_i, t'_i is either a variable, or a constant, or the special symbol ?.

Borrowing the notation for free variables in formulas, we write $\mathcal{O}(\vec{y})$ to stress that the (ordinary) variables $\vec{y}$ are all the variables that appear in the signature of an operation $\mathcal{O}$. We also say that an operation is *ground* if it contains only constant terms or the special symbol ?. When we need to emphasize this fact, we explicitly write $\mathcal{O}(\vec{c})$.

Definition 6: a *database rule* has the form $F(\vec{x}) \rightarrow \mathcal{O}(\vec{y})$, where $\vec{y}$ is a subset of $\vec{x}$.

In the sequel, we will also call $F(\vec{x})$ the Left Hand Side (LHS) or Condition Side of a rule and $\mathcal{O}(\vec{y})$ the Right Hand Side (RHS) or Action Side.

4.2 Semantics

The semantics of a RTS can be expressed either in a denotational style, as in [19] or operationally. We follow the latter option.

First, we specify the meaning of the elementary database operations.

Definition 7: given a *ground* database updating operation $\mathcal{O}(\vec{c})$, the meaning of $\mathcal{O}$ is a transformation from a database state S to a database state S', defined as follows:

- if $\mathcal{O}$ is insert($\mathrm{P}(\vec{c})$), then $S' = S \cup \mathrm{P}(\vec{c})^2$;

- if $\mathcal{O}$ is delete($\mathrm{P}(\vec{c})$), then $S' = S - \mathrm{P}(\vec{c})$;

- if $\mathcal{O}$ is replace($\mathrm{P}\ (t_1, \ldots, t_n,\ t_k \leftarrow t'_k)$), then $S' = S - \mathrm{P}(t_1, \ldots, t_n) \cup \mathrm{P}(t_1, \ldots, t_{k-1}, t'_k, t_{k+1}, \ldots, t_n)$

In the above definition, the presence of the special symbol ? in the signature of a ground operation is treated in a special way: the occurrence of ? in "op-name"($\mathrm{P}(\ldots, c_{i-1}, ?, c_{i+1}, \ldots)$)) is replaced by a constant value chosen randomly from the domain of the i-th field of relation P. An implementation of this mechanism could be a procedure that asks such a value to the user.

Definition 8: given a database state S and a database rule $R : F(\vec{x}) \to \mathcal{O}(\vec{y})$, an instantiation ϕ of R in S is a substitution of the variables $\vec{x}$ that makes F satisfied in S. The set of all instantiations of R in S is denoted by $\Phi_{S,R}$. $R\phi$ is called the instantiated rule.

A rule for which at least one instantiation exists in a given database state is said to be *triggered* in that state.

When a rule R is triggered, this defines bindings for the variables appearing in the RHS of R and yields the actual ground operation $\mathcal{O}(\vec{c})$ to be performed at rule execution.

Based on the above definitions, the operational semantics of a RTS is characterized in terms of *state transitions*[2, 9, 20]. Given an initial state S_0, denoted by a set of atomic ground formulas, called facts, all rules are evaluated in parallel to find those whose LHS is satisfied by S_0 (i.e., those that are triggered in S_0). Then, a state transition is performed, by applying the *deduction step*—defined below—to the set of triggered rules to generate new facts. These, "merged" with the pre-existing ones, yield a new state S_1. In this paper, we assume a very simple deduction step[3], which chooses from the set of triggered rules a single one, e.g., according to the total order $\prec_r$ of the RTS, and then executes one of its instantiations, selected randomly, and updates the database state according to the above illustrated operation semantics. This process continues until a state S_q is eventually reached in which the set of instantiated rules is empty.

This general mechanism is coupled with the database transaction mechanism as follows: state S_0 can be viewed as the database state resulting from the application of a user-supplied transaction, say T, to some original state S_{or}. Then, if the above described process applied to S_0 leads to a final state S_q, an all-inclusive transaction T' is generated bringing from S_{or} to S_q. In case of (presumed) non-termination or of an explicit command, a rollback can be issued to the original state S_{or}.

---

[2] $\mathrm{P}(\vec{c})$ denotes a tuple of relation P

[3] In [9] we report on a prototypical implementation of the run-time part of the Integrity Maintenance System on top of Starburst, a full-fledged active database.

5 Automatic generation of compensating actions from constraints

We now turn to the problem of deriving production rules from constraints, with the goal of generating a rule set which is sufficient to restore correctness and contains all the possible compensating actions that can be implemented through the available database updating operations. We also look for compensating actions that do not require the deletion or insertion of entire tuples, but repair a violation by replacing a tuple field that violates the constraint. Unfortunately, in the general case, this is achieved to the price of loosing the property that a compensating action restores correctness in any case, independently of the content of the database state in which the violation occurs.

First, the concept of database rule has to be related to that of compensating action.

Definition 9: a database rule R *uniformly compensates* a constraint C iff, for every database state S such that the violation set $\Theta_{S,C}$ of C is not empty, we have that $\Theta_{S,C} \supset \Theta_{S',C}$, where S' is the database state generated by the execution of R in S.

The property of *uniform compensation* says that a rule R uniformly compensates a constraints C if, whenever a violation of C occurs, R is triggered and each firing of R removes at least one violation of C.

Uniform compensation is a fundamental property for the correctness of a set of compensating actions: in [7] it is demonstrated that, if the rule set $\mathcal{R}$ comprises at least one uniformly compensating action per constraint and the initial database state contains a finite number of violations, then, if the computation eventually terminates, the final state is correct with respect to all constraints.

5.1 Insert/Delete actions

The simplest kinds of compensating actions are defined by the following basic results [5]:

Proposition 1: given a constraint C, a positive database literal p of the violation condition $C^\star$, such that $C^\star$ does not contain another negative literal p' built from the same predicate, a rule $R : F(\vec{x}) \rightarrow \mathcal{O}(\vec{y})$ *uniformly* compensates C, if F is $C^\star$ and $\mathcal{O}(\vec{y})$ is delete($\text{P}(\vec{y})$), where each y_i in $\vec{y}$ matches a free variable of p.

Proposition 2: given a constraint C, a negative database literal q of $C^\star$, such that $C^\star$ does not contain another positive literal q' built from the same predicate, a rule $R : F(\vec{x}) \rightarrow \mathcal{O}(\vec{y})$ *uniformly* compensates C, if F is $C^\star$ and $\mathcal{O}(\vec{y})$ is insert($\text{Q}(\vec{y})$), where each y_i in $\vec{y}$ either matches a free variable of q or is the special symbol ?.

Proof: straightforward, considering the semantics of insert and delete operations. The restriction on the occurrence of the same predicate in literals of different sign is due to possibility that a deletion (insertion) may remove an existing violation and introduce a new one at the same time.

As an example, consider the following constraint.

Constraint 2: referential integrity on the `wire-type` field of the relation WIRE.

```
∀* ∃ max-volt, max-pow, wire-section
  ¬(WIRE(wire-type, ...) ∧
    ¬WIRE-TYPE(wire-type, max-volt, max-pow, wire-section))
```

In case of violation, to restore the database to a correct state, two alternatives are available: either deleting the tuple of WIRE that determines the violation, or inserting a new tuple in WIRE-TYPE, with the value of the `wire-type` field imposed by the violation and arbitrary values of `max-volt`, `max-pow` and `wire-section`. These are exactly the alternatives captured by the two following rules, generated according to Proposition 1 and 2:

```
RULE 2-1
∀ max-volt, max-pow, wire-section
  WIRE(w-id, fr, to, wire-type, voltage, power) ∧
  ¬WIRE-TYPE(wire-type, max-volt, max-pow, wire-section)
→ delete(WIRE(w-id, fr, to, wire-type, voltage))
```

```
RULE 2-2
∀ max-volt, max-pow, wire-section
  WIRE(w-id, fr, to, wire-type, voltage, power) ∧
  ¬WIRE-TYPE(wire-type, max-volt, max-pow, wire-section)
→ insert(WIRE-TYPE(wire-type, ?, ?, ?))
```

These rules uniformly compensate Constraint 2, since they are triggered whenever the constraint is violated and they are always assured to remove the triggering violation.

5.2 Replacement Operations

Using delete compensating actions, whenever an incorrect tuple is introduced in the database by a user-supplied transaction, all the information it contains is rejected as a whole by the RTS. Clearly, it would be desirable for the RTS to discriminate the wrong pieces of information from the correct ones and supply (or ask) alternative data only for the defective part. This requires a finer granularity in the analysis of the constraint, to identify not only which relations, but also which attributes are relevant to compensate a violation. A benefit of providing replacement rules is that the probability that a compensating action can produce violations of other constraints is lower, if one performs modifications at the attribute level. On the other hand, unlike delete and insert compensating actions, replacement rules may lack the nice property of uniformly compensating a constraint, since their possibility to be fired may be conditioned by the existence in the database of appropriate values to be used in the replacement. In general, replacement rules alone are not sufficient to guarantee the correctness of the final state with respect to the constraint they enforce and are preferably used in conjunction with uniformly compensating rules.

As an example, consider the constraint below:

Constraint 3: the power of each wire does not exceed the maximum for its wire type

```
∀* ¬(WIRE(wire-type, power ...) ∧
    WIRE-TYPE(wire-type, max-pow, ...) ∧
    (power > max-pow))
```

Whenever a violation occur, the uniformly compensating actions that can be generated according to Proposition 1 are:

- delete(WIRE(...))

- delete(WIRE-TYPE(...))

Clearly, the most desirable compensating action would be to replace the type of the violating wire, searching a wire-type in table WIRE-TYPE that fits the power value *of the violating wire*. However, this action might be non-applicable, depending on the actual database state in which the violation occur. This shows that replacement rules in general do not compensate uniformly.

Since replacement rules cannot assure to compensate a constraint in any occasion, we will look for a property weaker than uniform compensation.

Definition 10: a database rule R *compensates* a constraint C iff, for every database state S such that the violation set $\Theta_{S,C}$ of C is not empty, we have that, if R is triggered in S, then $\Theta_{S,C} \supset \Theta_{S',C}$, where S' is the database state generated by the execution of R in S.

The property of (non-uniform) compensation requires only that, *if a rule is triggered in a given database state*, then its execution removes at least one violation. However, there might be cases in which a non-uniformly compensating rule is not triggered in a database state that does contain violations of the constraint enforced by the rule.

Now, we will look for the set of replacement compensating actions that can be derived for a given constraint. Since this set is infinite, we will generate only a finite number of compensating rules, choosing the most "general" representatives.

First, it is necessary to introduce a notion of *rule subsumption*.

Definition 11: a database rule R' *subsumes* another rule R'' if

- $\text{LHS}(R'') \Rightarrow \text{LHS}(R')$

- for every database state S and substitution pair θ', θ'' such that $\text{LHS}(R'\theta')$ and $\text{LHS}(R''\theta'')$ are satisfied in S, it holds that $\text{RHS}(R'\theta') \equiv \text{RHS}(R''\theta'')$.

Clearly, any rule R'', subsumed by a rule R' which compensates a constraint C, also compensates C. In fact, whenever R'' can fire, R' could also be fired and R'' performs the same action as R'.

We now introduce the fundamental result about replacement compensating actions:

Proposition 3: given a constraint $\mathcal{C}$, a literal p appearing positively in the violation condition $C^\star$, such that there is no other positive literal in $C^\star$ built from the same predicate, and a variable x_{h_i} of p, a replacement rule $R : F \rightarrow$ replace($\mathrm{P}(\vec{x_p}), x_{h_i} \leftarrow z_{h_i}$) compensates $\mathcal{C}$ if and only if R is subsumed by a rule having the following LHS:

$$\hat{F}(\vec{x} \cup z_{h_i}) \stackrel{\text{def}}{=} C^\star(\vec{x}) \wedge C^{\star\star}(\vec{z})\alpha.$$

In the definition above:

- $\vec{x}_p$ is the subset of variables $\vec{x}$ that appear in the literal p;

- $\vec{z}$ is a set of $|\vec{x}_p|$ auxiliary variables;

- $C^{\star\star}$ is the formula obtained from the s.c.f. of $\mathcal{C}$, by freeing all the variables $\vec{x}_p$ and dropping the literal p.

- α is a variable substitution $\{\vec{z} - z_{h_i} \mid \vec{x}_p - x_{h_i}\}$

Proof: see [10].

The formula $\hat{F}(\vec{x} \cup z_{h_i})$ is the conjunction of two subformulas: the violation condition $C^\star$ and the subformula $C^{\star\star}\alpha$. The former subformula is satisfied, by definition, by every substitution that defines a constraint violation; the latter is used to extract from the database a new value to be employed in the replacement operation.

The replacement value is chosen in a way that guarantees that the tuple produced by the replacement operation, say $\mathrm{P}(\vec{c})$, does not introduce violations of the same constraint. To do so, it is necessary to state that the constraint formula is satisfied by every substitution that binds the values of $\mathrm{P}(\vec{c})$ to the corresponding constraint variables.

Considering that the variable substitution α is used to pass variable bindings from $C^\star$ to $C^{\star\star}$ and that $\mathrm{P}(\vec{c})$ is formed by keeping all the values that violated the constraint except that of the replaced field, it is easy to see that the second part of the conjunction is nothing else than the correctness condition for $\mathrm{P}(\vec{c})$. In particular, the subformula $C^{\star\star}$ can be viewed as a specialized version of the constraint, that is evaluated under the assumption that $\mathrm{P}(\vec{c})$ holds.

The rationale of Proposition 3 is that the set of replacement rules that compensate a constraint through a single-attribute replacement is characterized by a "fundamental" rule, having $\hat{F}$ as its LHS. By Proposition 3, every element of this set is subsumed by such a "fundamental" rule. Therefore, $\hat{F}$ can be viewed as the less restrictive requirement that a database state must satisfy for a given compensating replacement to be applicable.

In the case of Constraint 3, the fundamental condition is:

```
WIRE(w-id, from, to, wire-type, power, voltage) ∧
WIRE-TYPE(wire-type, max-volt, max-pow, wire-section) ∧
(power > max-pow) ∧
∀max-pow", max-volt", wire-section"
  ¬(WIRE-TYPE(wire-type", max-volt", max-pow", wire-section") ∧
    (power > max-pow"))
```

In this case, $C^{\star\star}$ specializes the constraint in such a way that the new wire-type employed—namely wire-type"— must be compatible (only) with the wire that does violate the constraint. Note that this formula still lacks the property of safeness, since it is possible to satisfy it by choosing a value for wire-type" that does not exist in the database.

Now that we have stated a necessary and sufficient condition for a compensating replacement to be applicable, we use it to identify the subset of all the constraint variables that can be fruitfully employed to obtain compensating actions. Such variables are exactly those that are common to two or more literals (or a literal with itself) in the constraint, and will be called *join-variables*.

Definition 12: given a constraint C in s.c.f., a free variable x_i in $C^\star$ is a *join-variable* if it appears as an argument of a *database* literal m and at least of another literal m' of C, with $m \neq m'$. [4]

In Constraint 3 the join-variables are:

- wire-type appearing in literals WIRE, WIRE-TYPE;

- power appearing in literals WIRE, (power > max-pow);

- max-pow appearing in literals WIRE-TYPE, (power > max-pow);

We now show that the join-variables of a constraint C are the only ones relevant to the compensation of C through single-attribute replacement operations.

Proposition 4: the "fundamental" formula $\hat{F}(\vec{x} \cup z_{h_i}) \overset{\text{def}}{=} C^\star(\vec{x}) \wedge C^{\star\star}(\vec{z})\alpha$ for the compensation of a constraint C through the replacement of the value of variable x_{h_i} of literal p is satisfiable only if x_{h_i} is a join-variable of C.

Proof: obtained by applying the General Resolution Method to the s.c.f. of a generic constraint [10].

Propositions 1 through 4 identify all the possible ways to generate compensating actions from constraints through the permitted database updating operations, that can be summarized in the Rule Generation Algorithm, sketched below.

---

[4]The case of a variable occurring more than once in a literal is omitted, since $m(x,x) \equiv m(x,y) \wedge (x = y)$.

```
FOR EACH constraint DO
        FOR EACH negative database literal qᵢ in C*
                such that no positive literal q'ᵢ exists in C*
                built from the same predicate DO
                Generate an Insert Rule on qᵢ
        END (* FOR *)
        FOR EACH positive database literal pⱼ in C*
                such that no negative literal p'ⱼ exists in C*
                built from the same predicate DO
                Generate a Delete Rule on pⱼ;
        END (* FOR *)
        FOR EACH positive database literal pₖ in C*
                such that no positive literal p'ₖ exists in C*
                built from the same predicate DO
                FOR EACH join-var xₕᵢ in pₖ DO
                        Generate a Replacement Rule on xₕᵢ, pₖ
                END (* FOR *)
        END (* FOR *)
END (* FOR *)
```

However, the rule set derived according to these results requires further analysis to provide for efficient implementation of rules and to individuate redundant or misbehaving compensating actions.

5.3   Safeness Considerations on Automatically Generated Replacement Rules

We now turn to the problem of finding under what conditions the satisfaction of the formula expressing the fundamental condition for replacement can be determined based only on the actual content of the database state, since this is a necessary prerequisite for the property of safeness, which ensures an efficient implementation of the rule evaluation mechanism of the RTS, e.g., in Relational Algebra.

Since $\hat{F}(\vec{x} \cup z_{h_i}) \overset{\text{def}}{=} C^\star(\vec{x}) \wedge C^{\star\star}(\vec{z})\alpha$ and $C^\star$ is safe by definition, problems can only arise due to the presence of the additional free variable z_{h_i}.

We rewrite $C^{\star\star}$ as: $\neg p_1(\ldots) \vee \ldots \neg p_{i-1}(\ldots) \vee \neg p_{i+1}(\ldots) \vee \ldots \vee \neg p_n(\ldots) \vee q_1(\ldots) \vee \ldots \vee q_m(\ldots) \vee g(\ldots)$, where z_{h_i} occurs at least in one literal. Unless $C^{\star\star}$ contains only literals of the form $q_j(\ldots, z_{h_i}, \ldots)$, it is always possible to satisfy the formula by choosing an arbitrary value for z_{h_i}, contradicting the safeness requirement.

To avoid this, one can simply add an explicit existence condition that restrains the search of an admissible value of the replacement variable only to some fixed domain. This domain can be built by exploiting the relations used in the constraint.

To ensure that the "safe" rule still compensates the constraints, it is sufficient to show that it is subsumed by another rule, which is guaranteed to compensate, though possibly in an unsafe way.

In the case of Constraint 3, a restraining condition for the replacement value must be conjuncted to the fundamental formula to enforce safeness, as illustrated in the example below:

```
RULE 3
WIRE(w-id, from, to, wire-type, power, voltage) ∧
WIRE-TYPE(wire-type, max-volt, max-pow, wire-section) ∧
(power > max-pow) ∧
∃ max-pow', max-volt', wire-section'
   WIRE-TYPE(wire-type", max-volt', max-pow', wire-section') ∧
∀ max-pow", max-volt", wire-section"
   ¬(WIRE-TYPE(wire-type", max-volt", max-pow", wire-section") ∧
   (power > max-pow"))
→ replace(WIRE(w-id, ...), wire-type ← wire-type"))
```

The LHS of Rule 3 is obtained by adding the condition:

```
∃max-pow', max-volt', wire-section'
 WIRE-TYPE(wire-type", max-volt', max-pow', wire-section')
```

to restrain the binding of the free variable `wire-type"` to a value contained in relation WIRE-TYPE and thus ensure safeness. In addition, since the LHS of Rule 3 logically implies the fundamental condition, Rule 3 is subsumed by a rule that is assured to compensate the constraint, as required.

5.4 Ad-hoc Treatment of Built-In Constraints

From the example of Constraint 3, it is possible to see that the automatic generation of compensating actions from constraints leads to a number of alternatives that quickly renders the management of the RTS impractical. One of the sources of such combinatorial explosion is that the rule generation relies only on the specified constraints and does not consider information already existing or efficiently computable in most database systems, that could be employed to prevent undesirable compensating actions from being created. One such source of knowledge is the specification of constraints that are already dealt with by the underlying DBMS, and thus are not explicitly mentioned in the constraint set used for rule generation.

Constraints as read-only restrictions on tables, referential integrity and unique keys are commonly enforced at a lower level and their specification can be employed to prevent the generation of rules whose execution would be inhibited by the run-time system (e.g. rules manipulating read-only tables, updating variables belonging to a table key or deleting entries in a table with a referential integrity link).

As an example of the advantage of taking into account built-in constraints prior to Rule Analysis, consider the constraint below.

Constraint 4: each wire must have a cross-section not exceeding that of the tube(s) that contains it.

```
∀* ¬(WIRE(fr, to, wire-type, ...) ∧
    WIRE-TYPE(wire-type, wire-section, ...) ∧
    TUBE(fr, to, tube-type, ...) ∧
    TUBE-TYPE(tube-type, tube-section, ...) ∧
    ¬(wire-section < tube-section))
```

The 14 alternative compensating actions are:

- deleting a tuple from relation WIRE, TUBE, WIRE-TYPE and TUBE-TYPE

- updating field `wire-type` in table WIRE or WIRE-TYPE

- updating field `tube-type` in table TUBE or TUBE-TYPE

- updating field `wire-section` in table WIRE-TYPE

- updating field `tube-section` in table TUBE-TYPE

- updating field `from/to` in table WIRE or TUBE.

Knowing that tables WIRE-TYPE and TUBE-TYPE are read-only and that `from+to` is a secondary key for tables WIRE and TUBE, the number of compensating actions generated reduces to 4.

Another approach to further reduce the number of automatically generated compensating actions would be to incorporate in the derivation process semantic knowledge about data and constraints. However, we chose to perform rule generation on a lexical basis and to allow only general-purpose meta-information (as that on built-in constraint) to be mixed-in in the rule derivation process. In this way, the use of semantic information is confined to the subsequent phase of Rule Analysis, in which the user can interact with the system, controlling and possibly augmenting the knowledge employed to refine the rule set.

6 The Integrity Maintenance System

We faced the problem of reactive enforcement of database integrity in the context of a broader research on Integrity Maintenance Systems, i.e., automated systems that support the whole activity of integrity maintenance in (active) databases, from constraint specification to transaction execution time. Details of this work are contained in [3, 8, 9]. The solution we propose enables effective constraint maintenance even in presence of potentially non-terminating rule sets, to the price of an acceptable analysis effort at compile-time and of a reasonable sophistication of the run-time system that controls rule execution.

The general architecture of an Integrity Maintenance System consists of the components illustrated in Fig. 1.

Figure 1: Architecture of the Integrity Maintenance System

The *Constraint Editor* is used for collecting constraints definitions.

The *Rule Generator* automatically translates constraints into the complete set of production rules that enforce them, based on the results illustrated in the previous Section.

The *Rule Set Analyzer* is a component, possibly interactive, that analyzes and resolves situations in which rules may trigger each other in cycle, so that the termination of constraint-enforcing rules can be ensured. The actual product of this component is a partial order on the constraint set.

The *Rule Selector* provides a total order on the rule set, by identifying the compensating actions that should be used to maintain database integrity.

The *Run-time System* is responsible of execution control after a user-supplied transaction. It should either be built on top of an existing active DBMS, or be provided by the run-time system of an active DBMS by writing rules appropriately.

6.1   Rule Analysis

Section 5 has addressed the problem of generating compensating actions that are correct for a single constraint.

However, the set of constraints may be such that the enforcement of one constraint leads to violating other constraints. When this causes mutual triggering of compensating actions, the rule set is said to be *cyclic*.

Cyclicity is a potential source of non-termination, since rules lying on a cyclic path may trigger each other indefinitely.

It is then necessary to explicitly address the issue of making the rule set terminating, without loosing the capability of enforcing all the defined constraints.

To this end, the Rule Analyzer assists the user in the analysis of compensating actions, to ensure that rule execution after a possibly faulty transaction does terminate and restore the database to a correct state.

In the general case, the anomalous behavior of rules can be detected only by looking at their execution. However, compile-time analysis plus run-time monitoring can prevent such undesired situations and allow integrity maintenance even in presence of cyclic rules.

Rule Analysis is based on a tool called the Triggering Hypergraph—THG, for short. This is a directed labeled hypergraph, in which nodes represent constraints and hyperarcs are labeled by rule identifiers. The semantics of the THG is such that an hyperarc, labeled R, connects constraint C to a set of constraints $\{C_1 \ldots C_n\}$ if and only if R is a rule that enforces C and that can violate all the constraints listed in $\{C_1 \ldots C_n\}$.

Due to the above definition, hyperarcs of a THG have only one starting node and zero or more arrival nodes. The case of an hyperarc with zero arrival nodes represents a rule that cannot violate any constraint. Potential violation is statically detected by matching the standard conjunctive form of constraints to the signature of the database updating operations contained in the action side of rules.

The criteria adopted in the matching are the following [5, 9]:

- a delete operation on a relation P can violate a constraint C if and only if a database literal p, corresponding to P, appears negated in the violation query C^* of C (e.g., delete(WIRE-TYPE(...))) can violate Constraint 2 on referential integrity between relations WIRE and WIRE-TYPE).

- An insert operation on a relation P can violate a constraint C if and only if a database literal p, corresponding to P, appears positively in the violation query C^* of C (e.g., insert(WIRE(...))) can violate Constraint 2).

- The replacement of attribute a in relation P can violate a constraint C if and only if a matches a constraint variable that appears as an argument of a database literal p, corresponding to P, and at least of another literal p' of the violation query C^* of C, with $p \neq p'$ (e.g., replace(WIRE(..., wire-type $\leftarrow$ wire-type'))) can violate Constraint 2).

Since the above criteria do not use run-time information on the database state and the transaction, they are pessimistic: an action considered likely to violate a constraint, due to its signature, can still behave correctly at run-time, depending on the actual values of its variables (e.g., deleting a wire-type which is not used by any wire does not violate Constraint 2).

Once the THG is known, potential sources of non-termination are readily detected, as they correspond to cycles in the THG. Therefore, the task of ensuring termination reduces to that of eliminating such cycles, i.e., to the task of extracting an acyclic subgraph from the THG.

Cycle removal could be done manually by the user, but the complexity of the THG, even with few constraints, makes this approach unfeasible.

Thus, we have developed an automated tool to support Rule Analysis, which can run unassisted or interact with the user to achieve a better solution.

The outcome of the Rule Analyzer is a DAGH, i.e., a directed acyclic hypergraph derived from the original THG, by "marking as removed" a set of compensating actions. Marked rules are not physically removed from the rule set, but they will be monitored in a special, and costly, way by the run-time system.

To ensure that only the less preferable compensating actions are "marked" during Rule Analysis, a *weight function* is defined, which assigns to each compensating action a numerical index that reflects its semantic adequacy. In [9] we discuss the issue of defining rule's weight so to reflect at best the semantic adequacy of compensating actions and claim that *constraint classification* and the definition of standard *compensation policies* for classes of constraints are powerful means to increase the quality of Rule Analysis.

Semantic rule marking is then formulated as an optimization problem on a *weighed* THG. In [8], we demonstrate that the optimization problem is NP-complete and discuss alternative approximate solutions with polynomial complexity.

6.2   Rule Selection and Run-Time Control

The DAGH computed as the result of Rule Analysis defines a partial order $\prec_c$ on the constraint set, defined as follows: $C \prec_c C'$ if and only if the DAHG contains a path from C to C'.

This order defines a notion of priority on constraints. High priority is given to those constraints whose enforcement is likely—according to static analysis— to produce violations of the largest number of other constraints.

Then, if the run-time system tackles constraint violations in decreasing order of priority and uses only those rules that appear in the DAGH, termination is assured, since no compensating action can introduce violations of constraints that have already been repaired. Indeed, rules that can violate constraints with a priority higher than that of the one they enforce no longer appear in the DAGH.

Unfortunately, there is no guarantee that the compensating actions in the DAGH are still sufficient to repair all the defined constraint. In the general case, the compensating actions in the DAGH may be insufficient to restore correctness for some constraints and redundant for some others.

Therefore, Rule Selection is needed, to identify the rules to be made available at run-time, either by reintroducing compensating actions discarded by Rule Analysis or by pruning redundant rules to increase run-time efficiency. The more liberal the selection of available rules, the more flexible the compensation, but also the greater the run-time overhead.

Reintroducing rules that can violate higher priority constraints requires a special monitoring. The solution we implemented is to simulate the execution of possibly non-terminating rules to see if they actually violate higher priority constraints. If this does not happen, then the results of the rule's execution are made permanent. Otherwise, the compensation is terminated by issuing a roll-back to the original database state prior to the user's faulty transaction.

Therefore, the rule execution policy of the run-time system can be summarized as follows:

- tackle constraint violations in decreasing order of constraint priority; in case of violated constraints with the same priority, choose randomly—or according to a heuristic criterion.

- When more than one compensating action for the violated constraint is triggered, look for a rule that has not been discarded during Rule Analysis. A such rule can still collide with other rules but cannot violate already enforced constraints or constraints of higher or equivalent priority. In case of more than one choice, select randomly—or according to a heuristic criterion.

- if no "safe" rule is triggered, there must be one (or more) applicable compensating action that have been discarded during Rule Analysis. Since discarded rules are likely to produce cycles, simulate their execution—in any order or according to a heuristic criterion—until you find one that does not cause any violation of equivalent or higher priority constraints. If one is found, then make the effects of its execution permanent; otherwise, issue a rollback command to the original state prior to the user's transaction.

The proposed approach, to the price of a reasonable sophistication of the run-time system, retains the flexibility of alternative compensating actions for the same constraint, which is the main outcome of automatic rule generation. In addition, termination and correctness are guaranteed also for cyclic rule sets, though, in some cases, through a rollback statement.

7 Conclusions and Future Work

In this paper we have faced one of the core issues of integrity maintenance in active databases: the derivation of procedural compensating actions from declarative constraints. We have proposed an approach in which compensating actions are generated in a fully automated way, through a lexical analysis whose theoretical premises we have thoroughly discussed. Finally, we have widened the perspective, by collocating the problem of rule derivation in the broader context of Integrity Maintenance Systems.

Several lines of extension of the work herein described will be pursued in the next future:

- the constraint language needs to be enriched to capture real-world constraints; we are presently investigating the technical problems of extending the form of constraint formulas beyond the limitations of standard conjunctive form, to the full power of first order logic. As a first step toward this goal, we have added the possibility to use views in the definition of constraints, which greatly enhances the expressive power and clarity of the constraint language. After that, we will consider the introduction of aggregate functions and recursion.

- The rule based language will be improved as well, by extending the range of the permitted database updating operations (e.g. including multiple-fields update) and by allowing the RHS of rules to contain more than a single operation.

- The preceding points will require a thorough revision of the results underlying rule generation; in particular the problem of deriving compensating rules from constraints comprising aggregate functions will be carefully studied.

In the mid-term, we will also enhance the RTS model to capture more realistic semantics, e.g., set-oriented semantics [2, 18]. Finally, the research activity on the other tasks of integrity maintenance—namely, rule analysis and execution control—will be continued, by experimenting with different heuristics to obtain acyclic rule sets, by investigating alternative criteria for rule selection and by extending the present prototypical version of the Integrity Maintenance System.

References

[1] A. Aiken, J. Widom, J. M. Hellerstein, Behavior of database production rules: termination, confluence and observable determinism, in Proc. of ACM-SIGMOD, pp. 59-68, 1992.

[2] F. Cacace, S. Ceri, S. Crespi-Reghizzi, L. Tanca, R. Zicari, The Logres project: integrating object oriented data modeling with rule based programming paradigm, Tech. Rep. n. 89-039, Laboratorio di Calcolatori, Dipartimento di Elettronica, Politecnico di Milano, 1989.

[3] S. Ceri, P. Fraternali, S. Paraboschi, Integrity Maintenance Systems: an Architecture, Proc. 3th International Workshop on the Deductive Approach

to Information Systems and Databases, pp. 327-344, Rosas, Catalunia, Sept. 1992.

[4] S. Ceri, F. Garzotto, Specification and management of database integrity constraint through logic programming, Tech. Rep. n. 88-025, Laboratorio di Calcolatori, Dipartimento di Elettronica, Politecnico di Milano, 1988.

[5] S. Ceri, F. Garzotto, G. Gottlob, Specification and management of database integrity constraint through logic programming techniques, to be published as Tech. Rep. Laboratorio di Calcolatori, Dipartimento di Elettronica, Politecnico di Milano, 1992.

[6] S. Ceri, G. Gottlob, L. Tanca, **Logic programming and databases**, Springer Verlag, Surveys in Computer Science, Heidelberg, 1990.

[7] S. Ceri J. Widom, Deriving production rules for constraint maintenance, Proc. 16th Int. Conf. on VLDB, pp. 566-577, Brisbane, Australia, August 1990

[8] P. Fraternali, S. Paraboschi, Selecting Rules for Constraint Maintenance: Its Complexity and a Heuristic Solution, Tech. Rep. n. 92-057, Laboratorio di Calcolatori, Dipartimento di Elettronica, Politecnico di Milano, 1992.

[9] P. Fraternali, S. Paraboschi, L. Tanca, S. Ceri, Integrity Maintenance Systems, Tech. Rep. n. 92-054, Laboratorio di Calcolatori, Dipartimento di Elettronica, Politecnico di Milano, 1992 (submitted for publication).

[10] P. Fraternali, Automatic translation of database integrity constraints into compensating production rules, Tech. Rep. n. 92-055, Laboratorio di Calcolatori, Dipartimento di Elettronica, Politecnico di Milano, 1992.

[11] A. P. Karadimce, S. D. Urban, Diagnosing anomalous rule behavior in databases with integrity maintenace production rules, Proc. 3th Workshop on Foundations of Models and Languages for Data and Objects, pp. 77-102, Aigen, Austria, Sept. 1991

[12] J. M. Nicolas K. Yazdanian, Integrity checking in deductive databases, In **Logic and Databases**, H. Gallaire and J. Minker Eds., pages 325-344, Plenum, New York 1978.

[13] M. Stonebraker, A. Juingran, J. Goh, S. Potamianos, On rules, procedures, caching and views in database systems, In Proc. of ACM-SIGMOD, pp. 281-290, May 1990

[14] D. Stemple, S. Mazumdar, and T. Sheard, On the modes and meaning of feedback to transaction designer, In Proc. ACM-SIGMOD, pages 374-386, May 1987.

[15] B. Thalheim, **Dependencies in relational databases**, B G Teubner Verlgsgesellshaft, Stuttgart 1991

[16] J. D. Ullman, **Principles of database systems**, Computer Science Press, Potomac, Maryland, 1980 (rev. ed. 1982)

[17] S. Urban, L. Delcambre, Constraint analysis: a design process for specifying operations on objects, **IEEE Trans. on knowledge and data engineering**, Vol. 2 No. 4, Dec 1990.

[18] J. Widom S. J. Finkelstein, Set-oriented production rules in relational database systems, In Proc. of ACM-SIGMOD, pp. 259-270, May 1990.

[19] J. Widom, A denotational semantics for the Starburst production rule language, Research Report RJ 8581 (77360), SIGMOD Record, Vol. 21, No. 3, Sept. 1992.

[20] Y. Zhou, M. Hsu, A theory for rule triggering systems, in Advances in Database Technology - EDBT '90, LNCS 416, pp. 407-421. Springer-Verlag, Berlin, March 1990.

Integrity Enforcement in Object-Oriented Databases*

Klaus–Dieter Schewe[1], Bernhard Thalheim[2],
Joachim W. Schmidt[1], Ingrid Wetzel[1]

[1] University of Hamburg, Dept. of Computer Science,
Vogt-Kölln-Str. 30, D-W-2000 Hamburg 54, FRG
[2] University of Rostock, Dept. of Computer Science,
Albert-Einstein-Str. 21, D-O-2500 Rostock, FRG

Abstract. In contrast to the relational model methods in OODBs must enforce structurally defined constraints such as inclusion and referential constraints. It has been shown that this is possible for basic *generic update operations* that are determined by the schema. However, such operations only exist for value-representable classes.

In this paper we generalize this result and show that integrity enforcement is always possible. Given some arbitrary method S and some static or transition constraint $\mathcal{I}$ there exists a *greatest consistent specialization* (GCS) $S_{\mathcal{I}}$ of S with respect to $\mathcal{I}$. Such a GCS behaves nice in that it is compatible with the conjunction of constraints, inheritance and refinement.

Moreover, it is possible to derive simple representations of GCSs for basic update operations with respect to distinguished classes of explicitly stated static constraints. For the GCS construction of a user-defined operation, however, it is in general not sufficient to replace the involved primitive update operations by their GCSs.

1 Introduction

Consistency is a crucial property of database application systems. In general a database may be considered as a triplet $(S, \mathcal{O}, \mathcal{C})$, where S defines a structure, $\mathcal{O}$ denotes a collection of state changing operations and $\mathcal{C}$ is a set of constraints. Constraints can be classified into static, transition and general dynamic constraints describing legal states, state transitions or state sequences respectively. Then the *consistency problem* is to guarantee that each specified operation $o \in \mathcal{O}$ will never violate any constraint $\mathcal{I} \in \mathcal{C}$. *Integrity enforcement* aims at the derivation of a new set $\mathcal{O}'$ of operations such that $(S, \mathcal{O}', \mathcal{C})$ satisfies this property.

In this paper we address the integrity enforcement problem with respect to static and transition constraints. Our analysis will be based on the object oriented datamodel (OODM) introduced in [22] which is based on a clear distinction between *values* and *objects* as required e.g. in [6, 7]. In this model an object o consists of a unique identifier id, a set of (type-, value-)pairs (T_i, v_i),

* This work has been supported in part by research grants from the E.E.C. Basic Research Action 3070 FIDE: "Formally Integrated Data Environments".

a set of (reference-, object-)pairs (ref_j, o_j) and a set of methods $meth_k$. A type is defined algebraically by constructors, selectors, functions and axioms similar to [8, 18, 10, 12].

The class concept provides the grouping of objects having the same structure which uniformly combines aspects of object values and references. The extent of classes varies over time, whereas types are immutable. Relationships between classes are represented by references together with referential constraints on the object identifiers involved. Moreover, each class is accompanied by a collection of methods. A schema is given by a collection of class definitions together with explicit constraints. This datamodel is related to some other work on the foundations of object oriented databases [1, 7, 11, 15, 25], but it is distinct from existing systems [4, 2, 14]. The description of the OODM will appear in Section 3.

In general, verification techniques based on predicate transformers are applicable [20]. This includes to show that each update operation starting in a legal state with respect to the static constraints can only end up in legal states. This also comprises that methods on subclasses overriding inherited methods must be specializations. The latter proof obligation can be exploited to formalize the satisfaction of transition constraints, since each transition constraint can be regarded as a general predicatively specified method. Then a method satisfies a transition constraint iff it specializes the method associated with the constraint. In Section 2 we describe in part the theoretical background of consistency verification.

An obvious disadvantage of the verification approach is that it does not help the user in writing consistent operations. An alternative is to generate a *Greatest Consistent Specialization* (GCS) of a given method with respect to the given constraints. This comprises the following problems:

(i) Does a GCS exist in general? Is it compatible with the conjunction of constraints, optimization, inheritance and refinement?

(ii) How does a GCS look like in the OODM with respect to distinguished classes of constraints?

(iii) How to enforce integrity of general user-defined operations with respect to arbitrary constraints? Is it sufficient to replace involved primitive operations by their GCSs?

In Section 4 we address these problems for static constraints. We show the existence of GCSs and also discuss compatibility results with respect to the conjunction of constraints, specialization and refinement. These positive result set up a fundamental distinction to trigger approaches [13], where conjunctivity can not be guaranteed. In Section 5 we describe the structure of GCSs in the OODM with respect to specific classes of constraints. Moreover, we show that the general enforcement problem can not be reduced to primitive operations. In Section 6 we derive the existence of GCSs for transition constraints and also discuss compatibility properties. We conclude in Section 7 discussing some open problems concerning the handling of general dynamic constraints and the structure of GCSs in general.

2 Theoretical Background

For the moment let us abstract from the specific database context. Look at a database being defined as some *state space* X with typed state variables $x_1 :: T_1, \ldots, x_n :: T_n$. Then *state transitions* on X are expressible by (partial, non-deterministic) guarded commands with a sophisticated axiomatic semantics defined by predicate transformers. Formulae in first-order logic can be used to express both static and transition integrity *constraints* on X. We adopt this approach in order to formalize OODM as well as the integrity enforcement problem within a strict mathematical framework that will later be applied to the OODM.

2.1 Types

In general a type is specified by a collection of constructors, selectors and other functions – the signature of the type – and axioms defined by universal Horn formulae [23]. Now let N_P, N_T, N_F, and V denote arbitrary pairwise disjoint, countably infinite sets representing a reservoir of parameter-, type-, function-, and variable-names respectively.

Definition 1. A *type signature* Σ consists of a type name $t \in N_T$, a finite set of supertype-/function-pairs $T \subseteq N_T \times N_F$, a finite set of parameters $P \subseteq N_P$, a finite set of base types $B \subseteq N_T$ and pairwise disjoint finite sets C, S, $F \subseteq N_F$ of constructors, selectors and functions such that there exist predefined arities $ar(c) \in (P \cup B^* \cup \{t\})^* \times \{t\}$, $ar(s) \in \{t\} \times (P \cup B^* \cup \{t\})$ and $ar(f) \in (P \cup B^* \cup \{t\})^* \times (P \cup B^* \cup \{t\})$ for each $c \in C$, $s \in S$ and $f \in F$.

We write $f : t \rightarrow t'$ to denote a *supertype-/function-pair* $(t', f) \in T$. We write $c : t_1 \times \ldots \times t_n \rightarrow t$ to denote a *constructor* of arity $(t_1 \ldots t_n, t)$, $s : t \rightarrow t'$ to denote a *selector* of arity (t, t') and $f : t_1 \times \ldots \times t_n \rightarrow t'$ to denote a *function* of arity $(t_1 \ldots t_n, t')$. If $t_i = b_i^0 \ldots b_i^m \in B^*$, we write $b_i^0(b_i^1 \ldots b_i^m)$. We call $S = P \cup B \cup \{t\}$ the set of *sorts* of the signature Σ.

Definition 2. A *type declaration* consists of a type signature Σ with type name t such that there exists a type declaration for each $b \in B - \{t\}$ and a set Ax of Horn formulae over Σ. Moreover, if $b_i^0(b_i^1 \ldots b_i^m)$ with $b_i^j \in B$ occurs within a constructor, selector or function, then b_i^0 must have been declared as a parameterized type with m parameters. We say that (Σ, Ax) defines the *parameterized type* $t(\alpha_1, \ldots, \alpha_n)$, iff $P = \{\alpha_1, \ldots, \alpha_n\} \neq \emptyset$ or the *proper type* t respectively.
A *type* t is defined either by a type declaration or by mutually recursive equations involving t as a variable.

The semantics of a type is given by term generated algebras that are quotients of the term algebra defined by the constructors. Subtyping is modelled by the use of a continous function taking the subtype to the supertype. Recursive types are fixpoints of functors. It can be shown that even the guarded commands give rise to a type $GC(\alpha, \beta, \gamma)$, where α (β) is the type of the input (output) and γ is the type of the underlying state space. See [20] for more details.

2.2 State Transitions

In general non-deterministic partial state transitions S on a state space X can be described by a subset of $\mathcal{D} \times \mathcal{D}_\perp$, where $\mathcal{D}$ denotes the set of possible states on X and $\mathcal{D}_\perp = \mathcal{D} \cup \{\perp\}$, where $\perp$ is a special symbol used to indicate non-termination. It can be shown that this is equivalent to defining two predicate transformers $wp(S)$ and $wlp(S)$ associated with S satisfying the pairing condition $wp(S)(\mathcal{R}) \Leftrightarrow wlp(S)(\mathcal{R}) \wedge wp(S)(true)$ and the universal conjunctivity of $wlp(S)$. They assign to some postcondition $\mathcal{R}$ the *weakest (liberal) precondition* of S to establish $\mathcal{R}$. Informally these conditions can be characterized as follows:

- $wlp(S)(\mathcal{R})$ characterizes those initial states such that all terminating executions of S will reach a final state characterized by $\mathcal{R}$ provided S is defined in that initial state, and
- $wp(S)(\mathcal{R})$ characterizes those initial states such that all executions of S terminate and will reach a final state characterized by $\mathcal{R}$ provided S is defined.

Such operations S can be specified by guarded commands in the style of Dijkstra [9, 17]:

Definition 3. Let X be some state space. A *guarded command* S on X consists of a name S, a set of input-parameters $\{\iota_1, \ldots, \iota_k\}$, a set of output-parameters $\{o_1, \ldots, o_l\}$ and a body. To each input-parameter ι_i corresponds a type T_i and to each output-parameter o_j corresponds a type O_j. The *body* of S is recursively built from the following constructs:

(i)   assignment $x := E$, where x is a state variable in X or a local variable within S and E is a term of the same type as x,

(ii) *skip, fail, loop*,

(iii) sequential composition $S_1; S_2$, choice $S_1 \square S_2$, projection $x :: T \mid S$, guard $\mathcal{P} \to S$, restricted choice $S_1 \otimes S_2$, where $\mathcal{P}$ is a well-formed formula and x is a variable of type T, and

(iv) instantiation $x'_1, \ldots, x'_i \leftarrow S'(E'_1, \ldots, E'_j)$, where S' is the name of another operation ($S = S'$ is possible) on X with input-parameters $\iota'_1, \ldots, \iota'_j$ and output-parameters $o'_1, \ldots, o'_i$, such that the variables o'_f, x'_f have the same type and the term E'_g has the same type as the variable ι'_g.

Each variable occurring in the S has a well-defined scope. The scoping rules are omitted. Furthermore, we omit the detailed definition of the predicate transformers $wlp(S)$ and $wp(S)$ [17, 20]. We only give an informal description of the less usual operations *projection, guard* and *restricted choice*. Projection gives the introduction of a new local variable x of the given type. A guard $\mathcal{P} \to S$ gives a precondition $\mathcal{P}$ for S. If $\mathcal{P}$ is not satisfied, the whole operation is undefined. Restricted choice $S \otimes T$ means to execute S unless it is undefined in which case T is taken. The basic commands *skip, fail, loop* are only introduced for theoretical completeness: *skip* does nothing, *fail* is always undefined, and *loop* never terminates.

Here we dispense with any structuring of state spaces into modules. However, in order to define "extended operations" we need to know for each operation S the subspace $Y \subseteq X$ such that S does neither read nor change the values in $X - Y$. In this case we call S a Y-operation on X. We omit the formal details [17, 20].

2.3 Consistency Proof Obligations

General constraints and arbitrary operations on a state space X raise the problem whether consistency as defined by the constraints is always satisfied by the operations. One approach to address this problem is to use general verification techniques. The verification approach consists in the derivation (and proof) of general proof obligations expressed in the predicate transformer calculus.

The static constraints on a state space X, i.e. first-order formulae $\mathcal{I}$ with $fr(\mathcal{I}) \subseteq X$ partition the state space, i.e. the collection of the mutable classes into two distinguished subspaces. States not satisfying the constraints should never be reached.

In general inherited operations can be overwritten. Unless inheritance is simply regarded as a copying mechanism we should ensure that this can be done in a concise way, i.e., overriding should be restricted to "specialization". The intuition behind this definition is that whenever an execution of the specialized operation T establishes some post-predicate $\mathcal{R}$, then this execution should already be one of the general method S.

Transition constraints on X are expressible as first-order formulae $\mathcal{J}$ with $fr(\mathcal{J}) \subseteq X \cup X'$, where X' is a disjoint copy of X. We may then exploit a weak equivalence between guarded commands and predicative specifications. We may associate with the transition constraint $\mathcal{J}$ the guarded command $\Phi(\mathcal{J}) = x' \mid \mathcal{J} \rightarrow x := x'$ where x (x') is used as an abbreviation for the collection $x_1, \ldots, x_n$ $(x'_1, \ldots, x'_n)$ of (state) variables. Satisfying $\mathcal{J}$ is equivalent to each operation S specializing $\Phi(\mathcal{J})$. Hence the following formal definitions:

Definition 4. Let X be a state space, $Z \subseteq Y \subseteq X$ subspaces, $\mathcal{I}$ a static and $\mathcal{J}$ a transition constraint on X, S a Z-operation and T a Y-operation.

(i) S is *consistent* with respect to $\mathcal{I}$ iff $\mathcal{I} \Rightarrow wlp(S)(\mathcal{I})$ holds on X.

(ii) T *specializes* S iff $wp(S)(true) \Rightarrow wp(T)(true)$ and $wlp(S)(\mathcal{R}) \Rightarrow wlp(T)(\mathcal{R})$ hold for all Z-predicates $\mathcal{R}$ (denoted $T \sqsubseteq S$).

(iii) S is *consistent* with respect to $\mathcal{J}$ iff $\mathcal{R}$ $wlp(\Phi(\mathcal{J}))(\mathcal{R}) \Rightarrow wlp(S)(\mathcal{R})$ holds for all X-predicates.

Note that $\sqsubseteq$ defines a partial order on operations. There exists an equivalent characterization of transition consistency that avoids the quantification over all state predicates [19]. See [20] for more details.

3 Fundamentals of Object Oriented Data Modelling

In the following assume to be given a type system $\mathbf{T}$ as described e.g. in Section 2.1. Basically such a type system consists of some *basic types* such as $BOOL$, $\mathbb{N}, \mathbb{Z}, STRING$, etc., *type constructors* (parameterized types) for record, finite sets, lists, etc. and a *subtyping* relation. Moreover, assume that (mutually) *recursive types*, i.e. types defined by (a system of) domain equations, exist in $\mathbf{T}$. As an alternative to our definition of $\mathbf{T}$ in Section 2.1 we may restrict $\mathbf{T}$ being one of the type systems defined in [3]. In addition we suppose the existence of an abstract identifier type ID in $\mathbf{T}$ without any non-trivial supertype. Arbitrary *types* can then be defined by nesting. A type T without occurrence of ID will be called a *value-type*.

Now let $N_P, N_T, N_C, N_R, N_F, N_M$ and V denote arbitrary pairwise disjoint, denumerable sets representing parameter-, type-, class-, reference-, function-, method- and variable-names respectively.

3.1 The Concept of a Class

The OODM in [22] distinguishes between values grouped into types and objects grouped into classes. The extent of classes varies over time, whereas types are immutable. Relationships between classes are represented by references together with referential constraints on the object identifiers involved. Moreover, each class is accompanied by a collection of methods defined by deterministic guarded commands [17, 19, 20].

Each object in a class consists of an identifier, a collection of values and references to objects in other classes. Identifiers can be represented using the unique identifier type ID. Values and references can be combined into a representation type, where each occurence of ID denotes references to some other classes. Therefore, we may define the structure of a class using parameterized types.

Definition 5. (i) Let t be a value type with parameters $\alpha_1, \ldots, \alpha_n$. For distinct reference names $r_1, \ldots, r_n \in N_R$ and class names $C_1, \ldots, C_n \in N_C$ the expression derived from t by replacing each α_i in t by $r_i : C_i$ for $i = 1, \ldots, n$ is called a *structure expression*.

(ii) A *class* consists of a class name $C \in N_C$, a structure expression S, a set of class names $D_1, \ldots, D_m \in N_C$ (in the following called the set of *superclasses*), a set of static constraints $\mathcal{I}_1, \ldots, \mathcal{I}_k$ and a set of transition constraints $\mathcal{J}_1, \ldots, \mathcal{J}_l$. We call r_i the *reference* named r_i from class C to class C_i. The type derived from S by replacing each reference $r_i : C_i$ by the type ID is called the *representation type* T_C of the class C.

(iii) A *schema* $\mathcal{S}$ is a finite collection of classes $C_1, \ldots, C_n$ closed under references and superclasses together with a collection of static constraints $\mathcal{I}_1, \ldots, \mathcal{I}_n$ and a collection of transition constraints $\mathcal{J}_1, \ldots, \mathcal{J}_m$.

(iv) An *instance* $\mathcal{D}$ of a schema $\mathcal{S}$ assigns to each class C a value $\mathcal{D}(C)$ of type $PFUN(ID, T_C)$ such that all implicit and explicit constraints on $\mathcal{S}$ are satisfied.

Here we dispense with giving a concrete syntax for constraints and methods. On the representation level (see Section 3.2) we may use deterministic guarded commands for methods and first-order formulae for constraints. Distinguished classes of static constraints will be introduced in Section 5.1. Subclasses inherit the methods of their superclasses, but overriding is allowed as long as the new method is a specialization of all its corresponding methods in its superclasses.

3.2 The Representation of a Schema

We now associate with each schema $\mathcal{S}$ a state space X such that each class C in $\mathcal{S}$ is represented by a state variable $x_C :: PFUN(ID, T_C)$ in X called the *class type* of C. $PFUN(\alpha, \beta)$ is the type constructor for partial function from α to β with finite domain. Moreover, C gives rise to *referential constraints* defined by the structure S and *class inclusion constraints* defined by the set of superclasses of C. All other constraints on $\mathcal{S}$ and C are directly translatable in constraints on X. Methods on C are Y-operations on X with $Y = \{x_C\}$. Note that due to identifiers being only an internal concept, only value-defined operations, i.e. all input- and output-types are value types, are accessible to the user. Let us now formally describe the form of structurally defined inclusion and referential constraints.

Definition 6. Let C, C' be classes with representation types T_C and T'_C respectively and let $o : T_C \times ID \rightarrow BOOL$ be a function.

(i) If T_C be a subtype of T'_C via $f : T_C \rightarrow T'_C$, a *class inclusion constraint* on C and C' is a constraint in the form

$$\forall i :: ID.\, \forall v :: T_C.\, member(Pair(i, v), x_C) = true \implies$$
$$member(Pair(i, f(v)), x_{C'}) = true \;, \tag{1}$$

where $Pair$ is the constructor of $PAIR(\alpha, \beta)$ and $member$ is a function on finite sets $FSET(\alpha)$, hence also on the subtype $PFUN(\alpha, \beta)$.

In the general case a *class inclusion constraint* on C and C' has the form

$$\forall i :: ID.\, member(i, dom(x_C)) = true \implies member(i, dom(x_{C'})) = true \;.$$

(ii) A *referential constraint* on C and C' is a constraint in the form

$$\forall i, j :: ID.\, \forall v :: T_C.\, member(Pair(i, v), x_C) = true \land$$
$$o(v, j) = true \implies member(j, dom(x_{C'})) = true \;. \tag{2}$$

It is easy to see that each class D in the set of superclasses of C gives rise to an inclusion constraint. Moreover, each reference $r : E$ occurring in the structure expression S of C gives rise to a referential constraint with the function o determined by the type underlying S. Then $o(v, j) = true$ means that the identifier j occurs within v at a place corresponding to the reference.

3.3 Value Representability

Let us first concentrate on primitive update methods, i.e. insertion, deletion and update of a single object on a classes C. In contrast to the relational datamodel such update operations can not always be derived in the object-oriented case, because the abstract identifiers have to be hidden from the user. However, in [21, 22] it has been shown that for *value-representable* classes these operations are uniquely determined by the schema and consistent with respect to the implicit referential and inclusion constraints.

Definition 7. A class C in a schema S with representation type T_C is called *value-representable* iff there exists a proper value type V_C such that for all instances $\mathcal{D}$ of S there is a function $c : T_C \rightarrow V_C$ such that for $\mathcal{D}$

(i) the condition $\forall i, j :: ID.\, \forall v, w :: T_C.\, member(Pair(i, v), x_C) = true \land$
$member(Pair(j, w), x_C) = true \land c(v) = c(w) \implies i = j$ holds and

(ii) for each pair (V'_C, c') consisting of a proper value type V'_C and a function $c' : T_C \rightarrow V'_C$ such that property (i) is satisfied there exists a function $c'' : V_C \rightarrow V'_C$ that is unique on $c(codom_{\mathcal{D}}(x_C))$ with $c' = c'' \circ c$.

If only the first property holds, C is called *value-identifiable*.

Theorem 8. *Let C be a class in a schema S. Then there exist unique canonical update operations on C iff C and all its superclasses are value-representable.*

For details and proofs see [22].

3.4 An Example

Let us now finalize the presentation of the datamodel by a simple example.

Example 1. Assume the existence of a value type PERSON defined elsewhere. A class C named PERSONC may be defined as follows. Some details such as the definition of the method named "exists" are omitted, but we remark that the described insert-method is in fact the canonical one [22].

PERSONC ==
   Structure PAIR(PERSON , spouse : PERSONC)
   Constraints $\forall$ I,J :: ID . $\forall$ V :: T_C . member(Pair(I,V),x_C) = true $\wedge$
   member(Pair(J,V),x_C) = true $\Rightarrow$ I = J
   Methods
     insert(P :: V_C = PAIR(PERSON,V_C)) == I $\leftarrow$ insert$'$(P)
   (**hidden**)
   I :: ID $\leftarrow$ insert$'$(P :: $\overline{V_C}$ = PAIR(PERSON,UNION($\overline{V_C}$,ID))) ==
   B :: BOOL | (B $\leftarrow$ exists(P,x_C) ;
    B = true $\rightarrow$
     (I :: ID | (member(I,dom(x_C)) = false $\rightarrow$
       P$''$ :: T_C |
       ($\exists$ P$'$ :: T_C . P$'$ = P $\rightarrow$ P$''$:= P $\otimes$
       (J :: ID | J $\leftarrow$ insert$'$(substitute(P,I,second(P))) ;
       P$''$:= Pair(first(P),J))) ;
     x_C := union(x_C,single(Pair(I,P$''$)))))
    $\otimes$ skip
End PERSONC   □

4 Enforcing Static Integrity

An alternative to consistency verification is the computation of methods that enforce all constraints of a schema. We now address this problem first for static constraints and generalize Theorem 8. Our approach starts with a formalization of the integrity enforcement problem focussing on GCSs. We show that GCSs always exist and are unique (up to semantic equivalence). On this formal basis we are able to describe certain compatibility results and outline the structure of GCSs with respect to basic update operations and distinguished classes of static constraints.

4.1 The Problem

Suppose now to be given an update operation S and a static constraint $\mathcal{I}$. Assume that S is an X-operation, whereas $\mathcal{I}$ is defined on Y with $X \subseteq Y$. The idea is to construct a "new" Y-operation $S_{\mathcal{I}}$ that is consistent with respect to $\mathcal{I}$ and can be used to replace S. Roughly speaking this means that the effect of $S_{\mathcal{I}}$ on the state variables in X should not be different from the effect of S. Formally this is expressed by the specialization relation introduced in Definition 4. Clearly, if any there will be more than one such specialization. Hence the idea to distinguish one of them as the "greatest", i.e. all others should specialize it.

Before giving now the definition of a GCS let us first remark that for any predicate transformer f the *conjugate predicate transformer* f^* is defined by $f^*(\mathcal{R}) = \neg f(\neg\mathcal{R})$. Hence the following definition of a *greatest consistent specialization*:

Definition 9. Let $X \subseteq Y$ be state spaces, S an X-operation and $\mathcal{I}$ a static integrity constraint on Y. A Y-operation $S_{\mathcal{I}}$ is a *Greatest Consistent Specialization* (GCS) of S with respect to $\mathcal{I}$ iff

(i) $wlp(S)(\mathcal{R}) \Rightarrow wlp(S_{\mathcal{I}})(\mathcal{R})$ holds on Y for all formulae $\mathcal{R}$ with $fr(\mathcal{R}) \subseteq X$,
(ii) $wp(S(true) \Rightarrow wp(S)_{\mathcal{I}})(true)$ holds on Y,
(iii) $\mathcal{I} \Rightarrow wlp(S_{\mathcal{I}})(\mathcal{I})$ holds on Y and
(iv) for each Y-operation T satisfying properties (i) – (iii) (instead of $S_{\mathcal{I}}$) we have

    (a) $wlp(S_{\mathcal{I}})(\mathcal{R}) \Rightarrow wlp(T)(\mathcal{R})$ for all formulae $\mathcal{R}$ with $fr(\mathcal{R}) \subseteq X$ and
    (b) $wp(S_{\mathcal{I}})(true) \Rightarrow wp(T)(true)$.

Note that properties (i) and (ii) require $S_{\mathcal{I}}$ to be a specialization of S. Property (iii) requires $S_{\mathcal{I}}$ to be consistent with respect to the constraint $\mathcal{I}$. Finally, property (iv) states that each consistent specialization T of S with $T \sqsubseteq S$ also specializes $S_{\mathcal{I}}$.

Based on the formal definition of a GCS we can now raise the following questions:

- Does such a GCS always exist? If it does, is it uniquely determined by S and $\mathcal{I}$ (up to semantic equivalence)?
- Is the GCS $S_{\mathcal{I}}$ of a deterministic operation S itself deterministic? If not, how to achieve a deterministic consistent operation?
- Does a GCS $(S_{\mathcal{I}_1})_{\mathcal{I}_2}$ (provided it exists) with respect to more than one integrity constraint depend on the order of enforcement? Is it sufficient to take $(S_{\mathcal{I}_1})_{\mathcal{I}_2}$ in order to enforce integrity with respect to $\mathcal{I}_1 \wedge \mathcal{I}_2$?
- What is the relation between integrity enforcement and inheritance, i.e. is the GCS $T_{\mathcal{I}}$ of a specialization T of S a specialization of the GCS $S_{\mathcal{I}}$ of S?
- How does a GCS look like (if it exists)?

Partial results for these questions will be discussed in the next subsections.

4.2 Greatest Consistent Specializations

Let us first address the existence problem. Based on the axiomatic semantics via predicate transformers we can show that a GCS always exists and is uniquely determined up to semantic equivalence. First, however, we need some general properties concerning the specialization order $\sqsubseteq$.

Lemma 10. *Let $\mathcal{T}$ be a set of X-operations. Then there exists the least upper bound $S_0 = \bigsqcup_{S \in \mathcal{T}} S$ with respect to $\sqsubseteq$. S_0 is uniquely determined (up to semantic equivalence) and satisfies*

$$(i) \quad wlp(S_0)(\mathcal{R}) \Leftrightarrow \bigwedge_{S \in \mathcal{T}} wlp(S)(\mathcal{R}) \quad and \tag{3}$$

(ii) $wp(S_0)(\mathcal{R}) \Leftrightarrow \bigwedge_{S \in \mathcal{T}} wp(S)(\mathcal{R})$ (4)

for all formulae $\mathcal{R}$ with $fr(\mathcal{R}) \subseteq X$.

Proof. Let S_0 be defined (up to semantic equivalence) by (3) and (4). Then the universal conjunctivity and the pairing condition are trivially satisfied. It follows that S_0 is an X-operation.

Let $T \in \mathcal{T}$ and $\mathcal{R}$ be an arbitrary formula with $fr(\mathcal{R}) \subseteq X$. Then we have:

– $\bigwedge_{S \in \mathcal{T}} wlp(S)(\mathcal{R}) \Rightarrow wlp(T)(\mathcal{R})$ and

– $\bigwedge_{S \in \mathcal{T}} wp(S)(\mathcal{R}) \Rightarrow wp(T)(\mathcal{R})$.

Thus, S_0 is an upper bound of $\mathcal{T}$. If T_0 is any upper bound of $\mathcal{T}$, we get

– $wlp(T_0)(\mathcal{R}) \Rightarrow wlp(T)(\mathcal{R})$ and
– $wp(T_0)(\mathcal{R}) \Rightarrow wp(T)(\mathcal{R})$

for all $T \in \mathcal{T}$, hence also

– $wlp(T_0)(\mathcal{R}) \Rightarrow \bigwedge_{S \in \mathcal{T}} wlp(S)(\mathcal{R})$ and

– $wp(T_0)(\mathcal{R}) \Rightarrow \bigwedge_{S \in \mathcal{T}} wp(S)(\mathcal{R})$.

It follows that $S_0 \sqsubseteq T_0$, i.e. S_0 is the least upper bound.   □

Note that for $\mathcal{T} = \emptyset$ the least upper bound is *fail*. Now we are prepared to present our result concerning the unique existence of a GCS.

Theorem 11. *Let S be an X-operation, $X \subseteq Y$ and $\mathcal{I}$ a static integrity constraint on Y. Then there exists a greatest consistent specialization $S_{\mathcal{I}}$ of S with respect to $\mathcal{I}$. Moreover, $S_{\mathcal{I}}$ is uniquely determined (up to semantic equivalence) by S and $\mathcal{I}$.*

Proof. Let $\mathcal{T}$ be the set of Y-operations T satisfying (in place of $S_{\mathcal{I}}$ the properties (i) – (iii) of Definition 9 and let $S_{\mathcal{I}} = \bigsqcup_{T \in \mathcal{T}} T$. By definition of a least upper bound $S_{\mathcal{I}}$ satisfies properties (i), (ii) and (iv). Property (iii) follows from Lemma 10(i).   □

Although Theorem 11 states that there is always a (unique) solution of the integrity enforcement problem, it does not help us in constructing a GCS, since its proof is non-constructive. Another general problem is that there are usually more than just one static integrity constraint. If we successively build GCSs, can we guarantee that the final result will be independent of the order of constraints? Is the final result the same, if we simply take the conjunction of all constraints? We address these two problems next.

Theorem 12. *Let $\mathcal{I}_1$ and $\mathcal{I}_2$ be static constraints on Y_1 and Y_2 respectively. If for any operation S the GCS with respect to $\mathcal{I}_i$ is denoted by $S_{\mathcal{I}_i}$ $(i = 1, 2)$, then for any X-command with $X \subseteq Y_1 \cap Y_2$ the GCSs $(S_{\mathcal{I}_1})_{\mathcal{I}_2}$ and $(S_{\mathcal{I}_2})_{\mathcal{I}_1}$ are semantically equivalent.*

Proof. For symmetric reasons it is sufficient to show

$$(S_{\mathcal{I}_1})_{\mathcal{I}_2} \sqsubseteq (S_{\mathcal{I}_2})_{\mathcal{I}_1} \ .$$

We have $\mathcal{I}_2 \Rightarrow wlp((S_{\mathcal{I}_1})_{\mathcal{I}_2})(\mathcal{I}_2)$. Because of the transitivity of the implication $(S_{\mathcal{I}_1})_{\mathcal{I}_2}$ then satisfies properties (i) – (iii) with respect to S and $\mathcal{I}_2$, hence by property (iv) we get $(S_{\mathcal{I}_1})_{\mathcal{I}_2} \sqsubseteq S_{\mathcal{I}_2}$. We have

$$\mathcal{I}_1 \Rightarrow wlp(S_{\mathcal{I}_1})(\mathcal{I}_1) \Rightarrow wlp((S_{\mathcal{I}_1})_{\mathcal{I}_2})(\mathcal{I}_1) \ .$$

The first implication is the consistency of $S_{\mathcal{I}_1}$ with respect to $\mathcal{I}_1$, the second implication follows from property (i) for $(S_{\mathcal{I}_1})_{\mathcal{I}_2}$ with $\mathcal{R} = \mathcal{I}_1$.

Thus, $(S_{\mathcal{I}_1})_{\mathcal{I}_2}$ satisfies properties (i) –(iii) with respect to $S_{\mathcal{I}_2}$ and $\mathcal{I}_1$, i.e.

$$(S_{\mathcal{I}_1})_{\mathcal{I}_2} \sqsubseteq (S_{\mathcal{I}_2})_{\mathcal{I}_1} \text{ by property (iv)}.$$

$\square$

Theorem 13. *Let $\mathcal{I}_1$ and $\mathcal{I}_2$ be static constraints on Y_1 and Y_2 respectively. If for any operation S the GCS with respect to $\mathcal{I}_i$ is denoted by $S_{\mathcal{I}_i}$ ($i = 1, 2$), then for any X-command with $X \subseteq Y_1 \cap Y_2$ the GCSs $(S_{\mathcal{I}_1})_{\mathcal{I}_2}$ and $S_{(\mathcal{I}_1 \wedge \mathcal{I}_2)}$ coincide on initial states satisfying $\mathcal{I}_1 \wedge \mathcal{I}_2$, i.e., $\mathcal{I}_1 \wedge \mathcal{I}_2 \rightarrow (S_{\mathcal{I}_1})_{\mathcal{I}_2}$ and $\mathcal{I}_1 \wedge \mathcal{I}_2 \rightarrow S_{(\mathcal{I}_1 \wedge \mathcal{I}_2)}$ are semantically equivalent.*

Proof. From the transitivity of the implication and Definition 9 it follows that

$$(S_{\mathcal{I}_1})_{\mathcal{I}_2} \sqsubseteq S_{\mathcal{I}_1 \wedge \mathcal{I}_2} \text{ holds.}$$

Then also

$$\mathcal{I}_1 \wedge \mathcal{I}_2 \rightarrow (S_{\mathcal{I}_1})_{\mathcal{I}_2} \sqsubseteq \mathcal{I}_1 \wedge \mathcal{I}_2 \rightarrow S_{\mathcal{I}_1 \wedge \mathcal{I}_2} \text{ holds.}$$

We have to show the converse. Let

$$\bar{S}_{\mathcal{I}_1} = \mathcal{I}_1 \wedge \mathcal{I}_2 \rightarrow S_{\mathcal{I}_1 \wedge \mathcal{I}_2} \otimes S_{\mathcal{I}_1} \ .$$

Then we get $wlp(S)(\mathcal{R}) \Rightarrow wlp(\bar{S}_{\mathcal{I}_1})(\mathcal{R})$ and $wp(S)(\mathcal{R}) \Rightarrow wp(\bar{S}_{\mathcal{I}_1})(\mathcal{R})$ for all formulae $\mathcal{R}$ with $fr(\mathcal{R}) \subseteq X$.

Moreover, $\mathcal{I}_1 \Rightarrow wlp(\bar{S}_{\mathcal{I}_1})(\mathcal{I}_1)$ holds, hence by Definition 9 it follows that $\bar{S}_{\mathcal{I}_1} \sqsubseteq S_{\mathcal{I}_1}$.

If we define

$$\bar{S}_{\mathcal{I}_1, \mathcal{I}_2} = \mathcal{I}_2 \rightarrow \bar{S}_{\mathcal{I}_1} \otimes (S_{\mathcal{I}_1})_{\mathcal{I}_2} \ ,$$

then by analogous arguments we derive $\bar{S}_{\mathcal{I}_1, \mathcal{I}_2} \sqsubseteq (S_{\mathcal{I}_1})_{\mathcal{I}_2}$. In particular we conclude

$$\mathcal{I}_1 \wedge \mathcal{I}_2 \rightarrow \bar{S}_{\mathcal{I}_1, \mathcal{I}_2} \sqsubseteq \mathcal{I}_1 \wedge \mathcal{I}_2 \rightarrow (S_{\mathcal{I}_1})_{\mathcal{I}_2} \ ,$$

but $\mathcal{I}_1 \wedge \mathcal{I}_2 \rightarrow \bar{S}_{\mathcal{I}_1, \mathcal{I}_2}$ is semantically equivalent to $\mathcal{I}_1 \wedge \mathcal{I}_2 \rightarrow \bar{S}_{\mathcal{I}_1}$ and this to $\mathcal{I}_1 \wedge \mathcal{I}_2 \rightarrow (S_{\mathcal{I}_1})_{\mathcal{I}_2}$. Hence the theorem. $\square$

In Section 3.1 we required methods on subclasses that override inherited methods to be specializations. Since we regard methods as operations on some state space defined by the schema, the problem occurs, whether the GCS of a specialized operation T of S remains to be a specialization of the GCS of S. Fortunately this is also true.

Theorem 14. *Let $S_\mathcal{I}$ be the GCS of the X-operation S with respect to the static integrity constraint $\mathcal{I}$ defined on Y with $X \subseteq Y$. Let T be a Z-operation that specializes S. If $\mathcal{I}$ is regarded as a constraint on $Y \cup Z$, then the GCS $T_\mathcal{I}$ of T with respect to $\mathcal{I}$ is a specialization of $S_\mathcal{I}$.*

Proof. From the transitivity of the implication and the consistency of $T_\mathcal{I}$ with respect to $\mathcal{I}$ it follows that $T_\mathcal{I}$ satisfies properties (i) – (iii) of Definition 9, hence $T_\mathcal{I} \sqsubseteq S_\mathcal{I}$. □

In Section 3.1 methods were introduced as deterministic guarded commands. Hence the question whether this property is preserved under GCS construction. Unfortunately this is not true as the following example shows.

Example 2. Let x, y and z be state variables, all of type $FSETS(T)$, where $FSETS(\alpha)$ is the finite set constructor (see e.g. [20]) and T is any value type. Let $X = \{y\}$ and $Y = \{x, y, z\}$. Then we define an X-operation S by

$$S(t :: T) \;==\; y' :: FSET(T) \;|$$
$$y = Union(y', Single(t)) \land member(t, y') = false \;\rightarrow\; y := y'$$

and a static constraint $\mathcal{I}$ on Y by

$$x = Union(y, z) \;\land\; \forall t :: T.member(t, y) = true \Rightarrow member(t, z) = false\;.$$

Then the GCS $S_\mathcal{I}$ has the form

$$S_\mathcal{I}(t :: T) \;==\; \mathcal{I} \;\rightarrow\; S(t)\;;$$
$$(z := Union(z, Single(t) \;\square$$
$$x' FSET(T) \;|\; x = Union(x', Single(t)) \land member(t, x') = false \;\rightarrow$$
$$x := x')\; \otimes\; S(t)\;.$$

We omit the formal proof of the properties of Definition 9. □

A general approach to remove non-determinism is *operational refinement* as defined in [20]. However, operational refinement allows to "complete" a specification of an operation S whenever S is undefined are never terminating. In this paper we do not regard completion via refinement. Therefore, we regard the notion of specialization instead. Due to [20, Proposition 4.1] it is easy to see that whenever S is consistent with respect to a static constraint $\mathcal{I}$, then each specialization T of S does so, too.

Hence a deterministic specialization of $S_\mathcal{I}$ is still a consistent specialization of S with respect to $\mathcal{I}$. The next theorem states that we can choose a maximal one.

Theorem 15. *Let $S_\mathcal{I}$ be the GCS of a deterministic operation S with respect to the static constraint $\mathcal{I}$ and let T be some deterministic specialization of $S_\mathcal{I}$. Then T specializes S. Moreover, if T' is any deterministic specialization of S that is consistent with respect to $\mathcal{I}$, then T' also specializes some deterministic specialization T of $S_\mathcal{I}$.*

Proof. The first statement is trivial, since $\sqsubseteq$ is a partial order.

If T' is a deterministic specialization of S consistent with respect to $\mathcal{I}$, then according to Definition 9 T' must be a specialization of $S_\mathcal{I}$, hence the second statement. □

5 Enforcing Static Integrity in the OODM

Let us now apply the results of Section 4.2 to the OODM presented in Section 3. In this section we restrict ourselves to the basic update operations of Theorem 8 and describe the structure of their GCSs with respect to distinguished classes of static constraints. Moreover, we discuss whether the general problem of GCS construction could be reduced to these basic operations. Unfortunately this is not true.

5.1 Distinguished Classes of Static Constraints

Let us now introduce some kinds of explicit static constraints are generalizations of constraints known from the relational model, e.g. functional and key constraints, general inclusion and exclusion constraints, multi-valued dependencies and path constraints.

Definition 16. Let C, C_1, C_2 be classes in a schema S and let $c^i : T_C \to T_i$ ($i = 1, 2, 3$) and $c_i : T_{C_i} \to T$ ($i = 1, 2$) be functions.

(i) A *functional constraint* on C is a constraint of the form
$$\forall i, i' :: ID. \forall v, v' :: T_C. \; c^1(v) = c^1(v') \wedge member(Pair(i, v), x_C) = true$$
$$\wedge \, member(Pair(i', v'), x_C) = true \Rightarrow c^2(v) = c^2(v') \; . \qquad (5)$$
A functional constraint is called a *value constraint* iff neither T_1 nor T_2 contains ID.

(ii) A *uniqueness constraint* on C is a constraint of the form
$$\forall i, i' :: ID. \forall v, v' :: T_C. \; c^1(v) = c^1(v') \wedge member(Pair(i, v), x_C) = true$$
$$\wedge \, member(Pair(i', v'), x_C) = true \Rightarrow i = i' \; . \qquad (6)$$
A uniqueness constraint on C is called *trivial* iff $T_C = T_1$ and $c^1 = id$ hold.

(iii) A *general inclusion constraint* on C_1 and C_2 is a constraint of the form
$$\forall t :: T. \exists i_1 :: ID, v_1 :: T_{C_1}. \, member(Pair(i_1, v_1), x_{C_1}) = true \wedge c_1(v_1) = t$$
$$\Rightarrow \exists i_2 :: ID, v_2 :: T_{C_2}. \, member(Pair(i_2, v_2), x_{C_2}) = true \wedge c_2(v_2) = t. \, (7)$$

(iv) An *exclusion constraint* on C_1, C_2 is a constraint of the form
$$\forall i_1, i_2 :: ID. \forall v_1 :: T_{C_1}. \forall v_2 :: T_{C_2}. \, member(Pair(i_1, v_1), x_{C_1}) = true$$
$$\wedge \, member(Pair(i_2, v_2), x_{C_2}) = true \Rightarrow c_1(v_1) \neq c_2(v_2) \; . \qquad (8)$$

(v) An *object generating constraint* on C is a constraint of the form
$$\forall i_1, i_2 :: ID. \forall v_1, v_2 :: T_C. \, member(Pair(i_1, v_1), x_C) = true \wedge$$
$$member(Pair(i_2, v_2), x_C) = true \wedge c^1(v_1) = c^1(v_2) \Rightarrow$$
$$\exists i :: ID, v :: T_C. \, member(Pair(i, v), x_C) = true \wedge$$
$$c^1(v) = c^1(v_1) \wedge c^2(v) = c^2(v_1) \wedge c^3(v) = c^3(v_2) \; . \qquad (9)$$

Note that the definition of uniqueness constraints is a generalization of the key concept and object generating constraints are a straightforward generalization of multi-valued dependencies in the relational model [5, 24]. The following definition extends these constraints to path constraints.

Definition 17. (i) Let $C_1, \ldots, C_n$ be classes in a schema S with representation types $T_{C_1}, \ldots, T_{C_n}$ and let referential constraints on C_{i-1}, C_i be defined via $o_i : T_{C_{i-1}} \times ID \to BOOL$. Then $C_1, \ldots, C_n$ define a *path* in S and the corresponding *path expression* is given by
$$member(Pair(i_1, v_1), x_{C_1}) = true \wedge o_2(v_1, i_2) = true \wedge$$
$$member(Pair(i_2, v_2), x_{C_2}) = true \wedge \ldots \wedge o_n(v_{n-1}, i_n) = true \wedge$$
$$member(Pair(i_n, v_n), x_{C_n}) = true \; . \qquad (10)$$

(ii) Let C, C' be classes in a schema $\mathcal{S}$ and let $\mathcal{P}$ be a $\{$ (general) inclusion $|$ exclusion $|$ functional $|$ uniqueness $|$ object generating $\}$ constraint on C, C' or C respectively. If $C_1, \ldots, C_n$ and $C'_1, \ldots, C'_m$ are paths in $\mathcal{S}$ with $C_n = C$ and $C'_m = C'$, then replacing the corresponding path expressions for $member(Pair(i, v), x_C) = true$ and $member(Pair(i', v'), x_{C'}) = true$ respectively in $\mathcal{P}$ defines a *path constraint* $\mathcal{P}'$ on C_1 and C'_1. We assume all free variables in $\mathcal{P}'$ other than x_C and $x_{C'}$ to be universally quantified. More precisely we call $\mathcal{P}'$ a $\{$ *(general) path inclusion $|$ path exclusion $|$ path functional $|$ path uniqueness $|$ path object generating $\}$ constraint.*

5.2 Transforming Static Constraints into Primitive Operations

Let us now try to generalize the result of theorem 8 with respect to explicit static constraints. Let $\mathcal{S}$ be some schema and let $\mathcal{I}$ be an explicit static constraint on $\mathcal{S}$. We want to derive again insert-, delete- and update-operations for each class C in $\mathcal{S}$ such that these are consistent with respect to $\mathcal{I}$. Based on the Conjunctivity Theorem 13 we only approach the problem separately for the classes of constraints introduced in the previous subsection.

Moreover, we apply a specific kind of operational refinement in order to reduce the non-determinism of the resulting GCS. Whenever an arbitrary value of some proper value type is required, then we extend the input-type. However, this can not be applied to reduce the non-determinism arising from choice operations. In general, there exists a *choice normal form* for the GCS such that its components are the maximal deterministic operational refinements of the GCS that exist by Theorem 15.

In the following we restrict ourselves to the case of a single explicit constraint in addition to the one (trivial) uniqueness constraint that is required to assure value-representability and that has been used in [22] to construct *canonical update operations*. Then we look at an example with more than one constraint. We illustrate that although Theorem 13 holds, the structure of $S_{(\mathcal{I}_1 \wedge \mathcal{I}_2)}$ may be not at all obvious.

General (Path) Inclusion Constraints. Let $\mathcal{I}$ be a general inclusion constraint on C_1, C_2 defined via $c_i : T_{C_i} \rightarrow T$ $(i = 1, 2)$. Then each insertion into C_1 requires an additional insertion into C_2 whereas a deletion on C_2 requires a deletion on C_1. Update on one of the C_i requires an additional update on the other class.

Let us first concentrate on the insert-operation on C_1 (for an insert on C_2 there is nothing to do). Insertion into C_1 requires an input-value of type V_{C_1}; an additional insert on C_2 then requires an input-value of type V_{C_2}. However, these input-values are not independent, because the corresponding values of type T_{C_1} and T_{C_2} must satisfy the general inclusion constraint. Therefore we first show that the constraint can be "lifted" to a constraint on the value-representation types. Note that this is similar to the handling of IsA-constraints [22, Lemma 29].

Lemma 18. *Let C_1, C_2 be classes, $c_i : T_{C_i} \rightarrow T$ functions and let V_{C_i} be the value-representation type of C_i $(i = 1, 2)$. Then there exist functions $f_i : V_{C_i} \rightarrow T$ such that for all database instances $\mathcal{D}$*

$$f_1(d_1^{\mathcal{D}}(v_1)) = f_2(d_2^{\mathcal{D}}(v_2)) \Leftrightarrow c_1(v_1) = c_2(v_2) \tag{11}$$

for all $v_i \in codom_{\mathcal{D}}(x_{C_i})$ $(i = 1, 2)$ holds. Here $d_i^{\mathcal{D}} : T_{C_i} \rightarrow V_{C_i}$ denotes the function used in the uniqueness constraint on C_i with respect to $\mathcal{D}$.

Proof. Due to Definition 7 we may define $f_i = c_i \circ (d_i^{\mathcal{D}})^{-1}$ on $c_i(codom_{\mathcal{D}}(x_{C_i}))$ $(i = 1, 2)$.

Then we have to show that this definition is independent of the instance $\mathcal{D}$. Suppose $\mathcal{D}_1$, $\mathcal{D}_2$ are two different instances. Then there exists a permutation π on ID such that $d_i^{\mathcal{D}_2} = d_i^{\mathcal{D}_1} \circ \pi$, where π is extended to T_{C_i}. Then

$$c_i \circ (d_i^{\mathcal{D}_2})^{-1} = c_i \circ \pi^{-1} \circ (d_i^{\mathcal{D}_1})^{-1} = \pi^{-1} \circ c_i \circ (d_i^{\mathcal{D}_1})^{-1} ,$$

since c_i permutes with π^{-1}. Then the stated equality follows. □

Now let V_{C_1, C_2} be a subtype of $V_{C_1} \times V_{C_2}$ defined via the equality $f_1(v_1) = f_2(v_2)$, where $v_i :: V_{C_i}$ are the components of a value and f_i are the functions of Lemma 18. We omit the details. Then we can define the new insert-operation on C_1 by $(insert_{C_1})_{\mathcal{I}}(V :: V_{C_1, C_2}) ==$

$$insert_{C_1}(first(V)) \; ; \; insert_{C_2}(second(V)) . \tag{12}$$

Now we are able to generalize Theorem 8 with respect to general inclusion constraint.

Theorem 19. *Let $\mathcal{I}$ be a general inclusion constraint on C_1, C_2 defined via $c_i : T_{C_i} \rightarrow T$ and let $S_{\mathcal{I}}$ be the insert-operation of (12). Suppose that C_1 is not referenced by C_2. Then $S_{\mathcal{I}}$ is the GCS of the canonical insert-operation of Theorem 8 with respect to $\mathcal{I}$.*

Proof. We use the abbreviations $S_i = insert_{C_i}(V_i :: V_{C_i})$ $(i = 1, 2)$. Then

$$wlp(S_{\mathcal{I}})(\mathcal{R}) \equiv \{V_1/first(V)\}.wlp(S_1)(\{V_2/second(V)\}.wlp(S_2)(\mathcal{R}) .$$

Since S_i is total and always terminating, we have $wlp(S_i) = wp(S_i)$. Since C_1 is not referenced by C_2, we know that S_2 is a $\{x_{C_2}\}$-operation. Therefore, $wlp(S_2)(\mathcal{R})$ is a logical combination of $\mathcal{R}$ without any substitution, hence $wlp(S_1)(\mathcal{R}) \Rightarrow wlp(S_{\mathcal{I}})(\mathcal{R})$. This proves (i) and (ii).

In particular $wlp(S_{\mathcal{I}})(\mathcal{I}) \equiv$

$$\{ x_{C_1}/Union(x_{C_1}, Single(Pair(I_1, V_1))),$$
$$x_{C_2}/Union(x_{C_2}, Single(Pair(I_2, V_2))) \}.\mathcal{I}$$

with $I_1, I_2 :: ID$ and $V_i :: T_{C_i}$ with $c_1(V_1) = f_1(first(V))$ and $c_2(V_2) = f_2(first(V))$, where f_i are the functions of Lemma 18. Then property (iii) follows immediately. We omit the proof of (iv). □

Note there there is no need to require $C_1 \neq C_2$. Delete- and update-operations can be defined analogously to (12). Then a result analogous to Theorem 19 holds. We omit the details here. The generalization to path constraints is also straightforward.

(Path) Functional and Uniqueness Constraints. Now let $\mathcal{I}$ be a functional constraint on C defined via $c^1 : T_C \rightarrow T_1$ and $c^2 : T_C \rightarrow T_2$. In this case nothing is required for the delete operation whereas for inserts (and updates) we have to add a postcondition. Moreover, let $c^{\mathcal{D}} : T_C \rightarrow V_C$ denote the function associated with the value-representability of C and the database instance $\mathcal{D}$ and let all other notations be as before. Let us again concentrate on the insert-operation. Let $insert'_C$ denote the *quasi-canonical insert* on C [22]. Then we define

$$(insert_C)_{\mathcal{I}}(V :: V_C) ==$$

$$I :: ID \mid I \leftarrow insert'_C(V) \,;$$

$$V' :: T_C \mid member(Pair(I, V'), x_C) = true \rightarrow$$

$$(\,\forall J :: ID, W :: T_C. \, (\, member(Pair(J, W), x_C) = true$$

$$\land c^1(W) = c^1(V') \Rightarrow c^2(W) = c^2(V')\,) \rightarrow$$

$$skip \tag{13}$$

Note that in this case there is no change of input-type.

Theorem 20. *Let $\mathcal{I}$ be a functional constraint on the class C defined via $c^1 : T_C \rightarrow T_1$ and $c^2 : T_C \rightarrow T_2$ and let $S_{\mathcal{I}}$ be the insert-operation of (13). Then $S_{\mathcal{I}}$ is the GCS of the canonical insert-operation on C defined by Theorem 8 with respect to $\mathcal{I}$.*

Proof. The proof is analogous to the one of Theorem 19. □

For delete- and update-operations an analogous result holds. We omit the details. The generalization to path constraints is also straightforward.

A uniqueness constraint defined via $c^1 : T_C \rightarrow T_1$ is equivalent to a functional constraint defined via c^1 and $c^2 = id : T_C \rightarrow T_C$ plus the trivial uniqueness constraint. Since trivial uniqueness constraints are already enforced by the canonical update operations, there is no need to handle separately arbitrary uniqueness constraints.

(Path) Exclusion Constraints. The handling of exclusion constraints is analogous to the handling of inclusion constraints. This means that an insert (update) on one class may cause a delete on the other, whereas delete-operations remain unchanged.

We concentrate on the insert-operation. Let $\mathcal{I}$ be an exclusion constraint on C_1 and C_2 defined via $c_i : T_{C_i} \rightarrow T$ $(i = 1, 2)$. Let $f_i : V_{C_i} \rightarrow T$ denote the functions from Lemma 18. Then we define a new insert-operation on C_1 by

$$(insert_{C_1})_{\mathcal{I}}(V :: V_{C_1}) ==$$

$$insert_{C_1}(V) \,;$$

$$\mu S. \,((I :: ID \mid V' :: T_{C_2} \mid member(Pair(I, V'), x_{C_2}) = true$$

$$\land c^2(V') = f_1(V) \rightarrow delete_{C_2}(V') \,; S\,)$$

$$\otimes \; skip\,) \,. \tag{14}$$

Theorem 21. *Let $\mathcal{I}$ be an exclusion constraint on the classes C_1 and C_2 defined via $c_i : T_{C_i} \rightarrow T$ $(i = 1, 2)$ and let $S_{\mathcal{I}}$ be the insert-operation of (14). Then $S_{\mathcal{I}}$ is the GCS of the canonical insert-operation on C_1 defined by Theorem 8 with respect to $\mathcal{I}$.*

Proof. The proof is analogous to the one of Theorem 19. □

For delete- and update-operations an analogous result holds. We omit the details. The generalization to path constraints is also straightforward.

(Path) Object Generating Constraints. Let $\mathcal{I}$ be an object generating constraint on a class C defined via the functions $c^i : T_C \rightarrow T_i$ $(i = 1, 2, 3)$. Then integrity enforcement requires to add additional inserts (deletes, updates) to each insert- (delete-, update-) operation. Let us illustrate the new insert-operation. The handling of delete and update-operations is analogous. As in the case of inclusion constraints we need a preliminary lemma.

Lemma 22. *Let $c^i : T_C \rightarrow T_i$ be functions $(i = 1, 2, 3)$ such that $c^1 \times c^2 \times c^3$ defines a uniqueness constraint on the class C. Then there exist functions $f_i : V_C \rightarrow T_i$ such that $c^i = f_i \circ c^{\mathcal{D}}$ holds for all instances $\mathcal{D}$, where $c^{\mathcal{D}} : T_C \rightarrow V_C$ corresponds to the value-representability of C.*

Proof. Since $c^1 \times c^2 \times c^3$ defines a uniqueness constraint on C, it follows from Definition 7 that there exists some $f : V_C \rightarrow T_1 \times T_2 \times T_3$ with $c^1 \times c^2 \times c^3 = f \circ c^{\mathcal{D}}$. Then $f_i = \pi_i \circ f$, where π_i is the projection to T_i $(i = 1, 2, 3)$, satisfy the required property. $\quad\square$

Then we define a new insert-operation on C as follows:

$$(insert_C)_{\mathcal{I}}(V :: V_C) ==$$

$$\exists I' :: ID, V' :: T_C . \, member(Pair(I', V'), x_C) = true$$

$$\wedge\, c^1(V') = f_1(V) \;\rightarrow$$

$$(\, (\, V'' :: V_C \mid f_1(V'') = f_1(V) \,\wedge\, f_2(V'') = f_2(V)$$

$$\wedge\, f_3(V'') = c^3(V') \;\rightarrow\; insert_C(V'')\,)\,;$$

$$(\, V''' :: V_C \mid f_1(V''') = f_1(V) \,\wedge\, f_2(V''') = c^2(V') \,\wedge$$

$$f_3(V''') = f_3(V) \;\rightarrow\; insert_C(V''')\,)\,)\,;$$

$$\otimes\; skip\,)\,;$$

$$insert_C(V) \tag{15}$$

Theorem 23. *Let $\mathcal{I}$ be an object generating constraint on a class C defined via the functions $c^i : T_C \rightarrow T_i$ $(i = 1, 2, 3)$ such that $c^1 \times c^2 \times c^3$ defines a uniqueness constraint on the class C and let $S_{\mathcal{I}}$ be the insert-operation of (15). Then $S_{\mathcal{I}}$ is the GCS of the canonical insert-operation on C with respect to $\mathcal{I}$.*

Proof. The proof is analogous to the one of Theorem 19. $\quad\square$

For delete- and update-operations an analogous result holds. We omit the details. The generalization to path constraints is also straightforward.

Theorem 24. *Let S be a schema such that each class C in S is value representable. Suppose all explicit constraints in S are general inclusion constraints, exclusion constraints, functional constraints, uniqueness constraints, object generating constraints and path constraints. Then there exist generic update methods $insert_C$, $delete_C$ and $update_C$ for each class C in S that are consistent with respect to all implicit and explicit static constraints on S.*

Proof. The result has been shown above in the Theorems 19–23 for a single explicit constraint. Then the general result follows from Theorem 13. $\quad\square$

5.3   Transforming Static Constraints into Transactions

Let us now consider the case of arbitrary methods which can be used to model transactions. We concentrate on the question whether it is possible to achieve general consistent methods as combinations of consistent primitive operations as e.g. given by Theorem 24. Regard the following simple example:

Example 3.

ACCOUNTCLASS ==
     Structure TRIPLE(PERSON,NAT,NAT)
End ACCOUNTCLASS

Constraints
  $Pair(I, V) \in$ ACCOUNTCLASS $\Rightarrow second(V) + third(V) \geq 0$
  $Pair(I, V) \in$ ACCOUNTCLASS $\land Pair(I', V') \in$ ACCOUNTCLASS $\land$
     $first(V) = first(V') \Rightarrow I = I'$

The second component gives the account of a person and the third component gives his/her credit limit. Let

$transfer(P_1 :: PERSON, P_2 :: PERSON, T :: NAT)$ ==

$I_1, I_2 :: ID, N_1, N_2, M_1, M_2 :: NAT \mid$

$Pair(I_1, Triple(P_1, N_1, M_1)) \in$ ACCOUNTCLASS $\land$

$Pair(I_2, Triple(P_2, N_2, M_2)) \in$ ACCOUNTCLASS $\rightarrow$

$update_{AccountClass}(P_1, Triple(P_1, N_1 - T, M_1))$;

$update_{AccountClass}(P_2, Triple(P_2, N_2 + T, M_2))$

In this case the precondition to be added is simply the weakest precondition, i.e. $N_1 + M_1 - T \geq 0$. Now regard the operation

$S = transfer(P_1, P_2, T_1)$; $transfer(P_2, P_1, T_2)$.

The precondition to be added to S in order to enforce the first constraint simply is $N_1 + M_1 - T_1 + T_2 \geq 0 \land N_2 + M_2 - T_2 + T_1 \geq 0$, which is trivially satisfied if $T_1 = T_2$. However, for large values of $T_1 = T_2$ this condition is weaker then adding three precondition separately.   □

Theorem 25.   *Let S be a method and let $S_1 \ldots S_n$ be canonical update operations on a schema S occurring within S. Let S' result from S by replacing each S_i by its GCS $(S_i)_{\mathcal{I}}$ with respect to some static constraint $\mathcal{I}$. Then $S_{\mathcal{I}}$ and S' are in general not semantically equivalent.*

Proof.   A counterexample has been given in Example 3.   □

As a consequence of this theorem it is even not sufficient to know explicitly the GCS of basic update operations with respect to a single constraint. Although Theorem 13 allows the GCS with respect to more than one constraint to be built successively, we have seen in Theorems 19–23 that the GCS with respect to one constraint is no longer a basic update operation. Let us illustrate this open problem by a simple example.

Example 4.   Let C_1, C_2, C_3 be classes and $c_i : T_{C_i} \rightarrow T$ $(i = 1, 2, 3)$ be functions and suppose there are defined

 − a general inclusion constraint $\mathcal{I}_1$ on C_1 and C_2 via c_1 and c_2,
 − a general inclusion constraint $\mathcal{I}_2$ on C_1 and C_3 via c_1 and c_3 and
 − an exclusion constraint $\mathcal{I}_3$ on C_2 and C_3 via c_2 and c_3.

Clearly, the GCS of the insert-operation on C_1 with respect to $\mathcal{I}_1 \land \mathcal{I}_2 \land \mathcal{I}_3$ is *fail*, which is hard to build successively.   □

6 Enforcing Transition Integrity

In Section 4 we discussed integrity enforcement in a general framework with respect to static constraints. Let us now try to generalize the results for transition constraints. Thus, let S be an X-operation and J a transition constraint on Y with $X \subseteq Y$. The idea is again to construct a "new" Y-operation S_J that is consistent with respect to J and specializes S. Again this leads to the idea to construct a *Greatest Consistent Specialization* of S with respect to J. The difference to the case of static constraints is the use of a different proof obligation for consistency according to Definition 4.

6.1 GCSs with Respect to Transition Constraints

We start giving a formal definition of a *Greatest Consistent Specialization* (GCS) of an operation S with respect to a transition constraint J.

Definition 26. Let $X \subseteq Y$ be state spaces, S an X-operation and J a transition integrity constraint on Y. A Y-operation S_J is a *Greatest Consistent Specialization* (GCS) of S with respect to J iff

(i) $wlp(S)(\mathcal{R}) \Rightarrow wlp(S_J)(\mathcal{R})$ holds on Y for all formulae $\mathcal{R}$ with $fr(\mathcal{R}) \subseteq X$,
(ii) $wp(S)(true) \Rightarrow wp(S_J)(true)$ holds on Y,
(iii) $wlp(\Phi(J))(\mathcal{R}) \Rightarrow wlp(S_J)(\mathcal{R})$ holds on Y for all formulae $\mathcal{R}$ with $fr(\mathcal{R}) \subseteq Y$ and
(iv) for each Y-operation T satisfying properties (i) – (iv) (instead of S_J) we have

    (a) $wlp(S_J)(\mathcal{R}) \Rightarrow wlp(T)(\mathcal{R})$ for all formulae $\mathcal{R}$ with $fr(\mathcal{R}) \subseteq X$ and
    (b) $wp(S_J)(true) \Rightarrow wp(T)(true)$.

Note that properties (i), (ii) and (iii) say that $S_J \sqsubseteq S$, where $\sqsubseteq$ is the specialization order of Definition 4. Property (iv) requires S_J to be consistent with respect to the constraint J. Finally, property (v) states that each consistent specialization T of S with $T \sqsubseteq S$ also specializes S_J.

Based on this formal definition of a GCS we can now raise the same questions as in the static case. Before we state the result on the (unique) existence of GCSs, let us first examine the relation between static and transition constraints. Suppose I is a static constraint on Y, then we may regard I also as a transition constraint. Let I' result from I by replacing each state variable x_i occurring freely in I by x_i'. Then $I \Rightarrow I'$ defines the *corresponding transition constraint* denoted as J_I. Then we know that consistency with respect to I is equivalent to consistency with respect to J_I. This implies the following result:

Theorem 27. *Let S be an X-operation and I a static constraint on Y with $X \subseteq Y$. If S_I and S_{J_I} are the GCSs of S with respect to I and the transition constraint J_I respectively, then these two GCSs are semantically equivalent.*

Proof. This follows directly from Definitions 9 and 26. Using the equivalence of consistency proof obligations with respect to I and J_I implies the two definitions to coincide. $\qquad\qquad\square$

Next, we are able to proof the (unique) existence of a GCS also for transition constraints. As in the static case the proof will be non-constructive, hence does not help to construct a GCS.

Theorem 28. *Let S be an X-operation, $X \subseteq Y$ and $\mathcal{J}$ a transition integrity constraint on Y. Then there exists a greatest consistent specialization $S_{\mathcal{J}}$ of S with respect to $\mathcal{J}$. Moreover, $S_{\mathcal{J}}$ is uniquely determined (up to semantic equivalence) by S and $\mathcal{J}$.*

Proof. The proof is analogous to the one of Theorem 11. □

6.2 Compatibility Results

Let us now address the compatibility problems with respect to the conjunction of constraints, inheritance and refinement. Note that due to Theorem 27 some of the results in Section 4.2 occur as special cases of the results here.

Theorem 29. *Let $\mathcal{J}_1$ and $\mathcal{J}_2$ be transition constraints on Y_1 and Y_2 respectively. If for any operation S the GCS with respect to $\mathcal{J}_i$ is denoted by $S_{\mathcal{J}_i}$ ($i = 1, 2$), then for any X-command S with $X \subseteq Y_1 \cap Y_2$ the GCSs $(S_{\mathcal{J}_1})_{\mathcal{J}_2}$ and $(S_{\mathcal{J}_2})_{\mathcal{J}_1}$ are semantically equivalent.*

Proof. The proof is analogous to Theorem 12. □

Theorem 30. *Let $S_{\mathcal{J}}$ be the GCS of the X-operation S with respect to the transition constraint $\mathcal{J}$ defined on Y with $X \subseteq Y$. Let T be a Z-operation that specializes S. If $\mathcal{J}$ is regarded as a constraint on $Y \cup Z$, then the GCS $T_{\mathcal{J}}$ of T with respect to $\mathcal{J}$ is a specialization of $S_{\mathcal{J}}$.*

Proof. The proof is analogous to the one of Theorem 14. □

Theorem 31. *The GCS $S_{\mathcal{J}}$ of a deterministic X-operation S with respect to a transition constraint $\mathcal{J}$ is in general non-deterministic.*

Proof. This follows from Theorem 27, since determinism is not even preserved by GCSs with respect to static constraints as shown by the counter-example in Example 2. □

Hence the problem remains to remove the non-determinism. Due to [20, Proposition 4.2] it is easy to see that whenever S is consistent with respect to a transition constraint $\mathcal{J}$, then each specialization T of S does so, too.

Theorem 32. *Let $S_{\mathcal{J}}$ be the GCS of a deterministic operation S with respect to the transition constraint $\mathcal{J}$ and let T be some deterministic operational refinement of $S_{\mathcal{J}}$. Then T specializes S. Moreover, if T' is any deterministic specialization of S that is consistent with respect to $\mathcal{J}$, then T' also specializes some deterministic operational refinement T of $S_{\mathcal{J}}$.*

Proof. The proof is analogous to Theorem 15. □

7 Conclusion

In this paper we addressed the problem of integrity enforcement in object-oriented databases. First we introduced a formally defined object-oriented data-model (OODM) that includes inclusion and referential constraints implicitly in a schema and allows in particular explicit static and transition constraints to be defined. We gave formally defined general proof obligations for static and transition consistency. Using a general purpose theorem prover to prove these formulae gives a verification based approach to consistency.

However, the verification approach does not help in writing consistent methods. Hence the idea to replace each update operation (methods in the OODM) by a *Greatest Consistent Specialization* (GCS). We show that such GCSs always exist and are uniquely determined by the operation and the constraints up to semantic equivalence. Moreover, they are compatible with the conjunction of constraints, inheritance and refinement.

An unsolved open problem is the general structure of a GCS including the problem of its computation. One idea is to exploit the structure of a constraint that must involve constructor- and selector-expressions on state vaiables (classes in the OODM). However, this idea is still two vague to be discussed in this paper. Another open problem concerns the generalization to arbitrary dynamic constraints. Lipeck has shown in [16] that dynamic constraints expressed in some generalized propositional temporal logic give rise to transition graphs. It should be possible to derive a suitable proof obligation in the predicate transformer calculus also for such constraints. Then the idea of GCS construction should carry over even to this class of constraints that comprises static and transition constraints.

For the case of the OODM we achieve more specific results for a wide class of static constraints that occur as generalizations of kinds of constraints known from the relational model. We show that integrity enforcement for primitive update operations is possible. Moreover, part of the non-determinism can be removed in a canonical way by extension of the required input-type. In general, however, this is not sufficient, since it is not possible to construct the GCS as a combination of the GCSs of primitive operations.

References

1. S. Abiteboul: *Towards a deductive object-oriented database language*, Data & Knowledge Engineering, vol. 5, 1990, pp. 263 – 287

2. S. Abiteboul, P. Kanellakis: *Object Identity as a Query Language Primitive*, in Proc. SIGMOD, Portland Oregon, 1989, pp. 159 – 173

3. A. Albano, A. Dearle, G. Ghelli, C. Marlin, R. Morrison, R. Orsini, D. Stemple: *A Framework for Comparing Type Systems for Database Programming Languages*, in Type Systems and Database Programming Languages, University of St. Andrews, Dept. of Mathematical and Computational Sciences, Research Report CS/90/3, 1990

4. M. Atkinson, F. Bancilhon, D. DeWitt, K. Dittrich, D. Maier, S. Zdonik: *The Object-Oriented Database System Manifesto*, Proc. 1st DOOD, Kyoto 1989

5. S. Al Fedaghi, B. Thalheim: *Fundamentals of databases - The key concept*, submitted for publication, 1990

6. C. Beeri: *Formal Models for Object-Oriented Databases*, Proc. 1st DOOD 1989, pp. 370 – 395

7. C. Beeri: *A formal approach to object-oriented databases*, Data and Knowledge Engineering, vol. 5 (4), 1990, pp. 353 – 382

8. C. Beeri, Y. Kornatzky: *Algebraic Optimization of Object-Oriented Query Languages*, in S. Abiteboul, P. C. Kanellakis (Eds.): Proc. ICDT '90, Springer LNCS 470, pp. 72 – 88

9. E. W. Dijkstra, C. S. Scholten: *Predicate Calculus and Program Semantics*, Springer-Verlag, 1989

10. H.-D. Ehrich, M. Gogolla, U. Lipeck: *Algebraische Spezifikation abstrakter Datentypen*, Teubner-Verlag, 1989

11. H.-D. Ehrich, A. Sernadas: *Fundamental Object Concepts and Constructors*, in G. Saake, A. Sernadas (Eds.): Information Systems – Correctness and Reusability, TU Braunschweig, Informatik Berichte 91-03, 1991

12. H. Ehrig, B. Mahr: *Fundamentals of Algebraic Specification*, vol.1, Springer 1985

13. P. Fraternali, S. Paraboschi, L. Tanca: *Automatic Rule Generation for Constraint Enforcement in Active Databases*, in U. Lipeck, B. Thalheim (Eds.): Proc. 4th Int. Workshop on Foundations of Models and Languages for Data and Objects "MODELLING DATABASE DYNAMICS", Volkse (Germany), October 19-22, 1992, in this issue

14. A. Heuer: *Objektorientierte Datenbanksysteme*, Addison Wesley, 1992

15. S. Khoshafian, G. Copeland: *Object Identity*, Proc. 1st Int. Conf. on OOPSLA, Portland, Oregon, 1986

16. U. W. Lipeck: *Dynamische Integrität von Datenbanken* (in German), Springer IFB 209, 1987

17. G. Nelson: *A Generalization of Dijkstra's Calculus*, ACM TOPLAS, vol. 11 (4), October 1989, pp. 517 – 561

18. G. Saake, R. Jungclaus: *Specification of Database Applications in the TROLL Language*, in D. Harper, M. Norrie (Eds.): Proc. Int. Workshop on the Specification of Database Systems, Glasgow, 1991

19. K.-D. Schewe, J. W. Schmidt, I. Wetzel, N. Bidoit, D. Castelli, C. Meghini: *Abstract Machines Revisited*, FIDE Technical Report 1991/11, February 1991

20. K.-D. Schewe, I. Wetzel, J. W. Schmidt: *Towards a Structured Specification Language for Database Applications*, in D. Harper, M. Norrie (Eds.): Proc. Int. Workshop on the Specification of Database Systems, Springer WICS, 1991, pp. 255 – 274

21. K.-D. Schewe, B. Thalheim, I. Wetzel, J. W. Schmidt: *Extensible Safe Object-Oriented Design of Database Applications*, University of Rostock, Report CS - 09 - 91, September 1991

22. K.-D. Schewe, J. W. Schmidt, I. Wetzel: *Identification, Genericity and Consistency in Object-Oriented Databases*, in J. Biskup, R. Hull (Eds.): Proc. ICDT '92, Springer LNCS 646, 1992, pp. 341 – 356

23. K.-D. Schewe: *Class Semantics in Object Oriented Databases*, submitted 1992

24. B. Thalheim: *Dependencies in Relational Databases*, Teubner Leipzig, 1991

25. J. Van den Bussche, Dirk Van Gucht: *A Hierarchy of Faithful Set Creation in Pure OODBs*, in J. Biskup, R. Hull (Eds.): Proc. ICDT '92, Springer LNCS 646, 1992, pp. 326 – 340

Monitoring Temporal Permissions using Partially Evaluated Transition Graphs

Scarlet Schwiderski

Computer Laboratory, University of Cambridge

Cambridge, CB2 3QG, UK

Gunter Saake

Informatik, Abt. Datenbanken, Technische Universität Braunschweig

D–W 3300 Braunschweig, FRG

Abstract

The conceptual design of a database application includes not only the design of its static structure but also the design of its dynamic behaviour. Temporal permissions are one of several concepts which can be used to specify dynamic database behaviour. They are used as enabling conditions for the occurrence of specific state-changing operations. Temporal permissions refer to the whole past life cycle of a database and are therefore specified in a past tense temporal logic. An efficient method for monitoring past tense temporal formulae, presented in this paper, avoids storing the whole past life cycle of the database. Instead, past tense temporal formulae are partially evaluated during database runtime using special evaluation schemes (so-called transition graphs). Necessary information about the database history is represented as a non-temporal predicate logic formula. The actual evaluation of a past tense temporal formula can then be reduced to evaluating this non-temporal formula.

1 Introduction

The design of database applications is an increasingly important field of today's database research. Apart from a static structure, database applications have a dynamic behaviour which has to satisfy certain criteria. For that reason, appropriate design methods must have special concepts dealing with the specification of dynamic properties. One of these concepts is the specification of certain conditions to ensure the integrity of the stored data, so-called integrity constraints.

Static database integrity deals with the integrity of the stored data in a single database state. Formulae of first order predicate logic are used to specify such conditions, so-called static integrity constraints.

Dynamic database integrity deals with the integrity of the stored data in a sequence of database states. This so-called state sequence describes the dynamic behaviour of the database over the course of time. Formulae of temporal logic are used to specify such conditions, so-called dynamic integrity constraints [1-10].

Straightforward monitoring of static integrity constraints during database runtime is in principle comparatively easy. The database contents must be checked after each state transition. If there is one constraint violated in the new state, the state transition can be withdrawn and the old state is recovered. Nevertheless, efficient methods for monitoring static integrity constraints are still lacking.

Monitoring dynamic integrity constraints is much more difficult. Dynamic integrity constraints are formulae of temporal logic, which is first order predicate logic extended by temporal quantifiers like "always" and "sometime". Temporal quantifiers can be related either to the future database development (future tense temporal logic : FTTL) or to the past database development (past tense temporal logic : PTTL) [11]. In both cases temporal formulae are evaluated in state sequences; the future state sequence in the case of FTTL and the past state sequence in the case of PTTL.

Monitoring future-directed dynamic integrity constraints has already been discussed in several papers [4, 9, 10]. The methods proposed make use of special evaluation schemes, so-called transition graphs, for the stepwise evaluation of temporal formulae. The subject of this paper is monitoring past-directed dynamic integrity constraints. Temporal permissions are past-directed dynamic integrity constraints and are used as enabling conditions for the occurrence of specific state-changing operations, for example in the TROLL language [12]. This paper especially deals with monitoring temporal permissions of TROLL, although the results can be used for all past-directed dynamic integrity constraints.

An algorithm for monitoring temporal permissions during database runtime is developed in this paper. Transition graphs similar to those of FTTL are used for the stepwise evaluation of temporal permissions.

The fundamental idea of the developed monitoring algorithm is shown in the next chapter with the help of a simple example. Before the algorithm itself is discussed in chapter 6 the main foundations about past tense temporal logic (chapter 3), transition graphs (chapter 4) and temporal permissions (chapter 5) are introduced briefly. The conclusions follow in chapter 7.

2 Principal Idea

The principal idea of the proposed method is introduced with the help of a simple example:

A person (p) can only get his PhD certificate (get_PhD(p)), if he has submitted his thesis some time in the past (sometime_past(submit_thesis(p))).

$$\{ \text{ sometime\_past(submit\_thesis(p)) } \} \qquad ** = \varphi **$$
$$\text{get\_PhD(p)}$$

The past tense temporal formula φ is a temporal permission of the so-called event get_PhD(p).

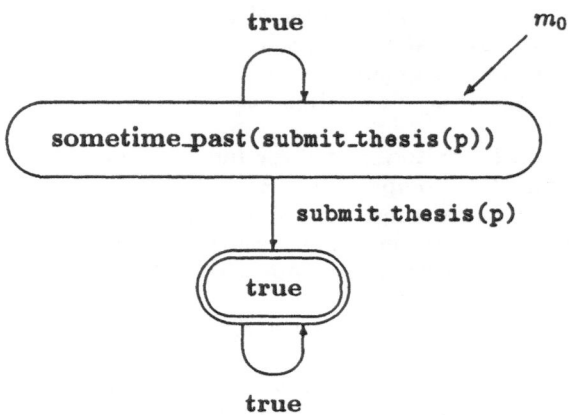

Figure 1: Transition graph of φ

An evaluation scheme, a so-called *transition graph*, can be constructed from φ using generally applicable construction algorithms. This transition graph (figure 1) allows the stepwise evaluation of φ, starting at node m_0 in the current state, evaluating edges in corresponding states of the past state sequence while going backwards in time and ending at the initial state of the database life cycle. In this way either the validity or invalidity of φ can be derived.

However, there is a serious problem with applying this method directly: it implies storing the complete past state sequence of the database, that is, the whole database history. The permanently growing stored data and the more and more complex evaluation would not allow an efficient handling of monitoring temporal permissions.

The basic idea of the method proposed in this paper is to evaluate the transition graph in the reverse direction. This way, the evaluation starts at the "end nodes" (indicated by a double line) in the initial state, evaluating the state sequence going forward in time and ending at the current state of the database life cycle.

The catch with applying this idea to our example is that there is a free variable p in φ, whose value is not determined in the initial state of the database life cycle. All permitted values of p are therefore possible. The temporal permission φ must be evaluated in anticipation for all these possible values. The solution is to store information about all admissible values of p for which φ is valid. In our example, this simply means that the value of p is stored after the event submit_thesis(p) occurred.

        occurring event : submit_thesis(Tim)
        stored value :   p = Tim

In the following sections we present a formal algorithm realizing an evaluation following the sketched idea. This algorithm consists of three parts: the first part deals with the evaluation of a single edge of a transition graph in a certain database state (algorithm 6.5), the second part shows a method to store the derived edge-information with the nodes of the transition graph (algorithm 6.11) and the third part integrates the other parts to an algorithm for the complete evaluation of the transition graph (algorithm 6.12).

3 Past Tense Temporal Logic (PTTL)

PTTL is an extension of first order predicate logic (PL) [13]. Syntax and semantics correspond to known linear temporal logics [14, 15, 7, 6, 5, 8, 11]. These linear temporal logics are future-directed and will therefore be referred to as future tense temporal logic (FTTL) hereafter.

3.1 Syntax of PTTL

The syntax of a language of mathematical logic is given by the definition of its formulae. Symbols are the basic elements for building formulae. Therefore we first define the symbols of PTTL before defining the formulae of PTTL themselves.

Definition 3.1 The symbols of PTTL are

- a signature $\Sigma = (S, \Omega, \Pi)$ with

  - $S = \{s_1, s_2, \ldots\}$, a set of sorts
  - $\Omega = \{f_1 : s_{1_1} \times \ldots \times s_{1_{n_1}} \rightarrow s_{1_0}, f_2 : s_{2_1} \times \ldots \times s_{2_{n_2}} \rightarrow s_{2_0}, \ldots\}$,
    a set of function symbols
  - $\Pi = \{p_1 : s_{1_1} \times \ldots \times s_{1_{m_1}}, p_2 : s_{2_1} \times \ldots \times s_{2_{m_2}}, \ldots\}$,
    a set of predicate symbols

- a set of **variables** $X = \{x_1 : s_1, x_2 : s_2, \ldots\}$

- **special symbols** like $\neg, \wedge, \vee, \exists, \forall$, *previous, existsprevious, always_past, sometime_past, always...since_last, sometime...since_last*

  previous and *existsprevious* are called **previoustime operators**. *always_past, sometime_past, always...since_last* and *sometime...since_last* are called **(past tense) temporal quantifiers**.

  In addition to PL, PTTL formulae can be built by using the introduced previoustime operators *previous* and *existsprevious* and temporal quantifiers *always_past, sometime_past, always...since_last* and *sometime...since_last*.

Definition 3.2 The formulae of PTTL are built as follows:

- Each PL formula φ is a formula.

- If φ and ψ are formulae, then $\neg \varphi$ and $\varphi \vee \psi$ are formulae.

- If φ is a formula, then *previous* φ and *existsprevious* φ are formulae.

- If φ and ψ are formulae, then *always_past* φ, *sometime_past* φ, *always* φ *since_last* ψ and *sometime* φ *since_last* ψ are formulae.

3.2   Semantics of PTTL

The semantics of a language of mathematical logic is given by the definition of an interpretation structure, in which the symbols of the language are interpreted. In the case of PTTL we need state sequences as interpretation structures, because PTTL formulae are evaluated in a sequence of database states; as opposed to PL formulae, which are evaluated in a single database state.

Definition 3.3 An interpretation of a signature $\Sigma = (S, \Omega, \Pi)$ is a Σ-structure $A(\Sigma) = (A(S), A(\Omega), A(\Pi))$ where

- $A(S)$ a set $A(s)$ for each sort $s \in S$

- $A(\Omega)$ functions $A(f): A(s_1) \times \ldots \times A(s_n) \to A(s_0)$ for each
  $f: s_1 \times \ldots \times s_n \to s_0 \in \Omega$

- $A(\Pi)$ predicates $A(p) \subseteq A(s_1) \times \ldots \times A(s_m)$ for each $p: s_1 \times \ldots \times s_m \in \Pi$

The definition of an interpretation is the same as for PL.

Definition 3.4 A state sequence $\hat{\sigma} = \langle \sigma_0, \sigma_1, \ldots, \sigma_i \rangle$ is a non-empty sequence of Σ-structures $\sigma_j = A_j(\Sigma)$, where $0 \leq j \leq i$.
σ_{i-j}, where $0 \leq j \leq i$, denotes the partial sequence $\langle \sigma_0, \sigma_1, \ldots, \sigma_{i-j} \rangle$ of $\hat{\sigma}$.

In PL we are looking at single database states, that is, at single Σ-structures $\sigma = A(\Sigma)$. Here, however we are looking at sequences of database states and therefore at sequences of Σ-structures $\hat{\sigma} = \langle \sigma_0, \sigma_1, \ldots, \sigma_i \rangle = \langle A_0(\Sigma), A_1(\Sigma), \ldots, A_i(\Sigma) \rangle$. In this way we can evaluate formulae containing previoustime operators and temporal quantifiers.

Definition 3.5 A local substitution β_j of variables X is an assignment $\beta_j(x:s) \in A_j(s)$ for each variable $(x:s) \in X$. **A global substitution** $\hat{\beta}$ of variables X is a sequence $\langle \beta_0, \beta_1, \ldots, \beta_i \rangle$ of local substitutions, which satisfies the following condition for each $(x:s) \in X$ with $0 \leq m, n \leq i$.

$$\beta_m(x) \in (\sigma_m(s) \cap \sigma_n(s)) \Rightarrow (\beta_m(x) = \beta_n(x))$$

Most PL and PTTL formulae contain free variables, whose values must be determined before the formulae themselves can be evaluated. In case of PL we need one variable-value-mapping for one database state (local substitution). In case of PTTL we need a sequence of these mappings, one for each state of the state sequence. We demand that each of these local substitutions maps variables to the same elements as long as possible (global substitution) [10].

Lemma 3.6 For a given state sequence $\hat{\sigma} = \langle \sigma_0, \sigma_1, \ldots, \sigma_i \rangle$ and a given global substitution $\hat{\beta} = \langle \beta_0, \beta_1, \ldots, \beta_i \rangle$, the validity of PTTL formulae is derived by

$$(\hat{\sigma}, \hat{\beta}) \models \varphi \qquad \text{iff} \qquad (\sigma_i, \beta_i) \models \varphi \text{ for PL formulae } \varphi$$

$$(\hat{\sigma}, \hat{\beta}) \models \neg\varphi \qquad \text{iff} \qquad \text{not } (\hat{\sigma}, \hat{\beta}) \models \varphi$$

$$(\hat{\sigma}, \hat{\beta}) \models \varphi \vee \psi \qquad \text{iff} \qquad (\hat{\sigma}, \hat{\beta}) \models \varphi \text{ or } (\hat{\sigma}, \hat{\beta}) \models \psi$$

$$(\hat{\sigma}, \hat{\beta}) \models \text{existsprevious } \varphi \qquad \text{iff} \qquad |\hat{\sigma}| > 1 \text{ and } (\hat{\sigma}_{i-1}, \hat{\beta}_{i-1}) \models \varphi$$

$$(\hat{\sigma}, \hat{\beta}) \models \text{previous } \varphi \qquad \text{iff} \qquad |\hat{\sigma}| > 1 \text{ and } (\hat{\sigma}_{i-1}, \hat{\beta}_{i-1}) \models \varphi \\ \text{or } |\hat{\sigma}| = 1$$

$$(\hat{\sigma}, \hat{\beta}) \models \text{always\_past } \varphi \qquad \text{iff} \qquad (\hat{\sigma}_{i-j}, \hat{\beta}_{i-j}) \models \varphi \text{ for all } 0 \le j \le i$$

$$(\hat{\sigma}, \hat{\beta}) \models \text{sometime\_past } \varphi \qquad \text{iff} \qquad \text{there exists } j, \text{ where } 0 \le j \le i, \\ \text{such that } (\hat{\sigma}_{i-j}, \hat{\beta}_{i-j}) \models \varphi$$

$$(\hat{\sigma}, \hat{\beta}) \models \text{always } \varphi \text{ since\_last } \psi \qquad \text{iff} \qquad (\hat{\sigma}_{i-j}, \hat{\beta}_{i-j}) \models \varphi \text{ for all } 0 \le j < k, \\ \text{such that } k = min \\ \{\{m | (\hat{\sigma}_{i-m}, \hat{\beta}_{i-m}) \models \psi\} \cup \{i+1\}\}$$

$$(\hat{\sigma}, \hat{\beta}) \models \text{sometime } \varphi \text{ since\_last } \psi \qquad \text{iff} \qquad \text{there exists } j, \text{ where } 0 \le j < k, \\ \text{such that } (\hat{\sigma}_{i-j}, \hat{\beta}_{i-j}) \models \varphi, \\ \text{where } k = min \\ \{\{m | (\hat{\sigma}_{i-m}, \hat{\beta}_{i-m}) \models \psi\} \cup \{i+1\}\}$$

It should be noted that the state sequence $\hat{\sigma} = \langle \sigma_0, \ldots, \sigma_i \rangle$ is evaluated backwards starting at the last state σ_i.

4 Transition Graphs

The semantics of PTTL gives no hint on how PTTL formulae can be evaluated systematically. An evaluation method allowing a stepwise formulae evaluation is therefore needed. Transition graphs, whose construction and evaluation is discussed in this section, present such an evaluation method.

Lemma 4.1 For arbitrary PTTL formulae φ and ψ, the following **temporal recursion rules** are valid:

$$\text{always\_past } \varphi \iff \varphi \wedge \text{previous } (\text{always\_past } \varphi)$$

$$\text{sometime\_past } \varphi \iff \varphi \vee \text{existsprevious } (\text{sometime\_past } \varphi)$$

$$\text{always } \varphi \text{ since\_last } \psi \iff \psi \vee (\varphi \wedge \text{previous } (\text{always } \varphi \text{ since\_last } \psi))$$

$$\text{sometime } \varphi \text{ since\_last } \psi \iff (\neg\psi \wedge \varphi) \vee (\neg\psi \wedge \\ \text{existsprevious } (\text{sometime } \varphi \text{ since\_last } \psi))$$

These recursion rules (see also [4, 5]) allow the decomposition of a temporally quantified formulae into a non-temporal and a temporal part. The non-temporal part can be evaluated in the current database state. The evaluation of the temporal part is postponed until the previous database state.

Lemma 4.2 Every PTTL formula φ can be transformed into an equivalent formula φ' of the form

$$\varphi' = \bigvee_k (\zeta_k \wedge \text{previous } \gamma_k [\wedge \text{existsprevious } \delta_k])$$

such that

- each ζ_k is a conjunction of basic PL subformulae of φ or their negations,

- each γ_k, δ_k is a conjunction of basic PL subformulae of φ, subformulae of φ bounded by temporal quantifiers or their negations.

The structure of φ' is called **Disjunctive Past tense Temporal Normalform (DPTN)**.

PTTL formulae are transformed into their DPTN by using the above temporal recursion rules and the basic rules of PL.

Definition 4.3 A **transition graph** $T = (G, \nu, \eta, m_0, F)$ consists of

1. a directed graph $G = (N, E)$ with nodes N and edges E,

2. a **node labelling** $\nu: N \rightarrow PTTL$,

3. an **edge labelling** $\eta: E \rightarrow PL$,

4. a non-empty **initial marking** $m_0 \subseteq N$ and

5. a set of **final nodes** $F \subseteq N$.

A transition graph T_φ can be constructed from every PTTL formula φ using the following construction algorithm (see also [4, 5]).

Algorithm 4.4 For a given PTTL formula φ, the corresponding transition graph T_φ of φ is constructed as follows:

1. Initialize T_φ
   $E := \{\}$;
   $N := \{0\}$;
   $\nu(0) := \varphi$;
   $m_0 := \{0\}$;
   $F := \{\}$;

2. **for each** node $n \in N$ in T_φ
   do transform the node label $\nu(n)$ into its DPTN $\nu(n)'$;
       for each $(\zeta \wedge previous\ \gamma)$ in $\nu(n)'$
       do if $\nu(m) \neq \gamma$ for all $m \in F$
           then add a new node k with $\nu(k) = \gamma$ to N;
               $F := F \cup \{k\}$;
       fi;
       let k be the node in F with $\nu(k) = \gamma$;
       add a new edge (n, k) with $\eta((n, k)) = \zeta$ to E;
   od;
       for each $(\zeta \wedge previous\ \gamma \wedge existsprevious\ \delta)$ in $\nu(n)'$
       do if $\nu(m) \neq \gamma \wedge \delta$ for all $m \in N - F$
           then add a new node k with $\nu(k) = \gamma \wedge \delta$ to $N - F$;
       fi;
       let k be the node in F with $\nu(k) = \gamma \wedge \delta$;
       add a new edge (n, k) with $\eta((n, k)) = \zeta$ to E;
    od;

if there are several edges from n to k
then substitute these edges by one labelled with
      the disjunction of the old edge labels;
  fi;
od;

The transition graph T_φ of a PTTL formula φ is the basis for the stepwise evaluation of φ in a state sequence $\hat{\sigma} = \langle \sigma_0, \sigma_1, \ldots, \sigma_i \rangle$, starting in state σ_i and going backwards to state σ_0.

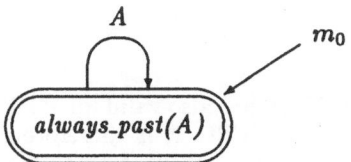

Figure 2: Transition graph of *always_past(A)*

The example in figure 2 shows the transition graph of the PTTL formula *always_past(A)*.

The basic idea of the following algorithm for the stepwise evaluation of a PTTL formula in a state sequence is to initially mark the initial nodes of the transition graph and to stepwise determine new markings in the currently observed states of the sequence. To do this, we evaluate the edge labels of the outgoing edges of the nodes of the current marking, which are simple PL formulae. If the edge label is valid in the current state, we unmark the start-node of the edge and mark the end-node. If all outgoing edge labels are invalid, we unmark the start-node only. After that, the current state is decreased and the procedure is repeated till the initial state σ_0. The PTTL formula is valid, iff there is a final node (indicated by a double line) marked in the last marking.

Definition 4.5 A **current marking** cm of a transition graph T_φ is a non-empty set of its nodes, $cm \subseteq N$.

Algorithm 4.6 Past-directed evaluation of a transition graph
For the given transition graph T_φ of a PTTL formula φ, a state sequence $\hat{\sigma} = \langle \sigma_0, \sigma_1, \ldots, \sigma_i \rangle$ and a global substitution $\hat{\beta} = \langle \beta_0, \beta_1, \ldots, \beta_i \rangle$ where $\beta_i(x : s) \in \sigma_j(s)$ for all x free in φ and $0 \leq j \leq i$, the transition graph is evaluated as follows:

```
begin
    ind := i;
    cm := m0;              (* cm : current marking *)
    while ind ≥ 0 do
        new_cm := {};
        for each (n1, n2) ∈ E with n1 ∈ cm and (σind, βind) ⊨ η(n1, n2)
        do
            new_cm := new_cm ∪ {n2};
        end
```

```
        cm := new_cm;
        if cm = {}
        then return ((σ̂, β̂) ⊭ φ);              (* φ is invalid *)
        fi
        ind := ind − 1;
    od
    if ∃n ∈ N : n ∈ {F ∩ cm}
    then return ((σ̂, β̂) ⊨ φ);                 (* φ is valid *)
    else return ((σ̂, β̂) ⊭ φ);                 (* φ is invalid *)
    fi
end
```

All properties of FTTL are also valid for PTTL, because PTTL is a directly reflected mirror image of FTTL. It is therefore not necessary to give proof of the lemmata and algorithms presented in this section. For further details of the theory and application of transition graphs see [4, 5, 9, 16, 17].

5 Temporal Permissions

The temporal permissions referred to in this paper are rooted in TROLL, which is a language for the object-oriented specification of information systems [12, 18, 19]. An information system in TROLL is a collection of interacting objects. A single object contains a static structure as well as a dynamic behaviour. The static structure is specified through typed attributes. The dynamic behaviour is specified through events, whose occurrence can depend on a number of conditions. Temporal permissions are one class of these conditions. They are enabling conditions for the occurrence of specific events and are specified as formulae of PTTL. A PTTL formula is evaluated in the past state sequence of the database and must be fulfilled (that is, valid) in the current state, if the corresponding event is to occur.

Example 5.1 An object, named PhD_students, is partially specified as follows:

```
object PhD_students
    . . .
    attributes
        students : set(name);
        . . .
    events
        submit_thesis(p:name);
        get_PhD(p:name);
        . . .
    permissions
        { p ∈ students } get_PhD(p);
        { sometime_past(submit_thesis(p)) } get_PhD(p); . . .
    . . .
    end object PhD_students;
```

The object **PhD_students** contains a set of student names. Two events are specified

- **submit_thesis(p)** : A PhD student submits a thesis.
- **get_PhD(p)** : A PhD student gets a PhD.

The event **get_PhD(p)** is only applicable to students p. This fact is expressed in form of a (simple) permission in the section **permissions**. This permission is called simple, because it is a formula of PL.

The event **submit_thesis(p)** must have occurred before the event **get_PhD(p)** can occur. This fact is expressed in form of a (temporal) permission in the section **permissions**. This permission is called temporal, because it contains a temporal operator.

Event terms, like **submit_thesis(p)** in our example, are predicates of the PTTL used here; and attributes, like **students**, are terms of the PTTL.

A state of an object life cycle is characterized by the current attribute values and an occurring event.

The syntax of the PTTL used here is slightly different from original **TROLL**.

6 Monitoring Temporal Permissions

Now we will discuss the question of how temporal permissions can be monitored efficiently during database runtime.

Temporal permissions are formulae of PTTL. Therefore a transition graph can be constructed from every temporal permission (algorithm 4.4). This transition graph allows the stepwise evaluation of the temporal permission in the past state sequence of the database, going backwards to the initial state (algorithm 4.6). Using this method directly would imply storing the past state sequence, that is, the whole database history. This way, we cannot monitor temporal permissions efficiently.

The single steps in our method for monitoring temporal permissions are illustrated by the following example.

Example 6.1 The following condition expresses that a person p can only start a PhD course at the university u (**start_PhD(p,u)**), if he first applied for admission (**apply_for_admission(p,u)**) and afterwards got admission (**get_admission(p,u)**).

{sometime_past(apply_for_admission(p,u)) and
  sometime(get_admission(p,u))since_last(apply_for_admission(p,u))}
start_PhD(p,u)

The PTTL formula { φ } is a temporal permission of the event start_PhD(p,u). The transition graph T_φ of φ is shown in figure 3.

The crucial step in our method is to evaluate the transition graph in the reverse direction. That is, the evaluation starts in the initial state and goes forward to the current state of the database life cycle.

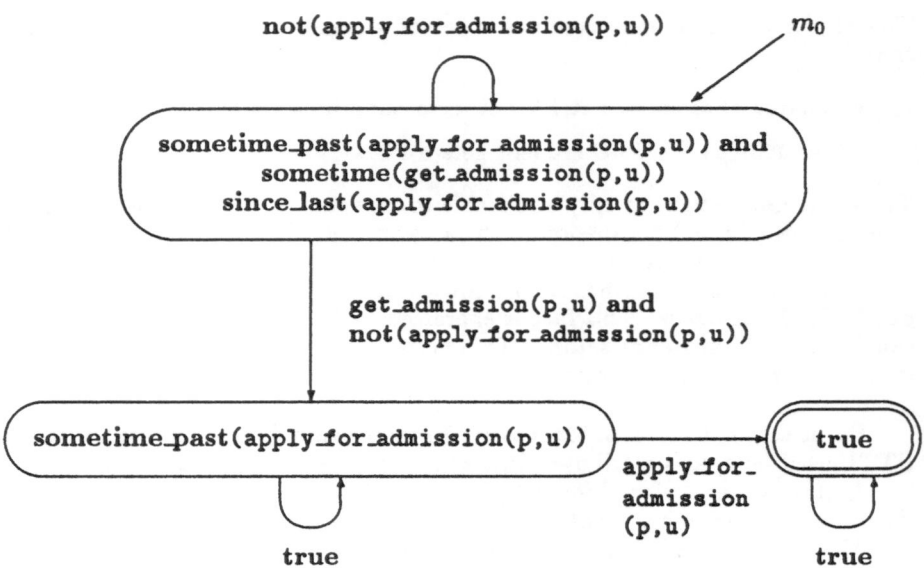

Figure 3: Transition graph T_φ

6.1 Reversed Transition Graphs

A reversed transition graph is defined as follows:

Definition 6.2 If $T_\varphi = \langle G = (N, E), \nu, \eta, m_0, F \rangle$ is the transition graph of a temporal permission φ, then T_φ^{-1} is called **reversed transition graph** of φ, iff

$$T_\varphi^{-1} = \langle G' = (N, E'), \nu, \eta', m_0, F \rangle$$

where E' with $(n_2, n_1) \in E'$ iff $(n_1, n_2) \in E$ and
$\eta' : E' \to PL$ with $\eta'(n_2, n_1) = \eta(n_1, n_2)$

For the construction of the reversed transition graph T_φ^{-1} of a temporal permission φ, we simply reverse the edges of the transition graph T_φ.

Example 6.3 The reversed transition graph T_φ^{-1} of φ is shown in figure 4.

The reversed transition graph T_φ^{-1} of φ is the basis for the stepwise evaluation of φ in a state sequence $\hat{\sigma} = \langle \sigma_0, \sigma_1, \ldots, \sigma_i \rangle$, starting in state σ_0 and going forward to state σ_i.

Algorithm 6.4 Future-directed evaluation of a reversed transition graph

For a given reversed transition graph T_φ^{-1} of a temporal permission φ, a state sequence $\hat{\sigma} = \langle \sigma_0, \sigma_1, \ldots, \sigma_i \rangle$ and a global substitution $\hat{\beta} = \langle \beta_0, \beta_1, \ldots, \beta_i \rangle$ where $\beta_i(x : s) \in \sigma_j(s)$ for all x free in φ and $0 \leq j \leq i$, the reversed transition graph is evaluated as follows:

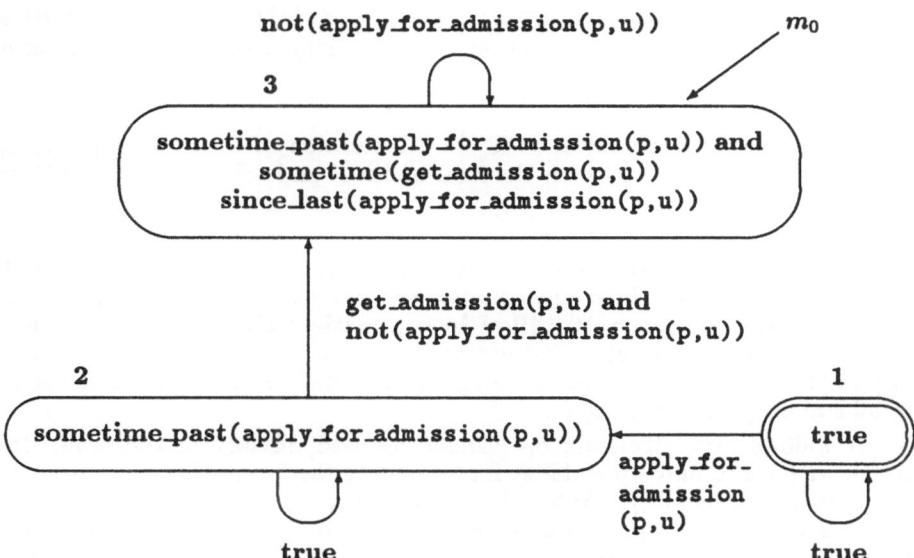

Figure 4: Reversed transition graph T_φ

```
begin
    ind := 0;
    cm := F;                        (* cm : current marking *)
    while ind ≤ i do
        new_cm := {};
        for each (n₁, n₂) ∈ E' with n₁ ∈ cm and
                (σ_ind, β_ind) ⊨ η'(n₁, n₂)
        do
            new_cm := new_cm ∪ {n₂};
        end
        cm := new_cm;
        if cm = {}
        then return ((σ̂, β̂) ⊭ φ);    (* φ is invalid *)
        fi
        ind := ind + 1;
    od
    if ∃n ∈ N : n ∈ {m₀ ∩ cm}
    then return ((σ̂, β̂) ⊨ φ);        (* φ is valid *)
    else return ((σ̂, β̂) ⊭ φ);        (* φ is invalid *)
    fi
end
```

It can be shown that the past-directed evaluation (algorithm 4.6) and the future-directed evaluation (algorithm 6.4) are equivalent [20]. The differences between the past- and future-directed evaluation are:

Past-directed evaluation of T_φ: Evaluation of $\hat\sigma = \langle \sigma_0, \sigma_1, \ldots, \sigma_i \rangle$ starting at state σ_i with the nodes of the initial marking m_0 and going backwards to state σ_0.

Future-directed evaluation of T_φ^{-1}: Evaluation of $\hat\sigma = \langle \sigma_0, \sigma_1, \ldots, \sigma_i \rangle$ starting at state σ_0 with the final nodes F and going forwards to state σ_i.

A given global substitution $\hat\beta = \langle \beta_0, \beta_1, \ldots, \beta_i \rangle$ is a precondition in the algorithm for the future-directed evaluation of a reversed transition graph. **This precondition cannot be fulfilled in a practical situation.** In the final analysis, we need the local substitution β_i in state σ_i, because the free variables of φ are bounded to these values throughout the whole evaluation and therefore in all states σ_j with $0 \le j \le i$.

It follows that algorithm 6.4 cannot be used directly in this way. Instead, we have to find a possibility for evaluating the reversed transition graph substitution-independent. What does that mean? There may be edges in a reversed transition graph, whose labels do not contain variables. An example is an edge with the simple edge label **true**. These edges can be evaluated in the normal way. The other edges, whose labels contain variables, have to be evaluated in a different way. The solution is to divide the evaluation into two steps.

1st step: Substitution-independent evaluation of an edge label in a current state σ_j, where $0 \le j < i$, to derive a "conditional validity" or invalidity of the edge label.

2nd step: Final evaluation of a "conditionally valid" edge label in state σ_i, when the local substitution β_i and therefore the global substitution $\hat\beta$ are given, to derive the validity or invalidity of the edge label.

6.2 Substitution-independent Evaluation of an Edge Label

The idea of the following algorithm is to substitute state-dependent elements of an edge label, namely attributes and events, by their interpretations in the current state and then to simplify this formula as far as possible. The resulting formula, the so-called state information (SI), contains the minimal information about the current state necessary to finally evaluate the edge label in any later state.

Algorithm 6.5 Substitution-independent evaluation of an edge label
For a given edge (n_1, n_2) of a reversed transition graph T_φ^{-1}, a current state $\sigma_{ind} \in \hat\sigma$ and a currently occurring event $event\_id_{cur}(par_{cur_1}, \ldots, par_{cur_n})$, the edge label $\eta'(n_1, n_2)$ of (n_1, n_2) is evaluated as follows:

begin
  $SI_{ind}(n_1, n_2) := \eta'(n_1, n_2);$
  for each attribute *attribute_id* in $SI_{ind}(n_1, n_2)$ **do**
    substitute
      attribute_id
    by
      $\sigma_{ind}(attribute\_id)^1;$
  end
  for each event *event_id* $(par_1, \ldots, par_m)$ in $SI_{ind}(n_1, n_2)$ **do**
    if *event_id* $=$ *event_id*$_{cur}$ **and** $m = n$
    then substitute
        event_id $(par_1, \ldots, par_m)$
      by
        true $\wedge$ $par_1 = par_{cur_1} \wedge \ldots \wedge par_m = par_{cur_n};$
    else substitute
        event_id $(par_1, \ldots, par_m)$
      by
        false;
    fi
  end
  Simplify $SI_{ind}(n_1, n_2);$
end

Definition 6.6 $SI_{ind}(n_1, n_2)$ is called state information of edge (n_1, n_2) in σ_{ind}.

Example 6.7 Algorithm 6.5 is presented for

- edge $(2, 3)$ of T_φ^{-1} with edge label
  $\eta'(2, 3) = \texttt{get\_admission(p,u)}$ **and** $\texttt{not(apply\_for\_admission(p,u))}$

- current state σ_2 with currently occurring event
  $\texttt{get\_admission(Tim,Cam)}$

begin
  $SI_2(2, 3) := \eta'(2, 3);$
  $\texttt{get\_admission(p,u)}$ in $SI_2(2, 3)$ substituted by
    true and $\texttt{p = Tim}$ **and** $\texttt{u = Cam}$;
  $\texttt{apply\_for\_admission(p,u)}$ in $SI_2(2, 3)$ substituted by
    false;
  $SI_2(2, 3) =$ **true and** $\texttt{p = Tim}$ **and** $\texttt{u = Cam}$ **and** $\texttt{not(false)}$
    $= \texttt{p = Tim}$ **and** $\texttt{u = Cam}$;
end

  The state information of an edge label can be **true** ($\equiv$ valid edge label), **false** ($\equiv$ invalid edge label) or a formula, which contains free variables of φ ($\equiv$ "conditionally valid" edge label). The state information contains the conditions about admissible values of the free variables of φ for which the edge label is valid in the current state.

---

[1] That means that the current interpretation of *attribute_id* (single values, lists, sets, tuples, etc.) is inserted, so it is available for later evaluation.

6.3   State Information Transfer

After having presented an algorithm for the evaluation of one edge label, we now present an algorithm for handling the state informations of several edge labels within the stepwise evaluation of a reversed transition graph.

State information is kept with the nodes of a reversed transition graph. The state information of a node can be **true** ($\equiv$ the node belongs to the current marking), **false** ($\equiv$ the node does not belong to the current marking) or a formula, which contains free variables of φ ($\equiv$ the node belongs to the current marking under certain conditions). The state information contains the conditions about admissible values of the free variables of φ for which the corresponding node belongs to the current marking.

Definition 6.8 $SI_{ind}(n)$ is called state information of node n in σ_{ind}.

Notation $ind(n)$ denotes the current index of the state information of node n, therefore the value of ind in $SI_{ind}(n)$.

Algorithm 6.9   Initialization of state information
For a given reversed transition graph T_{φ}^{-1} of a temporal permission φ, the state information is initialized as follows:

begin
    for each $n \in N$ **do**
        if $n \in F$
        then $SI_{-1}(n) :=$ **true**;
        else $SI_{-1}(n) :=$ **false**;
        fi
    end
end

Example 6.10   Initialization of state information for T_{φ}^{-1}:

$$SI_{-1}(3) := \textbf{false};\ SI_{-1}(2) := \textbf{false};\ SI_{-1}(1) := \textbf{true}$$

Algorithm 6.11   Transfer of state information
For a given reversed transition graph T_{φ}^{-1} of a temporal permission φ, a current state $\sigma_{ind} \in \hat{\sigma}$ and a currently occurring event $event\_id_{cur}(par_{cur_1}, \ldots, par_{cur_n})$, the state information is transferred as follows:

begin
    if $ind = 0$
    then Initialize the state information (algorithm 6.9);
    fi
    while $\exists n \in N$ such that $ind(n) = ind(n_{suc}) - 1$
          for all $n_{suc} \in N$ with $(n, n_{suc}) \in E'$ and $n_{suc} \neq n$ **do**
      $SI_{ind}(n) :=$ **false**;
      for each $(n_{pre}, n) \in E'$ **do**
          Derive the state information $SI_{ind}(n_{pre}, n)$
            of (n_{pre}, n) in σ_{ind} (algorithm 6.5);

$$SI_{ind}(n) := SI_{ind}(n) \vee (SI_{ind-1}(n_{pre}) \wedge SI_{ind}(n_{pre}, n));$$
end
Simplify $SI_{ind}(n)$;
Substitute $SI_{ind-1}(n)$ by $SI_{ind}(n)$;
   od
end

The state information transfer starts with the nodes of the initial marking and continues with corresponding predecessor nodes. This is, because the old state informations of the predecessor nodes are needed to derive the new state information of the currently evaluated node.

6.4 Substitution-independent Evaluation of a Reversed Transition Graph

Now we can integrate the derived results and present the main algorithm for the substitution-independent evaluation of a reversed transition graph, which is the revised version of algorithm 6.4 without a given global substitution $\hat{\beta} = \langle \beta_0, \beta_1, \ldots, \beta_i \rangle$.

Algorithm 6.12 Future-directed substitution-independent evaluation of a reversed transition graph

For a given reversed transition graph T_φ^{-1} of a temporal permission φ and a state sequence $\hat{\sigma} = \langle \sigma_0, \sigma_1, \ldots, \sigma_i \rangle$, the reversed transition graph is evaluated as follows:

begin
   $ind := 0$;
   $cm := F$;   (* cm : current marking *)
   while $ind \leq i$ **do**
       $new\_cm := \{\}$;
       for each $(n_1, n_2) \in E'$ with $n_1 \in cm$ and $SI_{ind}(n_1, n_2) \neq$ **false**
       do
          $new\_cm := new\_cm \cup \{n_2\}$;
       end
       $cm := new\_cm$;
       if $cm = \{\}$
       then return $(\neg \exists \hat{\beta} (\hat{\sigma}, \hat{\beta}) \models \varphi)$;   (* φ is invalid *)
       fi
       Transfer the state information of T_φ^{-1} w.r.t. σ_{ind}
          (algorithm 6.11);
       $ind := ind + 1$;
   od
   if $\exists n \in N : n \in \{m_0 \cap cm\}$
   then return $(\exists \hat{\beta} (\hat{\sigma}, \hat{\beta}) \models \varphi)$;   (* φ is conditionally valid *)
   else return $(\neg \exists \hat{\beta} (\hat{\sigma}, \hat{\beta}) \models \varphi)$;   (* φ is invalid *)
   fi
end

Definition 6.13 If $\exists \hat{\beta} \, (\hat{\sigma}, \hat{\beta}) \models \varphi$, then φ is called **conditionally valid in** $\hat{\sigma}$.

The main difference from the old algorithm is that we derive state informations of edges and nodes of T_φ^{-1} and keep the state informations of the nodes throughout the evaluation.

Example 6.14 Algorithm 6.12 is presented for the state sequence $\hat{\sigma} = \langle \sigma_0, \sigma_1, \ldots, \sigma_5 \rangle$ where the following events occur:

σ_0 : `apply_for_admission(Tim,Cam)`
σ_1 : `apply_for_admission(Jon,Ox)`
σ_2 : `get_admission(Tim,Cam)`
σ_3 : `get_admission(Jon,Ox)`
σ_4 : `get_admission(Tim,Ox)`
σ_5 : `apply_for_admission(Jon,Ox)`

begin
$ind := 0$
$cm := \{1\}$

$ind := 0$ / State σ_0 after `apply_for_admission(Tim,Cam)`

First we evaluate the edge labels of the outgoing edges of nodes of cm in the current state σ_0:
$SI_0(1,1) = \mathbf{true};$
$SI_0(1,2) = \text{p = Tim and u = Cam};$
The new current marking is:
$cm = \{1,2\}$
Then we derive the state informations of the nodes of the new current marking. These formulae are stored with the corresponding nodes.
$SI_0(2) = \mathbf{true}$ and p = Tim and u = Cam
$\qquad = \text{p = Tim and u = Cam}$
$SI_0(1) = \mathbf{true}$

$ind := 1$ / State σ_1 after `apply_for_admission(Jon,Ox)`

$SI_1(1,1) = \mathbf{true}$
$SI_1(1,2) = \text{p = Jon and u = Ox}$
$SI_1(2,2) = \mathbf{true}$
$SI_1(2,3) = \mathbf{false}$
$cm = \{1,2\}$
$SI_1(2) = (\mathbf{true}$ and (p = Jon and u = Ox)) or
$\qquad\quad ((\text{p = Tim and u = Cam}) $ and $\mathbf{true})$
$\qquad = (\text{p = Jon and u = Ox}) $ or $ (\text{p = Tim and u = Cam})$
$SI_1(1) = \mathbf{true}$

$ind := 2$ / State σ_2 after `get_admission(Tim,Cam)`

$SI_2(1,1) = SI_2(2,2) = \mathbf{true}$
$SI_2(1,2) = \mathbf{false}$
$SI_2(2,3) = \text{p = Tim and u = Cam}$
$cm = \{1,2,3\}$

$SI_2(3) = ((\text{p = Jon and u = Ox) or (p = Tim and u = Cam)) and}$
$\qquad \text{p = Tim and u = Cam}$
$\qquad = \text{p = Tim and u = Cam}$
$SI_2(2) = (\text{p = Jon and u = Ox) or (p = Tim and u = Cam)}$
$SI_2(1) = \textbf{true}$

$ind := 3$ / State σ_3 after get_admission(Jon,Ox)

$cm = \{1, 2, 3\}$
$SI_3(3) = (\text{p = Jon and u = Ox) or (p = Tim and u = Cam)}$
$SI_3(2) = (\text{p = Jon and u = Ox) or (p = Tim and u = Cam)}$
$SI_3(1) = \textbf{true}$

$ind := 4$ / State σ_4 after get_admission(Tim,Ox)

$cm = \{1, 2, 3\}$
$SI_4(3) = (((\text{p = Jon and u = Ox) or (p = Tim and u = Cam)) and}$
$\qquad \text{p = Tim and u = Ox) or}$
$\qquad (((\text{p = Jon and u = Ox) or (p = Tim and u = Cam)) and true)}$
$\qquad = (\text{p = Jon and u = Ox) or (p = Tim and u = Cam)}$
$SI_4(2) = (\text{p = Jon and u = Ox) or (p = Tim and u = Cam)}$
$SI_4(1) = \textbf{true}$
The event get_admission(Tim,Ox) has no effect on the state information of node 3, because the event apply_for_admission(Tim,Ox) had not occurred before.

$ind := 5$ / State σ_5 after apply_for_admission(Jon,Ox)

$cm = \{1, 2, 3\}$
$SI_5(3) = (((\text{p = Jon and u = Ox) or (p = Tim and u = Cam)) and false)}$
$\qquad \text{or (((p = Jon and u = Ox) or (p = Tim and u = Cam)) and}$
$\qquad \text{not(p = Jon and u = Ox))}$
$\qquad = \text{p = Tim and u = Cam}$
$SI_5(2) = (\text{p = Jon and u = Ox) or (p = Tim and u = Cam)}$
$SI_5(1) = \textbf{true}$
end

φ is conditionally valid in $\hat{\sigma}$, because node $3 \in \{m_0 \cap cm\}$. $SI_5(3)$ contains the necessary information about admissible values of the free variables in φ.

After having presented an algorithm for the substitution-independent evaluation of a reversed transition graph, we now present the second and, therefore, final step of monitoring temporal permissions. That is, the evaluation of a conditionally valid temporal permission in state σ_i of the state sequence $\hat{\sigma} = \langle \sigma_0, \sigma_1, \ldots, \sigma_i \rangle$ w.r.t. a global substitution $\hat{\beta} = \langle \beta_0, \beta_1, \ldots, \beta_i \rangle$.

Theorem 6.15 Evaluation of a conditionally valid temporal permission

Given are φ, a conditionally valid temporal permission in $\hat{\sigma} = \langle \sigma_0, \sigma_1, \ldots, \sigma_i \rangle$ and $\hat{\beta}$, a global substitution $\hat{\beta} = \langle \beta_0, \beta_1, \ldots, \beta_i \rangle$ where $\beta_i(x : s) \in \sigma_j(s)$ for all x free in φ and $0 \leq j \leq i$.

φ is valid in $\hat{\sigma}$ under $\hat{\beta}$, iff there is a state information $SI_i(n)$ with $n \in m_0 \subseteq N$ which is valid in σ_i under β_i, therefore

$$(\hat{\sigma}, \hat{\beta}) \models \varphi \Longleftrightarrow \exists\, n \in m_0\; (\sigma_i, \beta_i) \models SI_i(n).$$

Proof sketch

$\Longrightarrow$: $(\hat{\sigma}, \hat{\beta}) \models \varphi$ means that there is a path through T_φ^{-1} leading to a node $n \in m_0$, whose edges are evaluated to **true** in the corresponding states of $\hat{\sigma}$. Instead of evaluating an edge label all at once, the evaluation can be split into two steps:

1. The state-dependent elements of the edge label, namely attributes and events, are substituted by their current interpretations, and the resulting formula is simplified as far as possible.

2. The free variables of the derived formula are substituted by their current values, and the validity or invalidity of the edge label is derived.

The state information of the edge is obtained in the first step, before the edge label is finally evaluated in the second step. The conjunction of the corresponding state informations of the edges of the path is a subformula of $SI_i(n)$, which is valid in σ_i under β_i, because the free variables of φ are bounded to the same values in all β_j with $0 \leq j \leq i$.

$\Longleftarrow$: $\exists\, n \in m_0\; (\sigma_i, \beta_i) \models SI_i(n)$ means that there are paths through T_φ^{-1} leading to node $n \in m_0$, whose edges are conditionally valid in the corresponding states of $\hat{\sigma}$. $SI_i(n)$ is a disjunction of formulae. Each of these formulae is the conjunction of the corresponding state informations of a particular path. Since there is at least one of these conjunctions valid in σ_i under β_i and the free variables of φ are bounded to the same values in all β_j with $0 \leq j \leq i$, all edges of the corresponding path are evaluated to **true** and φ is therefore valid in $\hat{\sigma}$ under $\hat{\beta}$.

Example 6.16 The event `start_PhD(Tim,Cam)` is to occur in state σ_6. `start_PhD(Tim,Cam)` can only occur, if the temporal permission φ is valid under `p = Tim` and `u = Cam`.

φ is conditionally valid in $\hat{\sigma}$ (see above / example 6.14).
φ is valid in $\hat{\sigma}$ under `p = Tim` and `u = Cam`, because the state information
$$SI_5(3) = \texttt{p = Tim and u = Cam}$$
is valid/**true** under `p = Tim` and `u = Cam`.

The event `start_PhD(Tim,Cam)` can occur.

7 Conclusions

The algorithm presented in this paper can be used for monitoring temporal permissions during database runtime. The fundamental idea is to divide the evaluation of a temporal permission into two steps. The first step is to evaluate the corresponding reversed transition graph in the current state (where no variable-substitution is given) as far as possible. The derived state informations contain conditions about the admissible values of the free variables. These state informations are stored with the nodes of the reversed transition graph. This way, only the minimum necessary information about the database history is stored. The second step, the final evaluation of the temporal permission, can follow in any later state, at which time the temporal permission is checked and a variable-substitution is given. This final evaluation consists of the evaluation of a simple predicate logic formula.

The algorithm shown here is carried out prophylactically for all temporal permissions of the database during the whole database life cycle. The new state informations are evaluated after each state transition.

The final checking of a temporal permission is done independently of this monitoring procedure. This final checking consists of reading the state informations of certain nodes of the reversed transition graph and evaluating them under the given variable-substitution.

Originally this algorithm was meant to be used in the realization of temporal permissions of objects (specified in TROLL) in relational database systems [20]. It can, however, be used in all areas dealing with the monitoring of dynamic integrity constraints formulated in PTTL.

There is a closely related work of Chomicki [21, 22], which also deals with monitoring past-directed dynamic integrity constraints. As in our proposal, monitoring PTTL formulae (called Past TL formulae in his terminology) is reduced to checking simple predicate logic formulae. Chomicki's algorithm is used for monitoring past-directed dynamic integrity constraints in relational database systems.

It is even possible to use the proposed algorithm for monitoring formulae of a combined future tense and past tense temporal logic. The fundamental idea is to combine transition graphs of FTTL subformulae and reversed transition graphs of PTTL subformulae of a given formula and to evaluate the combined transition graph starting at the nodes of the initial marking and the final nodes respectively. The validity of the formula can be derived by checking the final nodes of FTTL subgraphs and the nodes of the initial marking of PTTL subgraphs.

References

[1] Sernadas, A., Temporal Aspects of Logical Procedure Definition, *Information Systems*, Vol. 5, 1980, pp. 167-187.

[2] Ehrich, H.-D., Lipeck, U.W. and Gogolla, M., Specification, Semantics, and Enforcement of Dynamic Database Constraints, in: *Proc. 5th Int. Conf. on Very Large Databases VLDB '84*, Singapore, 1984, pp. 301-308.

[3] Kung, C.H., A Temporal Framework for Database Specification and Verification, in: *Proc. 5th Int. Conf. on Very Large Databases VLDB '84*, Singapore, 1984, pp.91-99.

[4] Lipeck, U.W. and Saake, G., Monitoring Dynamic Integrity Constraints based on Temporal Logic, *Information Systems*, Vol. 12, No. 3, pp. 255-269, 1987.

[5] Saake, G., *Spezifikation, Semantik und Überwachung von Objektlebensläufen in Datenbanken*, Informatik-Skripten 20, TU Braunschweig, 1988.

[6] Saake, G. and Lipeck, U.W., Using Finite-Linear Temporal Logic for Specifying Database Dynamics, In: *Proc. CSL '88, 2nd Workshop Computer Science Logic*, (Börger, E.; Kleine-Büning, H.; Richter, M.M.), Duisburg 1988, LNCS 385, Springer-Verlag, 1989, pp. 288-300.

[7] Lipeck, U.W., *Zur dynamischen Integrität von Datenbanken: Grundlagen der Spezifikation und Überwachung*, Informatik-Fachbericht 209, Springer, Berlin, 1989.

[8] Arapis, C., Temporal Specification of Object Behaviour, in: Thalheim, B.; Demetrovics, J.; Gerhardt, H.-D. (eds.): *Proc. 3rd Symp. Mathematical Fundamentals of Database and Knowlede Base Systems MFDBS '91*, Rostock, 1991, LNCS 495, Springer-Verlag, pp. 308-324.

[9] Hülsmann, K. and Saake, G., Theoretical Foundations of Handling Large Substitution Sets in Temporal Integrity Monitoring, *Acta Informatica*, Vol. 28, 1991, Springer-Verlag, p. 365-407.

[10] Saake, G., Descriptive Specification of Database Object Behaviour, *Data & Knowledge Engineering*, Vol. 6 (1991), pp. 47-73.

[11] Manna, Z. and Pnueli, A., *The Temporal Logic of Reactive and Concurrent Systems, Vol. 1 : Specification*, Springer-Verlag, New York, 1991.

[12] Jungclaus, R., Saake, G., Hartmann, T. and Sernadas, C., Object-Oriented Specification of Information Systems: The TROLL Language, Informatik-Bericht 91-04, TU Braunschweig, 1991.

[13] Hermes, H., *Einführung in die mathematische Logik*, B.G. Teubner, Stuttgart, 3. Auflage, 1972.

[14] Kröger, F., *Temporal Logic of Programs*, Springer-Verlag, Berlin, 1987.

[15] Fiadeiro, J. and Sernadas, A., Specification and Verification of Database Dynamics, *Acta Informatica*, Vol. 25, No. 6, 1988, pp. 625-661.

[16] Lipeck, U.W., Transformation of Dynamic Integrity Constraints into Transaction Specification, *Theoretical Computer Science*, Vol. 76, 1990, pp. 115-142.

[17] Manna, Z. and Wolper, P., Synthesis of Communicating Processes from Temporal Logic Specifications, *ACM Transactions on Programming Languages and Systems*, Vol. 6, 1984, pp. 68-93.

[18] Jungclaus, R, Saake, G. and Hartmann, T., Language Features for Object-Oriented Conceptual Modeling, in: Teory, T.J. (ed.): *Proc. 10th Int. Conf. on the ER-Approach*, San Mateo, 1991, pp. 309-324.

[19] Saake, G. and Jungclaus, R., Specification of Database Dynamics in the TROLL Language, in: Harper, D. and Norrie, M. (eds.), *Proc. Int. Workshop on the Specification of Database Systems*, Glasgow, July 1991, pp. 228-245, Springer, London, 1992.

[20] Schwiderski, S., Realisation von Objekten in einem Relationalen Daten-banksystem, Diplomarbeit, TU Braunschweig, 1992.

[21] Chomicki, J., History-less Checking of Dynamic Integrity Constraints, in: *Proc. of the Eight IEEE Conference on Data Engineering*, F. Golshani, ed., February 1992, Phoenix, Arizona. pp. 557-564.

[22] Chomicki, J., Real-time Integrity Constraints, In: *Proc. 11th ACM SIGACT-SIGMOD-SIGART Symposium on Principles of Database Systems*, June 1992, San Diego, California.

[19] Sonnefeld, R., Klingbeil von Odhr, Werner Bourguin, Bernard, mechanische Eigenschaft 113 Brennstoffe.

[20] Grieser Anderson, Gallegoding, Gerhard, C. H. Silver P. and B. Tyst, IEEE Comput. Science, on Law degrees of Production of Information, Physics America, pp. 567-72.

[21] Grundy, J. L., Burbidge, engine engineering, LTUrev Sinno, D. K. H. Sompson, J. Rwys and Prono ord Agora Co., 1984-1986, Southern California.

Discussion Reports

Discussion Report: Update Languages

Catriel Beeri *

Fachbereich Informatik, Universität Hamburg

Hamburg, Germany

Abstract

This contribution presents basic issues of the discussion on update languages that followed the sessions on "Logic approaches to updates and constraints" and on "Rule-based updates of objects".

In the last five years, we have gained quite a deep understanding of the expressive power of database languages, both for queries and for updates. We now understand that both queries and updates are transformations, hence the tools used to investigate expressive power are often applicable to both cases. In this investigation, various extensions of Datalog have played a central role, particularly those that use negation with inflationary semantics. It was discovered that various control features can be coded in inflationary Datalog¬, so this language can express many interesting computation styles. An additional component that provides expressive power is that of invented values. In the context of object-oriented databases, new objects can play the role of invented values, hence the results about the expressive power in the presence of such values is particularly relevant.

In the talks we have seen several proposals for update languages for object-oriented databases. In contrast to the theoretical investigations that deal with expressive power, these proposals are intended to contribute to the development of practical languages. However, being 'rule-based' or 'logic-based' seems to be a central idea. In those that claim to be computationally complete, the expressive power is achieved by means that are similar to those mentioned above. The moderator of the discussion has therefore put forward for discussion the issue whether this is a good direction to follow. While the simulation of control structures by the various semantics, particularly the inflationary semantics, of deductive programs with negation is of theoretical interest, it is far from being a convenient or easy to understand programming style. If one considers carefully some of the 'deductive' update languages, it becomes obvious that they are not declarative, that they code ordering in time of actions by the ordering of literals in rules' bodies, and that their semantics may be quite difficult to understand.

The important point to keep in mind about updates is, indeed, that their order in time is extremely important. Every update changes the state of the database, and consequent updates must refer to the new state. Consequently, it was proposed that we should consider seriously that possibly the right approach

*Permanent Address: Department of Computer Science, The Hebrew University, Givat RAM, IL-91904 Jerusalem, Israel. E-Mail: beeri@cs.huji.ac.il

for the development of update languages is to follow the classical paradigms of programming: Whereas in the 'logical' languages order is represented in some fashion in the horizontal ordering of literals, this is not different from the vertical presentation used in classical programming languages, and the latter does not claim to be declarative — it admits to ordering actions in time. To that, one should add some of the classical control features, such as various forms of iteration, and packaging in procedures or modules. A program in such a language will show clearly the ordering in time of actions, and their packaging into meaningful units.

In the discussion that followed, some generally supported the opinion expressed above, while others felt is was not doing justice to the various goals of the research on update languages. Two points seemed to emerge from the discussion. First, as some participants observed, trying to express updates in logic is pushing too far the limits of what can be done in logic. That is, a logical framework is not necessarily best for the expression of updates. Logic is a good vehicle for expressing properties of a given state, or to state properties of the evolution of states over time. It is not necessarily a good vehicle for expressing the actions that need to be carried out and their order dependencies. Second, it was pointed out that the recently proposed update languages are not all the same. In particular, some have a bottom-up evaluation, or a fixed-point semantics, while others have a top-down semantics. This difference possibly reflects a fundamental difference in the goals and uses envisioned for the languages. A language that uses the top-down paradigm may for example be suitable for propagating an update from a view into a database, or specifying the updates that are needed for implementing a certain high-level action. The top-down evaluation paradigm does not use the inflationary semantics and its peculiar coding of control structures, and it actually offers a neat hierarchical structure on the actions that are executed.

In summary, it was agreed that we need to see more research into update languages, that such research should consider both 'declarative' and 'procedural' approaches, and importantly, that the application and mode of use of each language be carefully considered, in order to clarify the relationship between the paradigm underlying the language and how the language is being used.

Discussion Report:
Object Migration and Classification

Karen C. Davis*

University of Cincinnati, USA

Guozhu Dong[†]

University of Melbourne, Australia

Andreas Heuer[‡]

Technical University of Clausthal, Germany

Abstract

This contribution presents a summary of the discussions in the session on "Object migration and classification", and it includes the abstracts of two talks given in the session.

1 Introduction

One of the main topics in the research on modelling database dynamics is the specification and control of object life cycles. One basic requirement for an object to have a non-trivial life cycle is the possibility for the object to (i) change its state and (ii) change its class membership. In object-oriented models used in commercial object-oriented database systems, only the change of states is allowed. On the other hand, the object is fixed to the class where it is created over its complete life cycle.

To have non-trivial object life cycles, an object should have the possibility to *migrate* between classes, i.e. lose and gain memberships in classes. If object migration is allowed, class memberships can be determined dynamically by specifying object-oriented *views*. With this dynamic *classification* of objects, we have the two basic requirements always mentioned for classical database models: (1) generic update operations with object creation and migration, and (2) generic query operations defining views using classification techniques.

Within the discussion, no participant of the workshop accepted the model used in commercial object-oriented database systems. The features of object migration and classification seemed to be very important and had been implicitly assumed to be in all object-oriented models published so far. Some of the reasons why "commercial" object-oriented models (mostly originating from object-oriented programming languages) do not have both features are discussed in the last section of this paper.

---

*Electrical and Computer Engineering Department, University of Cincinnati, Cincinnati, OH, USA 45221-0030

[†]Computer Science Department, University of Melbourne, Parkville, Vic 3052, Australia

[‡]Institut für Informatik, TU Clausthal, Erzstr. 1, D-W3392 Clausthal-Zellerfeld, Germany

In the next two sections, we give abstracts of the presentations on object migration by G. Dong and object classification by K.C. Davis, both given in the session on "Object migration and classification". The last section summarizes some of the discussions and gives some references to related work.

2 Object Migration

In this section, we sketch an approach to object migration by special migration operations and an additional migration control specification which ensures that only meaningful migrations are allowed to happen. Details are given in a paper available from the authors [4].

Object migration modelling should satisfy the following requirements: the *identity conservation requirement* is that the identity of a migrating object be preserved during migration. The *behaviour transitional requirement* is that a migrating object be able to abandon old behaviour of the source class of the migration and to acquire new behaviour from the target class of the migration. The *information conservation requirement* is that information associated with a migrating object be preserved as much as possible, i.e. if an object O is to migrate from a source to a target class, then all the properties of O as a member of the source class that are applicable as a member of the target class should be retained.

Fundamental to object migration modelling is the ability of an object to dynamically change the class membership and to be a member of two or more classes. Multiple memberships of objects correspond to the notion of roles [6, 9]. Therefore, we distinguish between the *base class* where an object is created and the *residential classes* of an object where the object currently resides. Residential classes other than the base class correspond to roles of this object and can only result from object migrations.

The following migration operators are proposed:

- The RELOCATE operation relocates an object O from its residential class (if it is given) or otherwise its current base class to the specified target class. The relocated object will lose the old class membership.

- The PROPAGATE operation propagates an object from the current class (the residential class, if it is given in the operation, or the base class otherwise) to several target classes. The identity of the propagated object is copied to the target classes.

- The TRANSMIT operation transmits an object from its current class to several target classes and is equivalent to a PROPAGATE operation followed by a RELOCATE operation, where the target class of the RELOCATE is the most direct common superclass of the target classes of the PROPAGATE operation.

- The RETRACT operation allows an object to abandon dynamically any of its current residential classes but not a base class.

Note that object creation, object deletion and state changing operations are not considered as part of the migration operators while migration, creation, deletion and state changes together can be considered as a complete set of generic update operations for object-oriented databases.

In order to prevent meaningless object migrations from occurring, we define three kinds of migration paths as a migration control specification. They assert that object migration can and only can occur along the specified paths.

Migration paths are specified by triples *(source class, target class, mode)*, where the mode can be *relocational, propagational* or *transmittal.*

A migration control specification can imply another migration path. In the talk, a minimal sound and complete set of *inference rules* for migration paths was given. Additionally, the two sets of migration operators {*RELOCATE, PROPAGATE*} and {*PROPAGATE, RETRACT*} can be shown to be *complete* [4, 10]. In order to satisfy the information conservation requirement, the notion of completeness can be extended to information-preserving completeness, and it can be shown that that both sets of migration operators are information-preserving complete, that a migration transaction which is not information-preserving can be transformed into a information-preserving one, and that the information-preserving property is decidable for migration transactions [4].

3 Object Classification

In this section, we sketch an approach to object classification based on an object algebra with object-preserving operations. Details are given in a paper available from the authors [1].

To define views, an object classification mechanism is needed. To do dynamic object classification where the objects can reside in different classes (i.e., different views of the database), an object-function model with the following features is adopted: objects have an object identity, have properties, and can reference other objects through these properties. We distinguish between a type lattice (a subtype has more properties) and a collection lattice (a subclass has fewer objects). A class is a collection of objects and has a type. The class membership of objects may be defined by a predicate. This is the basic mechanism to define query subsumption, disjointness of collections, and the classification. The model is further described elsewhere [2].

Views are defined by queries. The query algebra used here consists of the subclass-forming (also called object-preserving [5, 7]) operators *union, intersection, difference, selection,* and *restriction,* and the class-forming (or object-generating [5, 7]) operators *project* and *product.* The difference between *selection* and *restriction* is the kind of quantification used for the predicates: *restriction* is universally quantified, *selection* is existentially quantified.

The classification technique uses a subsumption classifier which computes containment relationships between classes indicating a subclass-superclass relationship [3]. It determines subsumption and disjoint relationships for the object-preserving operations of the object algebra. To get a tractable classifier, the scope of the predicates defining class memberships is limited to property restrictions. Then, the class membership predicates are translated to a conjunctive normal form (called MNF for membership normal form).

This classifier is not only used to define views or to specify classes dynamically using predicates, but also to consider view materialization. Here it is important to detect irrelevant updates which are updates not affecting a specific view. It was discussed in the talk how to define views and updates using membership definitions, therefore casting the view materialization problem in terms of identifying disjointness [1].

4 Problems, Related Research and Discussions

During the discussion, some of the problems of the object migration technique that have been mentioned were related to the "operational" style of specification using migration paths instead of "descriptive" specifications. Why not use operations like create, delete, add, and remove as basic primitives and control migrations by integrity constraints like disjointness or covering constraints?

The discussion about the object classifier presented centered around the restricted set of operations used (no type-changing, object-preserving operators) and the restricted set of predicates allowed for class membership definitions. Clearly, generalizing both parameters of the technique too much can result in an intractable classifier.

Several notable contributions to object migration have been given in [6, 8, 9, 10]. Some research only allows the migration of objects from sub- to superclasses [8]. Other research considers migration constraints that represent the history of the valid roles [10]. A different approach allows arbitrary migrations that respect the subclass (i.e. inclusion) semantics after migration [7].

A bibliography of related work in the field of object classification is given by Davis [1]. Object-preserving operations of an object algebra are used as a basis for view definitions and updates of views [7]. In another research effort, a classifier takes into account the set operations union, intersection, and difference, and prevents intractable predicates by introducing class clusters representing several subclasses of a given class [5].

During the discussions, a lot of participants had not been aware that neither object migration nor object classification is available in existing object-oriented database systems — both techniques are even not applicable since objects are restricted to be in the class created and the subclass hierarchy is not understood as both a subtype hierarchy on the one hand and a collection hierarchy on the other hand.

Why do object-oriented models originating from object-oriented programming languages have such a restricted model? One of the answers is the wish to have strong typing in these languages besides dynamic aspects like method inheritance, overriding and late binding. If an object can reside in more than one class, there are additional problems in determining the class of an object which implies the method implementation to be executed. To this problem, there have been two replies by researchers interested in flexible object-oriented database models providing for object migration, classification, and creation: (i) we do not need the method overriding and late binding features and have no problems with object migrations, or (ii) the additional problems in strong typing while allowing object migration and late binding should be addressed. Object migration and dynamic classification seem to be so important for database models that no participant in the discussions wanted to eliminate them to conform to the programming language models used up to now.

References

[1] K.C. Davis. Object-oriented view materialization. Published in a technical report, 1992, available from the authors, 12 pages.

[2] K.C. Davis and L.M.L. Delcambre. A denotational approach to object-oriented query language definition. In *Proceedings of the International Workshop on the Specification of Database Systems*, 1991. Workshops in Computing, Springer-Verlag, 1992.

[3] K.C. Davis and L.M.L. Delcambre. A classifier for object-oriented schema and query processing. In *Progress in Object-Oriented Databases*, 1992. Volume 1, J.B. Prater, Editor, Ablex Publishing Corporation, to appear.

[4] G. Dong and Q. Li. Object migrations in object-oriented databases. Published in a technical report, 1992, available from the authors, 12 pages.

[5] A. Heuer and P. Sander. Classifying object-oriented query results in a class/type lattice. In *Proceedings of the 3rd Symposium on Mathematical Fundamentals of Database and Knowledge Base Systems (MFDBS 91)*, pages 14–28, Berlin, 1991. Springer, Lecture Notes in Computer Science 495.

[6] B. Pernici. Objects with roles. In *Proceedings of the ACM Conferences on Office Information Systems*, pages 205–215. ACM, 1990.

[7] M.H. Scholl, C. Laasch, and M. Tresch. Updatable views in object-oriented databases. In *Proceedings of the 2nd International Conference on Deductive and Object-Oriented Databases*, pages 189–207, Berlin, 1991. Springer, Lecture Notes in Computer Science 566.

[8] M. Schrefl and E. Neuhold. Object class definition by generalization using upward inheritance. In *Proceedings of the International Conference on Data Engineering*, pages 4–13. IEEE, 1988.

[9] E. Sciore. Object specialization. *ACM Transactions on Information Systems*, 7(2):103–122, April 1989.

[10] J. Su. Dynamic constraints and object migration. In *Proceedings of the International Conference on Very Large Databases*, pages 233–242, 1991.

Author Index

Published in 1990–91

AI and Cognitive Science '89, Dublin City
University, Eire, 14–15 September 1989
A. F. Smeaton and G. McDermott (Eds.)

**Specification and Verification of Concurrent
Systems,** University of Stirling, Scotland,
6–8 July 1988
C. Rattray (Ed.)

Semantics for Concurrency, Proceedings of the
International BCS-FACS Workshop, Sponsored
by Logic for IT (S.E.R.C.), University of
Leicester, UK, 23–25 July 1990
M. Z. Kwiatkowska, M. W. Shields and
R. M. Thomas (Eds.)

Functional Programming, Glasgow 1989
Proceedings of the 1989 Glasgow Workshop,
Fraserburgh, Scotland, 21–23 August 1989
K. Davis and J. Hughes (Eds.)

Persistent Object Systems, Proceedings of the
Third International Workshop, Newcastle,
Australia, 10–13 January 1989
J. Rosenberg and D. Koch (Eds.)

Z User Workshop, Oxford 1989, Proceedings of
the Fourth Annual Z User Meeting, Oxford,
15 December 1989
J. E. Nicholls (Ed.)

**Formal Methods for Trustworthy Computer
Systems (FM89),** Halifax, Canada,
23–27 July 1989
Dan Craigen (Editor) and Karen Summerskill
(Assistant Editor)

Security and Persistence, Proceedings of the
International Workshop on Computer
Architecture to Support Security and Persistence
of Information, Bremen, West Germany,
8–11 May 1990
John Rosenberg and J. Leslie Keedy (Eds.)

**Women into Computing: Selected Papers
1988–1990**
Gillian Lovegrove and Barbara Segal (Eds.)

3rd Refinement Workshop (organised by
BCS-FACS, and sponsored by IBM UK
Laboratories, Hursley Park and the Programming
Research Group, University of Oxford),
Hursley Park, 9–11 January 1990
Carroll Morgan and J. C. P. Woodcock (Eds.)

Designing Correct Circuits, Workshop jointly
organised by the Universities of Oxford and
Glasgow, Oxford, 26–28 September 1990
Geraint Jones and Mary Sheeran (Eds.)

Functional Programming, Glasgow 1990
Proceedings of the 1990 Glasgow Workshop on
Functional Programming, Ullapool, Scotland,
13–15 August 1990
Simon L. Peyton Jones, Graham Hutton and
Carsten Kehler Holst (Eds.)

4th Refinement Workshop, Proceedings of the
4th Refinement Workshop, organised by BCS-
FACS, Cambridge, 9–11 January 1991
Joseph M. Morris and Roger C. Shaw (Eds.)

AI and Cognitive Science '90, University of
Ulster at Jordanstown, 20–21 September 1990
Michael F. McTear and Norman Creaney (Eds.)

Software Re-use, Utrecht 1989, Proceedings of
the Software Re-use Workshop, Utrecht,
The Netherlands, 23–24 November 1989
Liesbeth Dusink and Patrick Hall (Eds.)

Z User Workshop, 1990, Proceedings of the Fifth
Annual Z User Meeting, Oxford,
17–18 December 1990
J.E. Nicholls (Ed.)

IV Higher Order Workshop, Banff 1990
Proceedings of the IV Higher Order Workshop,
Banff, Alberta, Canada, 10–14 September 1990
Graham Birtwistle (Ed.)